George Rogers Clark and William Croghan

George Rogers Clark *and* William Croghan

A Story of the Revolution, Settlement, and Early Life at Locust Grove

Gwynne Tuell Potts

UNIVERSITY PRESS OF KENTUCKY

Scholarly publisher for the Commonwealth,
serving Bellarmine University, Berea College, Centre
College of Kentucky, Eastern Kentucky University,
The Filson Historical Society, Georgetown College,
Kentucky Historical Society, Kentucky State University,
Morehead State University, Murray State University,
Northern Kentucky University, Transylvania University,
University of Kentucky, University of Louisville,
and Western Kentucky University.

Editorial and Sales Offices: The University Press of Kentucky
663 South Limestone Street, Lexington, Kentucky 40508-4008
www.kentuckypress.com

Unless otherwise noted, photographs are courtesy of Historic Locust Grove, Inc.

Library of Congress Cataloging-in-Publication Data

Names: Potts, Gwynne Tuell, 1948– author.
Title: George Rogers Clark and William Croghan : a story of the Revolution, settlement, and early life at Locust Grove / Gwynne Tuell Potts.
Description: Lexington : The University Press of Kentucky, [2020] | Includes index.
Identifiers: LCCN 2019037372 | ISBN 9780813178677 (hardcover) | ISBN 9780813178691 (pdf) | ISBN 9780813178684 (epub)
Subjects: LCSH: Clark, George Rogers, 1752–1818. | Croghan, William, 1752–1823. | United States. Continental Army—Biography. | Locust Grove (Louisville, Ky. : Estate)—History. | Pioneers—Kentucky—Biography. | Louisville (Ky.)—Biography. | Louisville (Ky.)—History—18th century. | United States—History—Revolution, 1775–1783.
Classification: LCC E207.C5 P68 2020 | DDC 973.3/3092 [B]—dc23
LC record available at https://lccn.loc.gov/2019037372

This book is printed on acid-free paper meeting the requirements of the American National Standard for Permanence in Paper for Printed Library Materials.

Manufactured in the United States of America.

Member of the Association of University Presses

Contents

Author's Note

This work is an extension of my long association with Locust Grove, Major William Croghan's Kentucky farm. Much of my initial understanding of George Rogers Clark's role in the Revolutionary West and his relationship with Croghan was the consequence of my conversations with Samuel W. Thomas and the absorption of his thorough research. Sam, clerk of the works during the site's restoration, devoted his life to the study, writing, and telling of Louisville's past. He and I produced a pictorial book for Historic Locust Grove, Inc., in 2006, which offered a survey of Clark's career and summarized the many stages of Locust Grove's development. The publication contained little historical context, as that was not its point, but it remains valuable to local historians who continue to clamor for Sam's detailed portrayals of early Louisville, and to the many interpreters who tell the stories connected to Clark. This book, too, contains much of Sam's research, cited through the many articles he published and the work he contributed to *George Rogers Clark & Locust Grove.* His gifts to Louisville, and to Historic Locust Grove in particular, remain timeless and treasured.

Prologue

George Rogers Clark's story is not understood today without some knowledge of the time and place in which he served as the military commander of the West. The time is simple to grasp—it was the American Revolution and its immediate aftermath—but because Clark chose to remain a westerner rather than join the Continental Army, the place is complicated to explain and was unknown to nearly all of Washington's troops. The discrepancies between the revolutions carried out on the Atlantic Coast and in the Ohio River valley are so great that many supporters of either sector appear, from time to time, to forget the other even existed. In fact, the two theaters operated tangentially, one under the financial control of the Continental Congress (for they offered Washington little else, and at that, inadequately), and the other directed by the governor of Virginia. That it worked cohesively at any level was the consequence of Washington's Virginia roots, which allowed Patrick Henry and Thomas Jefferson to communicate freely with the commander-in-chief with little regard to Congress.

The degree to which Clark was isolated and overworked in his attempts to eradicate British influence in the West invites few comparisons between the revolutionary experiences of Clark and any equal within the Continental ranks, and his postrevolution command is unique in American history. George Washington, the man who was tasked with defeating, or at least outlasting the British army on the eastern seaboard, was taxed beyond his known capabilities, but survived it surrounded by a coterie of admirers, a frequently disagreeable but unified officer corps that enjoyed regular periods of down time amid the chaos. Among that corps was Major William Croghan, who arrived in time to participate in Washington's disastrous New York campaign and stayed seven years to witness Cornwallis's surrender. His revolutionary career acts as a counterpoint to Clark's, and because their divergent paths eventually crossed, and later merged, his service offers an unparalleled complement to Clark's work in the West.

The young men met at Fort Pitt before either considered Britain his enemy. They again were together at Pitt nearly a decade later, one in exile from Washington's army as he awaited parole, the other attempting a near-impossible capture of Detroit. After they concluded their disparate war services honorably, Clark and Croghan arrived at the Falls of the Ohio River, where they worked together, later lived together, and finally died under a common roof as brothers.

At the end of their lives, Croghan achieved undisputed success in the new western country, while Clark failed to prosper in the land that he had defended and won. Yet, Clark died a conqueror, known even today to schoolchildren and scholars as a key figure in the American Revolution, while Croghan, wealthy and better connected, remains an obscure figure in his own home. Indeed, Croghan's house is a national landmark, not because of his own estimable achievements, but because of its association with Clark and his younger brother, General William Clark. By the standards of their time, each was a hero, but neither was an ideal man. Clark and Croghan employed men, women, and children as slave labor, and their lives reflected few of the philosophies that emerged from the Enlightenment they both admired. Neither moved far beyond the commonly held opinions of most westerners regarding Native American peoples, and they essentially died as they lived, as socially traditional men.

By nature a scientist and social historian, Clark was a regular reader of the *Spectator* and a voracious consumer of any material related to natural science and history. William Croghan, the rationalist, maintained a library of classical reading and kept meticulous financial and land survey records throughout his life, and ensured that his children were well educated and his debts paid. Together, Clark and Croghan knew most of the figures who led the American Revolution, those who subsequently settled the Ohio River valley, and of course, the first Americans to travel overland to the Pacific Ocean. Their personalities were distinctly contradictory, but their lives remarkably similar, and with their contemporaries, they created the United States of America.

Part I

Wilderness

1

George Croghan

The Buck

> Insofar as any man can influence history, [George] Croghan had much to do with laying the foundations upon which George Rogers Clark, the American diplomats at Paris in 1783, and the authors of the Ordinance of 1787 built. His dreams helped inspire such younger men as Daniel Clark, John Campbell, Barnard and Michael Gratz, and William Croghan to carry on similar work on more distant frontiers.
>
> —Albert T. Volwiler, *George Croghan and the Westward Movement, 1741–1782*

A decade before the outbreak of the American Revolution, the western boundary of Britain's thirteen North American colonies ran along the spine of the mountains that formed the Eastern Continental Divide. The frontier would have fluctuated, always pushing west, even without the interference of political considerations, because the population on each side of the divide was ephemeral—restless and always in need of sustenance. However, once colonists pushed beyond the great pass connecting the eastern Appalachians to the West, regular interaction between the few who risked the journey and the scarce but outraged native peoples who met them was inevitable.

It was the great waterway that poured from the Allegheny Range that created the irresistible pull westward. The Ohio River begins at Pittsburgh, home today to 2.5 million people who somewhat reluctantly embrace the sobriquet the "Paris of Appalachia." It is the second largest city in Pennsylvania and the largest in the Ohio River valley, but in 1772, it was the center of a transient regional population that numbered about five hundred persons, frequented by traders who plied the goods of eastern merchants to the Native Americans and European settlers who were their clientele. The community was a holding pen for eager frontiersmen who had gravitated west, but the heart of the settlement, Fort Pitt, was little more than an abandoned British outpost claimed by two colonies. Pennsylvania vaguely assumed that the area must fall within the Penn grant, but did little to assert its claim; Virginia forcibly placed a militia at the fort and seated a court. Therefore, such as it was, the only military and civilian jurisdiction recognized at the forks was Virginian, and as odd as it might seem to today's residents, the men of the Tenth Company of Virginia's Revolutionary Eighth Regiment were recruited from the Pittsburgh area four years later.[1]

Virginian George Rogers Clark and Dubliner William Croghan (*Crawn, Crohan*) were introduced to the West at the fort. This was fitting because the thick wilderness where the Monongahela and Allegheny rivers converge was a place where peace or war had been made for generations, and the early years of both men's adulthoods were consumed by war. Neither young man, however, might have been prepared for the American Revolution had "Colonel" George Croghan not first burst onto the frontier.

The elder Croghan wielded unprecedented influence in the area and knew Indian leaders and their lands in western Pennsylvania, New York, and the future state of Ohio as well as any man in North America. He owned tens of thousands of acres surrounding the fort, and his career, both notorious and illustrious, served as a metaphor for the colonial British experience in North America, embodying the events that led directly to the American Revolution in the West. No colonist owned more land or experienced the drive that ultimately pushed British interests down the Ohio and on to the Mississippi River more deeply than George Croghan.

Croghan left Ireland in 1741 and settled in Lancaster County, Pennsylvania, in the company of Scots-Irish and German immigrants, becoming an extraordinarily popular trader who provided Philadelphia goods to Indians in exchange for hides. By 1744, he had traveled into Iroquois territory as far as the mouth of the Cuyahoga River, the future site of Cleveland. Contemporary mapmaker Lewis Evans wrote that, of the hundred or so traders of his day, those few "of greatest respectability" included Thomas McKee, John Frasure, Edward Ward, and partners William Trent and George Croghan.

McKee, a Scots-Irish veteran who fought in the French and Indian War, had first married a Shawnee captive from North Carolina who was the mother of Col. Alexander McKee, and second, Margaret Tecumsapah Opessa, sister to Tecumseh's mother, Mary. Most biographers believe that Trent, the son of a Pennsylvania Supreme Court jurist and founder of Trenton, New Jersey, was Croghan's brother-in-law. Edward Ward was Croghan's younger half brother. Croghan initiated the first of a fabled series of land transactions in 1745 when he and Trent established Pennsboro near today's Harrisburg. Here, he housed his European-American first wife, whose identity is unknown, his mother, his stepfather Thomas Ward, several cousins, indentured servants, and enslaved Africans; and it was at Pennsboro that at least one child, Susanna, was born in 1750.[2]

The Six Nations' Onondaga Council awarded two hundred thousand acres to Croghan, known to them as the "Buck," in 1749 in appreciation of his "constant attention to the preservation of peace." The council's center of authority lay in New York's Mohawk River valley, where the Crown established diplomatic liaisons that were assumed in London to provide a dialogue with every Native American village between Virginia and lower Canada. Unknown to the Council or Croghan, the Onondaga gift overlapped a five-hundred-thousand-acre grant made weeks earlier to a Virginia-based land company. The prestige of the Ohio Company's members was fundamental to the government's approval of the patent, as its shareholders included Lawrence Washington, George Mason, and others so influential that the venture's objective to gain control of the Ohio River valley was assured. Of the many controversies that resulted from this land grant conflict, the most profound was its contribution to the Virginia–Pennsylvania boundary dispute, which would affect the course of the American Revolution's western campaigns.[3]

When the company hired Baltimore surveyor Christopher Gist to explore and map its land grant in 1750–1751, Gist noted the peaceful but complex economic and political relationships British colonists had established with frontier natives. After coming across Croghan, who was camped in today's northeastern Ohio, Gist convinced him to serve as guide through Delaware, Wyandot, Shawnee, and Twightwee villages, ostensibly spreading word of a Virginia conference meant to strengthen the British alliance with Native Americans. Gist's true objective in organizing the 1752 Logstown Conference was to certify the Six Nations' 1744 land grant to Virginia, to permit the Ohio Company to move ahead with its trading activities without fear of Indian reprisal.[4]

The conference concluded with the Six Nations' agreement to surrender a large area beyond the Appalachians as far south as Virginia to allow the Ohio Company to construct a western fort and trading post and, by extension, invite European settlement. The Logstown agreement marked the end of the Iroquois confederation's hold over the tribal peoples who lived beyond the Ohio River and provided impetus for trans-Appalachian colonization, but the British government failed to recognize this critical turn of events. Croghan knew better, and communicated his concern to Pennsylvania governor James Hamilton in May. "The government may have what opinion they will of the Ohio Indians, and think they are oblig'd to do what the Onondago Counsel will bid them, butt I ashure your honour they will actt for themselves att this time without consulting the Onondago Councel."[5]

The North American theater of the Seven Years' War, the European conflict known by Americans as the French and Indian War, began with a series of skirmishes rather than a declaration. A French unit had fired on a party of Virginians led by Gist and George Washington in 1753, moving the Virginia legislature to appropriate £10,000 to mount a retaliatory expedition. In anticipation of an opportunity to distribute arms and supplies to pro-British Indians, the Ohio Company quickly hired Trent to build Fort Prince George at the forks of the Ohio in the spring of 1754. Most of the construction work fell to young Edward Ward, who had not yet finished when a French army that Ward believed to be a thousand-men strong approached on 17 April. Ensign Ward's surrender foretold the early course of the French and Indian War; the French razed the Ohio Company's structure and built a new stockade yards away, soon christened Fort DuQuesne.

The Virginia House of Burgesses' reaction was to order its militia into motion with Washington at the lead. The House also approved construction of the aptly named Fort Necessity at nearby Great Meadows and hired Croghan to provide wheat and interpretive services for Washington. Croghan, whose trading business collapsed at the beginning of the war with a £16,000 loss, was prevented by the ongoing fighting from completing his obligation to Virginia, but he was present at Fort Necessity when Washington surrendered to the French on 4 July 1754. Citing inadequate supplies and support, Washington's complaints against Croghan were bitter and never fully rescinded. With no recourse, Croghan returned to his

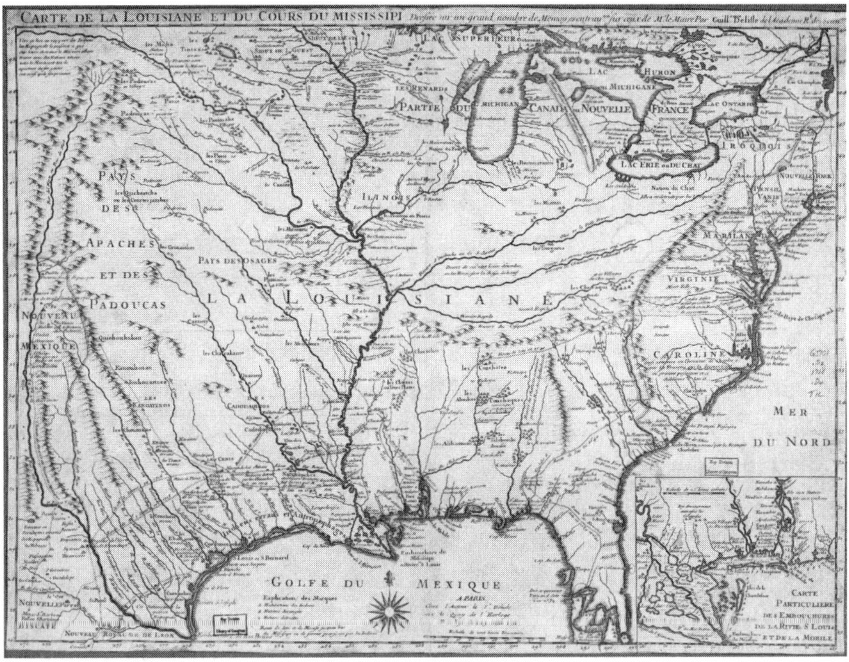

French Territory in North America, 1718. Map by L'Isle, Library of Congress.

new settlement at Aughwick (Fort Shirley) and lived on the frontier to escape his financial obligations, but he continued to volunteer as liaison between the British government and the region's Indians. His unpaid role as negotiator did not go unnoticed by the government, as British deputy Indian agent Conrad Weiser's letter to the governor recorded. "I counted above twenty cabbins about [Croghan's] house, and in them at least two hundred Indians, men, women and children, and a great many more scattered thereabouts, some two or three miles off, and frequently come to fetch meals at Mr. Croghan's."[6]

In recognition of the legitimate initiation of the war, British major general Edward Braddock was placed in command of the crown's forces in February 1755, after which military operations were coordinated with an authority and a sense of purpose that were lacking in the Virginia militia. Braddock's first objective was the capture of Fort DuQuesne, and without acquainting himself with native alliances or regional geography, he organized an army of more than two thousand regulars and militiamen on the

Potomac at Fort Cumberland. Since the frontier war had effectively put traders out of business, Croghan joined Braddock in June as an interpreter and spy, and when fourteen hundred men left camp with nine companies of Virginia militiamen, it did so with an interior map of Fort DuQuesne provided Croghan by a British prisoner of war.[7]

Drenching rain soon ruined most of the army's wheat and reduced the party to near starvation, and scarce forest forage, a circumstance unforeseen by Braddock, left the draught horses in the same condition. The march was slow. Braddock had not anticipated the difficulties associated with carving a road and moving artillery through the Alleghenies, and as the army neared Fort DuQuesne, Indian scouts harassed the fringes, killing and scalping men and women who managed the baggage and animals that trailed the procession. At 2 a.m. on 9 July, Lieutenant Colonel Thomas Gage, George Croghan, and three to four hundred advance guard troops rode to the Monongahela River to identify the two safe crossings Braddock's army would ford early in the afternoon. Despite the early hour, the guard did not go unnoticed.[8]

Later in the day, knowing the worst of the march was completed, Braddock's soldiers hugged "themselves with joy" and the drummers played the Grenadier's March as they approached the forks of the Ohio River. With ten miles to go, Gage led the convoy, Washington and Gist accompanied Braddock further back, and Daniel Boone and his cousin, Daniel Morgan, rode among the wagoners driving supplies at the rear. Without warning, nearly nine hundred French Canadians and their native allies sprang from the woods. The advance guard parted and dove for cover, as did the Virginia militiamen, who were accustomed to woodland fighting; but the red-jacketed British officers at the core of the march ordered their soldiers to remain in strict formation, which ensured that they would absorb the full impact of the attack. When it was over, Washington, who had not been mounted until the ambush began in deference to a stomach ailment, escaped without a wound after having two horses shot from under him, and Boone, having freed one of his packhorses, disappeared across the Monongahela with dozens of others. Twelve to twenty captives were stripped and taken to the fort, where they were tortured and burned at the stake on the lacrosse field where Indians and French soldiers competed. Braddock, who died four days after the attack, would become one of the 977 British soldiers killed or wounded, a number surpassed in the French and Indian War only by the Battle of Ticonderoga, which would be fought one day short of three years in the future.[9]

The people of the Shawnee nation, with villages extending through the Shenandoah Valley to the Potomac River, left their homes after the Logstown Conference. They had crossed the mountains to join a western tribe at Lower Shawneetown, where the Scioto and Ohio rivers met, and adopted the pro-British alliance of their predecessors. After Braddock's defeat, however, the Shawnee warriors, who had fought with the Delaware, Miami, Huron, Ottawa, and Mingo peoples, changed allegiances and began raiding Pennsylvania settlers, which prompted even the comfortably settled Aughwick community to melt into the woods. In addition to the natives' desire to align themselves with victors, Croghan's intuitive understanding of their alliances proved correct; western Indians were determined to establish their independence from the pro-British Onondaga Council because the hundreds of thousands of acres the Six Nations had ceded to Pennsylvania and Virginia in recent years had been their home.

The Pennsylvania Assembly responded to the Indian assaults by authorizing construction of a series of frontier fortifications, three of which Croghan was contracted to build. Chafed by the assembly's criticism of the expenses associated with the Cumberland County fort, he resigned his Pennsylvania commission and placed his cousin, Thomas Smallman, in charge of his personal matters. With Trent left to manage his business affairs, he traveled to Albany, New York, with a letter of introduction from Pennsylvania's governor to Sir William Johnson, "His Majesty's Sole Agent and Superintendent of Indian Affairs for the Northern Parts of North America and Colonel of the Six Nations." Croghan's career as diplomat and land speculator was about to begin.[10]

Johnson had been appointed to his new position by George II shortly before he arrived in New York and honored with a baronet's title in recognition of his successful command against the French in the Crown Point campaign. Croghan was hired as his deputy at their initial meeting at Johnson's Mohawk River fort, probably because Johnson viewed Croghan's years of interaction among the western natives as valuable experience, and he, like Croghan, regularly preferred the company of Indians to that of others on the frontier.[11]

Even at the edge of civilization, Johnson's lifestyle was unusual. Early on, he had struck a warm relationship with the Mohawk Turtle Clan sa-

Sir William Johnson by Reynolds.

chem, Brant Canagaradunck a, known simply as Brant. The chief had seen eastern cities and understood the benefits of a close association with Great Britain, so when his stepdaughter, Molly, gave birth in 1759 to the first of eight children fathered by Johnson, the bond between the British government and the Onondaga Council only was strengthened. The son and daughters of his first wife would inherit his title and homestead, but Johnson, who lived with Molly and her children until his death, ensured that she and each of her children would be provided large New York farms.[12]

Molly's younger brother, Joseph Brant (Thayendanegea, Tayadaneega), knew Johnson even before his sister moved to Fort Johnson. At the age of fifteen, he had accompanied Johnson's troops and four hundred Iroquois warriors to French Fort Carillon at the foot of Lake Champlain. From their defensive position on Mount Defiance on 8 July 1758, he, Johnson,

Joseph Brant after Romney. Courtesy of Yale University Art Gallery.

Croghan, and the others watched as Major General James Abercromby's British forces absorbed a savage defeat at the hands of Lt. General Louis Joseph Montcalm's outnumbered French army. Years later, long after Brant ended his personal campaign to kill George Rogers Clark, he remembered his first war experience, saying his fear had been so great it was necessary to hold a tree branch to steady his shaking body when the firing began.[13]

In January 1758, Croghan, now widowed and settled into a domestic relationship with the eldest daughter of another Mohawk clan sachem, relocated to German Flats to provide Johnson with intelligence from the Six Nations. Moving into a remote Mohawk River valley fort, he ordered supplies from Schenectady merchants and dug in for the season, mockingly declaring, "British officers are to delicatt to undertake a winter expedition." His second daughter, Adonwentishon, was born there in 1759 and was acknowledged throughout her life to be Catherine Croghan. Croghan's relationship with her mother might have been the most successful decision of his career, as it improved his image among the Indians with whom he worked, and brought him closer to the extended society of Johnson. And, as influential as Catherine's father had been within diplomatic circles, paternal connections meant little in the matrilineal Iroquois society. It was Adonwentishon, or Catherine Croghan, who would assume her mother's position among the Mohawks and determine who would lead her nation through the American Revolution. Catherine Croghan and Joseph Brant would be married at Fort Niagara in December 1779 in the midst of the Mohawk nation's flight ahead of the Continental Army, and Brant would live the remainder of his life with Catherine and their children. Believing the Americans would seize all Indian land should they achieve independence, and always faithful to his mentor, Johnson, Brant fought as a British officer from Long Island to Detroit to the Ohio River valley in an attempt to secure Mohawk claims in North America; and after the Revolution, he would lead the remaining 1,843 New York Mohawks to Ontario with the king's personal permission.[14]

In an effort to rebound from the defeat so vividly recalled by Joseph Brant, Major General Jeffrey Amherst, new British commander-in-chief, dispatched Brigadier General John Forbes to retake Fort DuQuesne in 1758. With Croghan working as his interpreter and negotiator, Forbes first made peace with the Iroquois, Shawnees, and Delawares, who consequently abandoned the French cause. The French army, in turn, set fire to the fort and disappeared. Forbes renamed the ashes Fort Pitt and left two hundred Virginians in charge of its reconstruction. French and Indian War momentum shifted permanently after the epic September 1759 battle for Quebec and the capture of Fort Carillon, renamed Ticonderoga, and the war in North America effectively ended in 1760 when Amherst seized Montreal.

By the terms of the Treaty of Paris, signed in February 1763, all of France's North American territory east of the Mississippi River, with the exception of New Orleans, now belonged to Britain. The treaty temporarily calmed tensions between London and Paris, but it created a long and bloody struggle in North America, where a succession of American Indian

Jeffrey Amherst. ©National Portrait Gallery, London.

leaders organized to halt the British occupation of French posts that lay between the Appalachian Mountains and the Mississippi River. Consequently, undeclared and unrecognized by Parliament, a war that would not cease until the end of the War of 1812 continued on the trans-Appalachian frontier.[15]

Under Ottawa chief Pontiac's direction, warriors crossed western Pennsylvania to create havoc within European settlements, randomly killing and burning as they went. Amherst ordered Croghan back to Fort Pitt to settle the uprising, but Johnson's deputy ignored the dispatch. He believed it had been Amherst's Indian policies and budget restrictions that had led Pontiac, whom he knew, to declare war. Croghan resigned his position as Johnson's deputy, but not before he made his own feelings for Amherst known in a public toast made at the fort.

> From evry generous noble passion free; As proud and ignorant as man can be Revengefull, avaritious, obstinate is he; Malicious, stupid and obdurate will ever be A fleeting consequence he's dully grave; Rest here my pen, enough—the man's a knave![16]

Swiss military officer Col. Henry Bouquet assumed command of the British Royal American Regiment (Sixtieth) in 1763, along with responsibility for crushing Pontiac's Rebellion. At the direction of Amherst, he distributed blankets discarded by the fort's smallpox victims to area natives with the intention of spreading the disease among the indigenous people. Had this tactic failed, Bouquet was told to initiate the Spanish method, and turn dogs on the Indians. Bouquet succeeded temporarily in ending attacks in the area, but could not make a treaty with Pontiac.

Croghan continued to disassociate himself from the British government in general, and Amherst's policies specifically, and focused his attention on the subject increasingly occupying American and British interest—western land speculation. Benjamin Franklin had proposed in 1754 that the territory west of the thirteen colonies be organized as self-directed governments, or charter colonies, under the authority of the Crown. Following Franklin's lead, Croghan and other former traders now appealed to London for reimbursement of income and inventory lost as a result of the French and Indian War, and suggested payment be made in the form of a western land charter, or, the fourteenth British colony.[17]

2

Land Mad

> Have it all, lose it all.
> —Lin-Manuel Miranda, *Hamilton*

William Trent and Philadelphia merchant Samuel Wharton coined the traders' organization the "Suffering Traders of 1754," but by the time Croghan left for England to present their case for compensation, subsequent frontier war losses were included in the application. Croghan placed Susanna in a Philadelphia boarding school and set sail aboard the ill-fated *Britannia* on 22 December 1763, carrying a notebook of tips for London visitors provided by a Fort Pitt officer. Although the *Britannia* was warned by the captains of two ships that were emerging from the English Channel in a 27 January gale, it ignored the warnings and slammed into the Guernsey Island rocks seven times. The evacuation of the ship, followed by a perilous struggle to reach the French shore, took place moments before the *Britannia* rolled onto land and fell to pieces with most of its cargo, including Croghan's personal baggage, destroyed. The nearly frozen passengers made their ways to Paris, and from there to port, finally landing at the Isle of Wight on 8 February 1764.[1]

After Croghan encountered unexpected expenses in France, and under the necessity of purchasing a new wardrobe, he at last set about in London to plead the traders' cause. Few of the city's "genteel" men would hear him, and he found no one in government who offered an audience, which led him to note that the members of the board of trade were "imensly ignerant." Croghan didn't care for the London ladies and was disappointed in his hope to travel to Ireland to recover an estate left by his grandfather, Edmund Croghan. He wrote Johnson: "I am Nott sorry I came hear as it will Larn Me to be Contented on a Litle farm in america if I can gett one

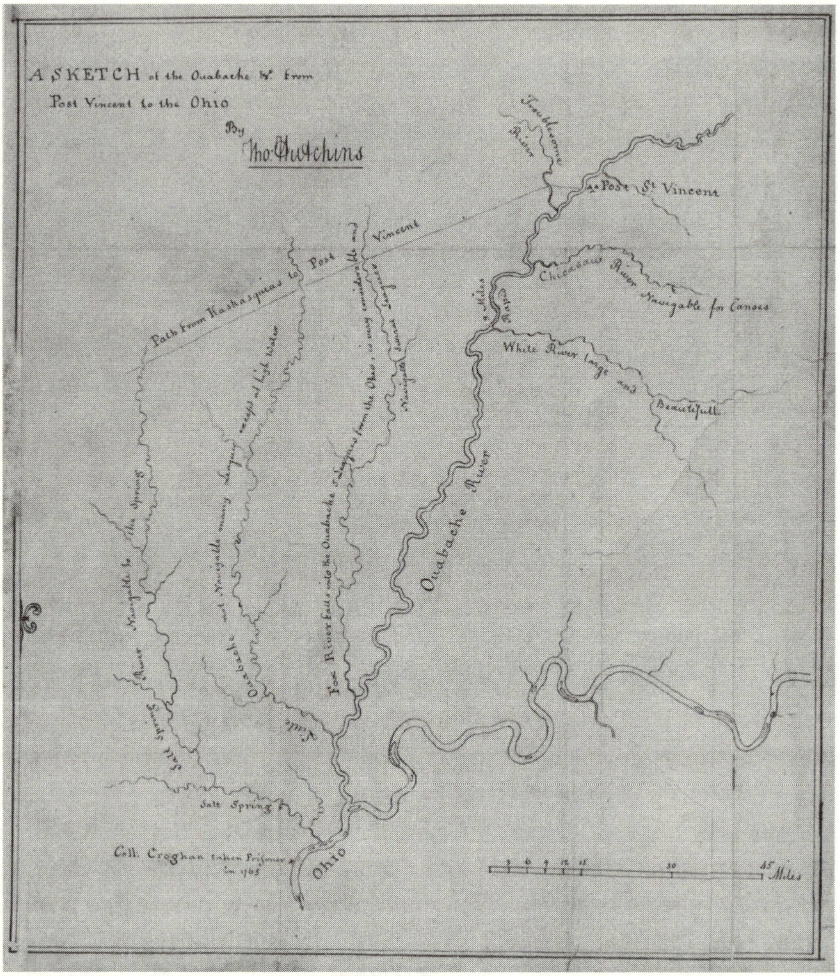

Hutchins's map of Quabache (Wabash). Map reproduction courtesy of British Library Collection.

when I go back Butt I ashure yr. Honor I am sick of London & harttily tierd of the pride and pompe of the slaves in power." When he reached New York and found that his resignation from government employ had not been registered by Johnson, he returned to work as Britain's deputy Indian supervisor, but continued to invest in western land companies.[2]

Croghan saw the Illinois territory for the first time in 1765. Again in the role of peace negotiator, the deputy superintendent had volunteered to travel to the Illinois to seal the peace achieved by Bouquet in 1764. The government, anxious to gain control of Ohio and Mississippi river posts, but loath to face hostile natives so far from supply lines, postponed a planned Illinois expedition to allow Croghan the "opportunity" to craft an agreement with the western nations. Bound for the Mississippi from Fort Pitt in May, Croghan kept an informative and ironic journal as the trip unfolded. His caravan included Thomas Smallman, servants, Shawnee deputies, and an attending physician, crowded into two boats already packed with presents for the Indians.[3]

Not long after seven French traders were captured operating among the Shawnee people, Croghan's party was attacked by Kickapoo and Mascouten warriors six miles below the mouth of the Wabash. Two servants and three Shawnee guides died, and Croghan, tomahawked, was forced to march forty-two miles to Vincennes. He soon described the event to Fort Pitt commander, William Murray, in self-effacing fashion. "I got the stroke of a hatchett on the head, but my scull being pretty thick, the hatchet would not enter, so you see a thick scull is of service on some occasions." Croghan's opinion of the citizens of Vincennes did not mirror the admiration he later expressed for the area. "The French Inhabitants hereabouts are an idle lazy people a Parcel of Renegades from Canada and are much worse than Indians." Lieutenant Alexander Fraser, who had followed Croghan from Fort Pitt, agreed. "The Illinois Indians are about Six hundred & fifty able to bear Arms, nothing can equal their passion for drunkeness, but that of the French Inhabitants, who are for the greatest part drunk every day."[4]

The Vincennes villagers had no reason to pity the English captives; neither did those living 180 miles further west, at Kaskaskia, where the population chose not to intervene in the native melee that followed the party's arrival. The murders of the luckless Shawnees, however, probably saved the lives of their companions. Fearful of reprisal, the Kickapoos and Mascoutens released their captives in exchange for sixty-four gallons of rum provided by Croghan and begged his intervention with the angry Shawnees who had arrived for revenge.

At Kaskaskia, Croghan received word that Pontiac was willing to discuss the English occupation of Illinois, and he agreed to meet with representatives from four Illini tribes who gave their consent to allow the English to occupy abandoned French posts. Later, Croghan described the chief ("an old acquaintance of mine") in a letter to Johnson: "Pondiac is a shrewd sensible Indian of few words & commands more respect amongst those nations than any Indian I ever saw." He then moved quickly to assemble a treaty with Ohio and Illinois natives, and rode to Detroit with Pontiac to announce the peace to an astonished assembly.[5]

Croghan returned east a hero and purchased a brick residence overlooking the Delaware River in Philadelphia's suburban district of Northern Liberties. He named the place Monckton Hall in honor of the man he hoped would replace Amherst and went about furnishing it in much the style he had come to appreciate at Johnson Hall, Sir William's new estate at Johnsontown, New York. The home was outfitted with "Scottish carpets . . . quantities of spirits and wine . . . Irish linen, china . . . candlesticks, and valuable furniture . . . a dozen mahogany chairs upholstered in green damask . . . tables, desks, bookcases, commodes, backgammon tables and . . . an expensive spinet," all of which suited one of the most important men in Philadelphia. Ensconced in his new setting, he left the Suffering Traders business to Trent and Wharton and began to organize an application for a second land charter.[6]

He had returned from London convinced a British colony was about to be established in the Illinois country. Certain that the territory's beaver trade alone would reap £100,000 annually, he wanted to acquire the formerly French fur-trading business in the Ohio and Mississippi river valleys. In a move that foreshadowed Virginia's next-decade diplomatic tactic, he wrote London to advocate for the establishment of an Illinois colony that would not only control western fur trade, but also provide food for all Louisiana, administer military affairs in the West, and keep an eye on French and Spanish activities. The company he imagined would, by use of the Penn model of proprietary colonization, receive a vast amount of land in the Illinois country and permission to organize and execute the king's law.[7]

In New York, Croghan soon visited Susanna, who was newly married to Royal American Regiment officer Lt. Augustin Prevost Jr.; and he brought Johnson, Benjamin Franklin, and his son, New Jersey governor William Franklin, into his scheme. The Illinois Plan, drafted by the younger Franklin, designated King George III as owner of an intended twelve-hundred-thousand-acre Illinois Colony. A "company of men of wealth" that was prepared to bring "2000 white Protestant settlers" to Illinois would administer the new colony. The first governor of the colony, Franklin continued, should be "a person experienced in the management of Indian affairs, and who has given proofs of his influence with the savages." Johnson tacitly acknowledged his willingness to participate in the company and support Croghan's effort to become the colony's governor when he permitted his deputy to return to the Mississippi the next year. In his response, Croghan congratulated his boss for his foresight and their good fortune, as "one half of England is Now Land Mad & Every body there has thire Eys fixt on this Cuntry," and the opportunity would not last. Although he claimed publicly to be acting only as an agent for the partnership, Croghan, in fact, owned a quarter of the newly formed Illinois Company.[8]

The announced purpose of Croghan's 1766 trip to the Illinois was to consolidate the agreements established with western Indians the year before, but the expedition's covert goals were to create English trading houses and map the Illinois country's new colony. With Croghan's assurance of business, the Philadelphia mercantile firm of Baynton, Wharton, and Morgan loaded its financial future into several longboats and set off from Fort Pitt in June. Along with Croghan, the party included Shawnee chiefs and enslaved Africans, ninety Senecas, Wharton's junior partner George Morgan, engineer Captain Harry Gordon, and cartographer Ensign Thomas Hutchins.

The expedition arrived at Fort de Chartres on the Mississippi in August, where Gordon's engineering skills were of use in repairing this fort and nearby Fort Kaskaskia, which, although equally dilapidated, had the advantage of a high situation above the Mississippi and the town below. Croghan soon realized that, although the British operated the former French forts, the French retained control of the territory's population. Working for Johnson, he brought representatives of the various Illinois tribes and the Ohio Shawnees together at Kaskaskia to ensure peace in the Northwest while he had the territory mapped with an eye to future development. He then traveled down the Mississippi to New Orleans and sailed back to Philadelphia early in 1767. The forts did not fare as well: Chartres was taken by flood before the Revolution, and the French citizens of Kaskaskia burned their fort down in October 1766, after the British unit departed.[9]

Once home, Croghan received a note from neighbor Benjamin Franklin, "You have doubtless render'd great service to Government by your negotiations among Indians. I take every opportunity of mentioning it, and

I hope you may in time obtain suitable reward." Franklin's son, Croghan, Trent, Wharton, and others reorganized the earlier Suffering Traders' land grant application into the Indiana Company with a claim that its members had lost £86,000 during the uprisings that followed the 1763 treaty. Although neither Croghan nor Franklin had been a trader in 1763, each was a stockholder in the newly created company, whose membership nearly duplicated that of the Illinois Company.[10]

The activity associated with preparations for the two new colonies caused Native Americans to put aside territorial differences to demand enforcement of the 1763 Proclamation Line that protected them from European encroachment west of the Appalachian Mountains. And while they were willing to offer land to ensure appeasement for the Suffering Traders, Indian leaders demanded payment for land taken from them within the former French territory. At the same time, Parliament was under pressure by merchants and developers on each side of the Atlantic to establish a government presence west of the mountains to combat France's cultural influence, and, since their 1763 acquisition of Louisiana, Spain's authority. Ultimately, it was the American West's commercial potential that convinced the Crown in 1768 to send Colonel John Wilkins from Philadelphia to Fort Pitt, and from there to the Illinois Territory, where Wilkins established a Spanish–British trade route between Illinois and New Orleans. Alarmed, Native Americans who lived between the Appalachians and the Mississippi River realized their lands were about to be wedged between two European civilizations and correctly foresaw the outcome.[11]

In one of his final acts as colonial office secretary, Lord Shelburne ordered Sir William Johnson to call a treaty conference at Fort Stanwix, New York, to sort out the chaotic North American land policy and create a tangible frontier barrier through the legitimate purchase of Native American lands. Simultaneously, the Suffering Traders' Indiana Company proposal moved slowly through the various stages of British bureaucracy while Croghan's Illinois Plan was coming together. It therefore was not surprising that the 1768 Fort Stanwix Treaty reflected the Suffering Traders' goals as well as the Crown's, because Wharton, Croghan, Trent, and Johnson had planned the conference and controlled the agenda. In addition to confirmation of all earlier land transactions between Native Americans and any individual (this included Croghan's 1749 gift from the Six Nations), the treaty minutes reflect a grant of twenty-five hundred thousand acres on the Ohio River to the king, who was a trustee for the Indiana Company. The company's organizers assumed that the nomination of the king as trustee would secure their claim against competing land companies, but paradoxically, the king's association soon proved fatal to the traders' planned colony.[12]

Reasonably, Shelburne's replacement received the Fort Stanwix Treaty with disbelief. Trent, Samuel Wharton, and Ben Franklin "immediately sailed for London" to lobby for the treaty's approval, but "four objections" within the treaty led the men to understand it was a lost cause. Trent wrote Croghan from London, pleading for assistance. "I beseech you by all the Ties of Friendship, Our Wives & our Children have all their Eyes fixed on you Our and their future happyness depending entirely Upon your bringing this affair to a happy Conclusion," but Croghan ignored Trent's cries as he prepared to move from Monckton Hall. His creditors had become nuisances in Philadelphia, and the remoteness of Lake Otsego, New York, where he had acquired another two hundred thousand acres, now appealed to him. He leased his Poplar Lane estate to Wharton's wife, packed up, and relocated on the New York frontier.[13]

Now well into middle age, he established Croghan's Forest at the foot of Lake Otsego, at the headwaters of the Susquehanna River and about nine miles across the lake from his elder daughter's home. James Fenimore Cooper later portrayed Croghan's Otsego home as "a rude dwelling," but in 1769, Richard Smith described the homestead as a sophisticated and diverse household. Croghan had constructed two log dwellings, one large enough to require six chimneys, and he wrote his brother in Ireland to request eight indentured servants and a bagpiper to supplement his existing staff. Figured wallpaper, damask cloths, thirty chairs, quantities of liquor and food, glass windowpanes, and brass locks were ordered. German frontiersmen, English officers, and area natives were welcomed equally by the Irish deputy and his Mohawk and British families, as a New Jersey traveler recorded in 1769. "At night a drunken Indian came and kissed Col. Croghan and me very joyously. Here are natives of different Nations almost continuously. They visit the deputy Superintendant as Dogs to the Bone."[14]

Croghan's dream of retiring to his forest retreat was short-lived. His unrestrained speculation in western land schemes had exhausted his financial resources, and when New York demanded patent fees on his Otsego property, his home was threatened. Reconciled to taking up the Indian trade again, Croghan purchased £1,000 of Philadelphia goods and planned to sell his 1749 land claims around Fort Pitt to pull himself out of debt while he awaited the approval of the Indiana and Illinois colonies. He rented a chaise to accommodate his gout in the spring of 1770 and traveled with his wife and Catherine to Fort Pitt to manage renewed unrest. Although he hoped to return to New York within weeks, this would be the last time George Croghan saw Lake Otsego.[15]

He put down an Iroquois conspiracy and began a new career as a realtor at the same time as George Washington began work as a de facto land broker for Virginia's French and Indian War veterans. Washington arrived at Fort Pitt in October and dined at Semple's Tavern with Croghan and Dr. John Connolly, "nephew to Colonel Croghan, a very sensible, intelligent man, who had traveled over a good deal of this country both by land and water." He later visited Croghan Hall, where Croghan attempted to sell him fifteen thousand acres of his 1749 grant, but Britain's unsurveyed western boundary, coupled with ongoing Indian skirmishes, diminished the value of the grant and influenced Washington against the purchase.[16]

General Thomas Gage had recommended the abandonment of Fort Pitt in 1768 after he identified its only remaining purpose as "a post of communications with the Illinois," but did not order the fort's evacuation until 31 August 1772. Croghan had resigned from government service for the last time in November 1771, to devote his attention to land investment, and had named Alexander McKee as his deputy Indian superintendent replacement. But, when the British garrison was withdrawn the following November, Gage made the best building at the fort available to Croghan in hopes that the retired deputy would continue to treat with the western nations as only he could do. Croghan agreed and soon found his duties were not significantly different from his early days as Johnson's deputy, when he had written, "You'l Excuse boath Writing and peper, and guess at my Maining, fer I have this Minnitt 20 Drunken Indians about me." Croghan did not disappoint his old friend, Gage, but combined his professional responsibilities with increased efforts to stabilize his financial situation.[17]

John Murray, Lord Dunmore, the newly appointed governor of Virginia, appeared at Fort Pitt in 1773, and it was then that he and Croghan agreed Virginia would acknowledge Croghan's 1749 grant in exchange for the trader's support of Virginia in its boundary dispute with Pennsylvania. When he learned that Dunmore was about to place a militia unit at the fort, Croghan suggested Connolly as the new commander. The long relationship between Connolly and Croghan soon dissolved, however, when Croghan joined forces with Pennsylvanian Arthur St. Clair to organize a united defense for Virginia and Pennsylvania settlers. In an episode that foreshadowed future conflicts in the Fort Pitt area, Connolly viewed Croghan's conciliatory position with the Pennsylvanian as a challenge to his Virginia-based military authority and sent Washington a blistering critique concerning his former guardian. Unbothered, Croghan left Pittsburgh to make a last attempt to secure peace with native warriors, which prompted St. Clair to write, "Mr. Croghan's views I do not pretend to see, but this you may be assured of, he is at present a friend of this country, and if it depends on him we shall have no war yet."[18]

While Croghan again was preoccupied with regional conflict, Philadelphia merchants Barnard and Michael Gratz, and their partner, David Franks, assumed much of the Illinois trading business formerly managed by the bankrupt Baynton, Wharton, and Morgan company. They were in association with a group of Lancaster fur traders, the most prominent of whom was Joseph Simon, and after 1768, this interrelated group of Jewish merchants, who had become Croghan's only mercantile suppliers, formed the Illinois and Ouabache land companies. The Gratzes employed former Fort Pitt commander William Murray as their Kaskaskia manager, and through William Franklin's intervention in London, Murray received permission to acquire two land parcels in July 1774 from Illinois natives. The company's stockholders consisted primarily of Lancaster merchants, but also involved the usual Croghan circle of friends and family, which kept Croghan's original ambitions for the Illinois country alive and officially established an English-speaking populace at Kaskaskia.[19]

In London, Trent and Wharton remained convinced their Suffering Traders' colony was about to be created even if the Fort Stanwix Treaty failed, and they, too, worked with Franklin to press for meetings with key government and commercial leaders. The huge Grand Ohio Company, which envisioned much of today's West Virginia and eastern Kentucky as a new colony known as Vandalia, was created from these talks. Vandalia's land would encompass Croghan's 1749 grant, the proposed Indiana grant, and most of the Ohio Company's grant, thereby satisfying hundreds of claimants. After Virginia ended its opposition to the grant a year later, when the company agreed to provide set-asides for the colony's French and Indian War veterans, development of the lands between the Ohio River and Great Lakes, from the Appalachian Mountains to the Mississippi River, seemed certain, regardless of earlier efforts to secure Native American territory.[20]

Unimaginably, in a season so full of turmoil that it inevitably concluded in war, Croghan's prosperity ended abruptly. He had returned from the West in the summer of 1774 with a temporary Indian truce; but with no news from Samuel Wharton, and hobbled by the continued threat of regional Indian unrest, his economic plans stalled. He considered abandoning Croghan Hall and Fort Pitt, renamed Fort Dunmore by Connolly, because he no longer could afford the food and presents demanded by the Indians who camped at his homes. His cheerless mood was compounded when his most important friend, Johnson, died in July the day before the local sheriff brought nearly fifty-one thousand acres of Croghan's New York land to the auction block.

In London, the British government was overwhelmed by competing western land grants and stymied by discord between land companies and Virginia's leaders, who clung to the colony's original charter. The solution was the 1774 Quebec Act, which annexed the territory lying north and west of the Ohio River to the province of Quebec. The act disappointed both the land companies and Virginians, but it succeeded in one critical aspect. Most wealthy Virginia landowners united against British policy for the first time.[21]

The April 1775 battles at Lexington and Concord made moot the Grand Ohio Company's attempts to gain the Crown's recognition as, at least temporarily, no directive emanating from London would carry the weight of law in Virginia. Now in control of its destiny, the colony would not permit the redistribution of its charter lands. Croghan's family and associates recognized Virginia as the only legitimate government in the West and joined him in placing all hope for the recognition of their western land proposals in Williamsburg. Virginia considered its West Augusta District to extend as far north as Fort Pitt, and so, to prove his allegiance to the dominion, Croghan became chair of West Augusta's Committee of Correspondence and hosted its first meeting at Croghan Hall. Pennsylvania responded with the creation of Westmoreland County, which overlapped much of West Augusta, including Fort Pitt. As the partisan division between the colonies intensified, extremists in each province accused Croghan not only of favoring the other government, but also of favoring the Indians and England above either. When the American Revolution erupted, Croghan was warned by British associates to abandon Fort Pitt or face arrest.[22]

Croghan's associations with Dunmore, Johnson, and Pennsylvania traders tarnished his reputation in Virginia, but it was his connections to land schemes that ruined him at the outbreak of the rebellion. He lived in obscurity and poverty at the end of his life, southwest of Philadelphia, at Passyunk. The Gratzes saved him from debtors' prison, and they accompanied him to Williamsburg in November 1779 to plead for recognition of his land titles. They were refused. After he sold and mortgaged most of his properties for Susanna's inheritance, Croghan became reclusive. "Pray, how is the old gentleman," nephew William Croghan wrote Barnard Gratz from Charleston, and Susanna Prevost forwarded £60 in the last known correspondence between father and daughter. "I have, my honoured parent, for a long time past been entirely ignerant in what place you had fixed your residence. . . . We are distressed beyond expression at the painful incertitude we are in on your account."[23]

Croghan Hall, once thought to be the "oldest and probably the largest [estate] in the Pittsburgh area, perhaps the most impressive west of the Alleghenies" was mortgaged to Joseph Simon. When creditors sacked the house in search of goods to serve as payment, they reported "one old axe, one old spade, one pitch fork, one small box of iron and old lanthorn and no more" as their reward. In his final correspondence with longtime friend Thomas Wharton, Croghan appeared at last to be resigned. "Heaven gives its blessings & takes away & we must submit."[24]

By his own estimation, the value of Croghan's estate exceeded £140,000. In his will, made on 12 June 1782, he devised twenty thousand acres to friends and family, with virtually everything else left to his "beloved daughter, Susanna, wife of Augustin Prevost." Croghan died 31 August 1782 at his Passyunk house, in possession of personal property that included an "antediluvian" carriage, but no horse, one old pinchbeck watch, a pair of buckles, ten pewter plates, and six silver spoons. Aside from the clothes in which he was buried, Croghan owned two pairs of stockings, five shirts, and a pair of breeches. His gardener brought the body to

Philadelphia, where the Christ Church sexton recorded his burial at St. Peter's graveyard, and it was here that his contributions to the expansion of British interests in North America lay virtually unrecognized for nearly two centuries.[25]

The validity of Croghan's Indiana Company and 1749 Iroquois land grants was under consideration by a congressional committee at the time of his death. Each soon was endorsed as bona fide and valid. Unfortunately for William Croghan and many others who had bought parcels of Croghan's property, most of it was held by the courts to offset debts. The Gratz brothers succeeded in keeping some acreage south of Fort Pitt, but Croghan's most cherished Otsego Lake property, meant for Susanna, was won by Andrew Craig and William Cooper. In the suit that followed, Cooper hired Alexander Hamilton to represent their interests, and Augustin Prevost hired Aaron Burr to represent Susanna's. Hamilton won, and Cooperstown, New York, today sits on the site of George Croghan's Forest.[26]

Part 2

Rise Up!

3

George Rogers Clark

Nature's Favorite

> O my dear honeys, heaven is a Kentucky of a place!
> —Isaac Reed, *The Christian Traveler,* 1828

The first recorded reference to the redheaded adolescent's presence at Fort Pitt comes from Baptist minister David Jones, who had enjoyed George Croghan's hospitality before he began an exploration of the Ohio River in 1772. Having dined with Croghan and received a bearskin, belt of wampum, and sixty pounds of biscuit for his journey, Jones left the fort "9 June in the company of George Rogers Clark, a young gentleman from Virginia, who, with others, inclined to make a tour of this new world." The group returned to Fort Pitt on 22 July, when Jones noted they "conversed with several principal Indians of different nations," before he returned home in August."[1]

Clark heard descriptions of the Illinois country here, in the company of Croghan, Murray, McKee, and others who first had seen the West when he was a child. Born in Albemarle County, Virginia, 19 November 1752, George Rogers Clark was the second son of second cousins John Clark and Ann Rogers. At the time of his birth, the family lived near the Rivanna River on a 410-acre tract near the Virginia frontier, about two miles east of the future Charlottesville. It is unlikely the Clark children had memories of this farm or its neighbors, the Jeffersons, because the family moved to the safety of Caroline County in the early years of the French and Indian War.[2]

Named for his mother's brother, Clark endured a brief formal education after he and older brother, Jonathan, moved to their maternal grandfather's

George Rogers Clark by John Buxton. Courtesy of John Buxton.

home in 1763. Jonathan soon was enrolled in the nearby school run by his Scottish uncle, Donald Robertson, and George Rogers followed in September 1766. He remained among the student body, which included James Madison, until May 1767, when he opted to conclude his school days at the age of fourteen. With Robertson in full agreement, Clark spent more time with his grandfather, learning the principles of surveying, before he decided to strike out on his own. He roamed the Blue Ridge, frequently visiting relatives, but was drawn west, where he moved among the itinerant population who looked to Fort Pitt for security. While his youth could have hindered his ability to survive, he was fortunate in his intelligence and preparation, and in addition to natural abilities recognized by his contemporaries, Clark benefited from the long-established relationships enjoyed by his family with Virginia planters—an advantage few western pioneers knew.[3]

He returned to Caroline County shortly after his adventure, but traveled back to the Ohio River in the autumn, this time with his father and neighborhood friend James Higgins. When the elder Clark turned for home, Clark and Higgins remained to build a cabin near Fish Creek in Virginia's West Augusta District, some forty miles from the nearest settlement. They farmed the land, producing a fine corn crop, as Clark ran surveys for area settlers and became well acquainted with the plentiful regional characters whose ambitions centered on the acquisition of land across the Ohio.[4]

Governor Dunmore had come to the frontier with a vastly different background than that known to most of the king's rural American subjects, but his interest in the acquisition of land was as keen as theirs. By the time of his Fort Pitt conference with George Croghan, Dunmore was an active speculator who veered publicly from the British policy that denied western land claims. He used his authority, if not the law, to send Thomas Bullitt to the Falls of the Ohio to survey for French and Indian War officers later that year, and Bullitt's first and most valuable survey grant was awarded to new Fort Pitt commander, John Connolly, who had served as a surgeon's mate in the recent war.[5]

Connolly's two-thousand-acre patent lay between those of Edward Ward and Charles DeWarrensdorff, and comprised most of today's downtown Louisville, Kentucky. After he appealed to former Croghan employee John Campbell for help in acquiring DeWarrensdorff's patent, Connolly reached an agreement in which he and Campbell purchased DeWarrensdorff's land and shared ownership of Connolly's original grant. From Lancaster, Joseph Simon joined the partnership when he supplied cash for the development of the combined grant lands. William Preston, who supervised the Kentucky territory's surveying activities, refused to enter most of Bullitt's surveys because they had not been made by his appointed deputies and lay beyond the settlement line. He retained the patents claimed by Connolly and Campbell, however, who already were advertising the sale of lots at the Falls, where they expected to establish a town that would in a "short Time be equaled by few inland Places on the American Continent."[6]

In violation of British law, the Ohio River valley experienced a land rush in the spring of 1774. Connolly and Simon soon were in negotiations with Dunmore to build a fort on the Ohio at Wheeling Creek; with Pittsburgh, Wheeling, and the Falls under their military and financial management, and through their connections to stockholders in the Illinois and Indiana land companies, the men envisioned their holdings extending to the Mississippi River. Patrick Henry, who attended a meeting between Dunmore and Connolly that year, later wrote that the British governor was obsessed with land acquisition, and would favor an Indian war to achieve his objective of driving natives from a piece of land he coveted. By that time, however, Henry's poor opinion of Virginia's governor was understood, as was Dunmore's estimation of Henry.[7]

The colony's legislature had formed a committee of correspondence in the spring of 1774 to communicate concerns connected to the Intolerable Acts, and they planned a day of fasts and prayers to demonstrate their objections. Outraged, Dunmore dissolved the House, which prompted "patriot" legislators to move to Richmond the first week of August to select delegates for the Second Virginia Convention. Scheduled to meet the following March, the convention would be dumbfounded when Patrick Henry concluded a thunderous speech with the plea, "Give me liberty, or give me death!"

Dunmore now wrestled with two objectives: he and his son hoped to secure enormous wealth through the acquisition of key western lands, and simultaneously, he had to put down the political unrest that threatened to erupt in open rebellion against his government. A military victory far from the center of population would remind Virginians of the necessity for British law and it would cost the Tidewater townspeople and Piedmont farmers nothing. Most importantly, it could conclude in an arrangement that would give Dunmore everything he wanted. Whether or not Henry's identification of the impetus for the campaign that is known as Dunmore's War was legitimate, it soon made no difference. At this moment, the inevitable firestorm between native and European-American peoples erupted along the Appalachian boundary that had been created to separate the antagonists, and the explosion was more violent and long-lasting than any skirmish Dunmore or Henry could have imagined.

South of the great Ohio River artery that was the focus of talks between Williamsburg and London, Daniel Boone had begun a journey to

Kentucky in September 1773. Boone's group of forty or so people were part of the first attempt to establish a colonial trans-Appalachian settlement in the Kentucky territory. As was usual with Boone, no permission had been sought or given before he left the Yadkin Valley of North Carolina to lead the party through Cherokee land and into Shawnee hunting grounds. His partner in the venture was Captain William Russell of Castle's Wood, Virginia, who planned to join Boone in a matter of days with additional men, horses, and supplies. When he realized his stock would run out before Russell's arrival, Boone sent his sixteen-year-old son, James, brothers John and Richard Mendinall, and the son of a fellow pioneer named Drake back to Russell's compound for additional provisions. Boone, meanwhile, slowly traveled on with his cumbersome convoy. Supplemented with fresh supplies and accompanied by two enslaved backwoodsmen named Charles and Adam, and Russell's son, Henry, and local sharpshooter, Isaac Crabtree, James Boone returned to the trail on 9 October and camped that evening at Wallen's Creek, three miles behind his father and a few miles ahead of William Russell. The small party was oblivious to the presence of fifteen Delaware, two Cherokee, and two Shawnee men who watched from the dark of the woods.

The Mendinall boys were the first to die, each taking a direct shot. Charles stood frozen while Adam dashed under a log at the edge of the camp. James Boone and Henry Russell were shot and on the ground, but alive and conscious, and the others, wounded, ran into the woods. Adam heard James call to Big Jim, a Cherokee man he and his father had known from earlier hunting trips, but rather than coming to the aid of the boys, the Cherokee and other men began stabbing the incapacitated victims before pulling out their finger and toe nails. James pleaded for his life, called for his mother, then begged to die, according to Adam, before other natives, having rounded up the animals young Boone had brought from Castle's Wood, called the tormenters away. Each boy received a death blow to the head before the raiders grabbed Charles and rode out of the camp, leaving only Adam to tell others what had happened. After Russell and Boone located and buried the bodies of their sons and the Mendinalls, they discovered the grisly remains of Drake's son and Charles. Adam wandered the forest for eleven days before he was rescued.[8]

Boone's tragic 1773 expedition ended abruptly when the survivors returned to safety east of the mountains. Dunmore called on the Cherokee chiefs with whom he treated to punish the offenders, but continued to have valuable land staked west of the mountains even as he spoke. Meanwhile, Crabtree, Russell, and others carried on successive raids of revenge after the October killings, which incited natives as far away as the Fort Pitt area.[9]

Yellow Creek flows into the west bank of the Ohio River four hundred or so miles north of Castle's Wood. It was here that Daniel Greathouse appeared with about twenty armed men after an area innkeeper, having been warned of approaching Indians in the spring of 1774, asked local settlers for help. When a small group of Mingos arrived for a day of drinking, Greathouse's men killed and scalped them, sparing only a young child. A pregnant woman in the party, said to be the wife of frontiersman John Gibson and sister of Cayuga chief Logan, was selected for particularly cruel treatment, forced to endure a fatal slashing and become a witness to her unborn child's murder as she lay dying near the river. Logan, who now lived among the Mingos, blamed Captain Michael Cresap and other Virginians for the murders and led a coalition of his warriors and area Shawnees in a series of attacks from Pittsburgh to Kentucky. The raids resulted in the sudden cessation of the sale of Connolly's Ohio River valley parcels and the initiation of the war (truly, more a campaign) Dunmore wanted.[10]

Clark and Michael Cresap were among dozens of frontiersmen to whom Dunmore issued military commissions in the name of George III, marking Clark's short career as a king's man. The 2 May 1774 appointment made by Lt. Col. Charles Lewis authorized the twenty-one-year-old Clark to serve as a captain in the Virginia militia, with duties that included the provision of arms and ammunition to his soldiers and obedience to orders issued by the governor. Far from Williamsburg, and with little talk of revolt yet on the minds of backwoodsmen, the private motivations of Dunmore's soldiers must have mirrored the governor's to some degree, which suggests that the action was less about defense than the control of western land. Dunmore, however, normally sheltered in Williamsburg's Governor's Palace, had little to fear from the natives, but his soldiers fought for their futures against men who lived among them, and each side was prepared to die to prevent the other's success.[11]

Within the year, Dunmore and British authority would be held in contempt throughout Virginia, and the colony's militia would drive the governor to the safety of a royal navy ship and, ultimately, New York. But, still secure on 24 July and eyeing a financial coup, Dunmore ordered forts built at the mouths of Wheeling Creek and the Kanawha River, and directed Shawnee villages to be raided through late summer. He planned to lead Major John Connolly's Fort Pitt regiments to the Scioto River, while Colonel Andrew Lewis would command a second thousand-man unit from the Greenbrier Valley to the Scioto by way of the Ohio. Once united, Dunmore would take charge of the full army in a combined attack on the Shawnee village at Chillicothe.[12]

The governor sent an advance guard down the Ohio as far as the newly constructed Fort Fincastle at Wheeling Creek, and led his remaining five-hundred-man force, including Clark, along the eastern bank of the river. The advance unit came under fire almost immediately, with the loss of four men before it joined Dunmore at Fincastle on 30 September, en route to the Scioto. Meanwhile, Lewis's army rested on 6 October at a place known as Point Pleasant, near the mouth of the Kanawha River. Three nights later, nearly a thousand Shawnee, Mingo, Wyandot, Ottawa, and Delaware warriors, led by Shawnee chief Hokoleskwa (loosely translated as "Cornstalk"), slipped silently across the Ohio to stage a dawn attack. Lewis lost more than sixty men in the 10 October fight, including his brother, Charles, with scores wounded; Indian losses included Pucksinwah, Tecumseh's father. The fighting was fierce, and through it all, Cornstalk could be heard encouraging his warriors to be strong. When it was over, the Virginians had held their ground and the natives silently withdrew into the woods.[13]

Nine days passed before Cornstalk realized Dunmore meant to attack the Shawnee families at Chillicothe, which forced him to sue for peace. Made to give up their ancient hunting rights in Kentucky, the Shawnees agreed through the Treaty of Camp Charlotte to relinquish forever their claims to land south and east of the Ohio River. Chief Logan refused to attend the negotiations. John Gibson, sent to encourage his participation, returned only with a declaration said to have been made by Logan, and later repeated by Jefferson.[14]

> I appeal to any white man to say if ever he entered Logan's cabin hungry, and he gave him not meat; if ever he came cold and naked, and he clothed him not. . . . Such was my love for the whites, that my countrymen pointed as they passed, and said, Logan is the

> friend of white men. . . . Col. Cresap . . . in cold blood and unprovoked, murdered all the relations of Logan, not sparing even my women and children. There runs not a drop of my blood in the veins of any living creature. Who is there to mourn for Logan? Not one.[15]

Two wars later, Dr. Samuel Brown, brother of future Kentucky senator John Brown, was asked by Thomas Jefferson to urge George Rogers Clark to write his own summary of the events that led to Dunmore's War. Jefferson had accepted Logan's point of view and blamed Cresap for the murders in his book, *Notes on the state of Virginia,* and consequently, his political opponents and Cresap's family were critical of the work. Clark's immediate response would defend Jefferson's error in naming Cresap, but correctly identify the culprit. "The conduct of Cresap I am perfectly acquainted with, he was not the Author of that murder, but a Family of the Name of Greathouse—But some Transactions that happened under the conduct of Captn. Cresap a few Days previous to the Murder of Logan's Family gave him sufficient Ground to suppose that it was Cresap who had done him the Injury." Jefferson published an *Appendix* to his original *Notes* in 1800, but failed to amend his initial version of the events that took place at Yellow Creek, although Clark's letter survives among his papers.[16]

Clark returned to Grave Creek after Point Pleasant, where he remained active in West Augusta affairs and was appointed county justice in 1775. He and David Rogers, William Harrod, and Hancock Lee were among the western men who volunteered to lead a campaign against Detroit after they heard of the battles at Lexington and Concord, but, with a year to pass before Virginia fully mobilized its military forces, these hungry young men began another adventure in the interim. Clark left the area for Kentucky late in the spring, informing Jonathan he had been appointed deputy surveyor for the Ohio Company under Hancock Lee for "ye priviledge of Taking what Lands I want." The West Augusta men had tabled Detroit in favor of opportunity.[17]

From Wheeling, Clark traveled with Nicholas Cresswell, an Englishman hired by London investors to examine land options in the Illinois country. On opposite sides of the rising political divide, the party nevertheless found subjects of common interest as they spent three weeks studying ancient mounds, various plant species, and the "Elephant Bone" lick specimens found along the Ohio River. Cresswell's 7 May journal entry recorded, "This morning Captn. Clark (whom I find is an intelligent man), showed me a root that the Indians call pocoon, good for the bite of a Rattle Snake," and after Clark left the group to meet Lee, a cryptic journal note suggested his traveling companion's spirited nature already was known on the frontier. Clark surveyed in the Leesburg area of the Kentucky River throughout the autumn and associated with settlers at Harrodsburg and other stations before he returned to his parents' home for the winter.[18]

Meanwhile, in Philadelphia, the second Continental Congress agreed to a declaration of independence from British authority on 2 July 1776 and announced the decision two days later. The organization of military and civil institutions became the immediate focus of Congress's work, which resulted in the geographic division of territory from the Atlantic to the Mississippi into three districts. George Morgan, as manager of the Middle District, went about the work of planning the American occupation of the first Northwest of the "United Colonies." In the belief that the area's French settlers would support the Americans against the British, he encouraged Congress to look further west and form an alliance with Spain, who owned the land beyond the Mississippi River. Congress delayed action, but Morgan and Patrick Henry, who was inaugurated as Virginia's first "Patriot" governor on 29 June, proceeded and initiated a series of events that made the Revolution in the West possible. Their plan closely resembled the strategy proposed more than a decade earlier by Illinois Company directors, Benjamin and William Franklin, George Croghan, and Morgan himself.[19]

Fifteen years later, George Rogers Clark would write that his 1776 decision to challenge the Virginia Convention to recognize its claim to Kentucky was made only as a result of settlers' pleas for protection. His initial thinking evolved, however, and he soon believed that if the convention were unwilling to protect its western population, Kentucky should "establish an Independent Government, and by giving away a great part of the Lands, and disposing of the Remainder . . . we could not only gain great numbers of Inhabitants but in good measure protect them." He had come to the conclusion that the protection of trans-Appalachian settlers was more important than the claims of any one state, and had decided to forgo temporarily the pursuit of personal wealth in favor of ensuring the safety of these settlers. "The whole of my time . . . was devoted to reflecting upon things in general: particularly whether or not it accorded with the interest of the United States to support Kentucky. This led me to . . . lay aside every private view and engage seriously in the war, having the interest and the welfare of the public my only concern until the fate of the continent could be known."[20]

He later wrote that it had not crossed his mind that he and John Gabriel Jones would represent Kentucky at Virginia's fifth, and last, revolutionary convention, when he announced a general meeting for 6 June 1776 in Harrodsburg. Arriving late to the meeting, he found "the people had been in some confusion" as to the purpose of the gathering, and had determined in his absence to elect delegates to go to Williamsburg as their representatives, thereby formally connecting Kentucky's Harrodsburg settlement to Virginia's new government. Clark and Jones accepted their charge, and after a harrowing trip across the mountains, arrived too late in Williamsburg to attend the convention, which had approved an independent constitution before it inaugurated Patrick Henry. Unperturbed, Clark rode on to Scotchtown, home of the ailing governor, whom he knew as his family lawyer, and it was there he pressed his challenge on the subjects of Kentucky's defense and its future. Henry consequently offered support for Clark's request of five hundred pounds of gunpowder for use in the district.[21]

The governor forwarded his decision to Virginia's executive council, who, Clark wrote, "agreed to furnish the supply but as we [Kentucky] ware a detached people not yet united to the state of Virginia . . . they could only lend us the amunation as to Frends in distress." After the council stipulated that Clark assume responsibility for the powder's transportation, he declined the offer, "informing them that I had weighed the Matter and found that it was out of my power to convey those stores at my own Expence such a distance through an Enemies Cuntrey [and] that I was sorry to find that we should have to seek protection else whare which I did not doubt of getting [and] that if a Cuntrey was not worth protecting it was not worth Claiming &c &c." In other words, if Virginia were not prepared to defend Kentucky, another government might be willing to do so.[22]

Clark's audacious response initiated a meeting of the minds among the executive council, and the creation of Kentucky County, effective 31 December 1776, is viewed as his achievement. Insiders, however, understood

Virginia's claim to Kentucky was about something more than protection. British treaties and land grants had been annulled by the Revolution, and in the vacuum that replaced British authority, Virginia's prosperous planters, who constituted much of its legislative assembly, along with some of its more radical western representatives, sought to establish a western empire. The new assembly members, however, realized that their goals would be achieved only if they could eliminate Native American land claims beyond the Appalachians, and their decision represented a critical turning point in a newly declared nation that had not yet codified its laws. There is no evidence that Virginia's legislators were committed to a Detroit campaign in 1776, or through most of 1777, although Henry, at least, entertained the possibility. The assembly nevertheless conflated its legislative responsibility and personal welfare, and determined to have the flag of Virginia planted on the eastern bank of the Mississippi River before young Clark was invited into the larger conversation. Because his proposal answered many needs, it was accepted. As for Clark, he agreed to Virginia's support without questioning the motivations of his employers, because he, not Henry, knew the terror of the West.[23]

Patrick Henry, already a western diplomat before Clark appeared, began an international dialogue three weeks after he became governor. Now, on his 23 August 1776 orders, George Gibson, a newly commissioned captain in the First Virginia Regiment, started down the Ohio River with Lieutenant William Linn and a company of former West Augusta militiamen disguised as traders. The company, facetiously known as "Gibson's Lambs," were camp brawlers who were considered better suited to the wilderness than to Williamsburg and were well matched for the dangerous mission. Gibson carried a letter from Henry to Spanish governor Don Luis de Unzaga y Amezega requesting that Spain allow former Pennsylvania merchant Oliver Pollock to furnish American troops with ten thousand pounds of gunpowder. Henry wisely added that the Americans were prepared to attack British outposts in West Florida in exchange for the gunpowder. Although Spain had adopted a neutral policy regarding the Revolution, Unzaga had been alerted to the mission and was ordered to receive Gibson cordially. By agreement, in a move designed to placate British forces in Florida, Unzaga temporarily jailed Gibson while Linn and the remaining company secretly loaded the gunpowder and left New Orleans under the protection of the flag of Spain.[24]

After wintering at Arkansas Post, Linn arrived at the mouth of the Ohio on 3 March 1777, presumably to deliver goods to Illinois traders, but in reality, to exchange information with Thomas Bentley, a Kaskaskia merchant who would become critical to Virginia's later success there. Linn continued up the Ohio with the ammunition Clark would need to mount an American defense of the frontier, around the Falls of the Ohio and on to forts Fincastle and, finally, Pitt. Clark implied in his *Memoir* that he had seen the value of an "understanding" between Spain and Virginia independently of Henry's private correspondence, but the extent of his early knowledge, if any, of Gibson's mission is unknown.[25]

Before Henry's diplomacy delivered any relief to Kentucky, Clark and the clusters of settlers who survived there spent much of 1777 fighting for their lives. Clark had received his commission as a major in the Virginia militia on 5 March and, at twenty-four years old, officially assumed charge of Kentucky's defense. He confirmed Simon Kenton, Michael Stoner, and other rugged frontiersmen as his scouts (spies), and appointed Daniel Boone, James Harrod, Benjamin Logan, and John Todd—the most respected men in the West, and each Clark's elder—as his captains. "From this period we may date the commencement of that Blody war in Kentucky that have continued ever since with savage fury," Clark would recall. "On a moderate calculation, upwards of two thousand souls have perished on our soil." His diary entries were specific and haunting: "24 Ap 1777: 40 or 50 Indians attacked Boonesborough, killed and scalped Danl Goodman, wounded Capt Boone, Capt Todd, Mr Hite and M. Stoner," and "22 June 1777: Ben Linn & Saml Moore arr[ived] from Illenois. Barney Stagner senr. Killed and beheaded." Linn and Moore were two of his scouts, and had returned with affirmation of support on the Mississippi. When he again left Harrodsburg for Williamsburg on 1 October 1777, the fort's inhabitants apparently believed Clark might not return. "I left them with Reluctance," he later wrote, "promising that I would certainly Return to their assistance, which I had predetermined."[26]

Fueled by his knowledge of British Detroit's organization of Kentucky Indian raids, Clark improvised a proposal for the military invasion of Britain's western territory, but it was not until 10 December that he approached

Henry with the plan. As he mixed among Williamsburg's society, he first weighed the Tidewater's political climate before steeling himself to make the proposition to the governor. Afterward, Henry held private meetings with men who questioned the proposed campaign's possibilities of success, and, when he assured them that Clark intended to cross the Mississippi to seek protection in New Spain should things go awry, "the Expedition was resolved on."[27]

In proposing Kaskaskia as his expedition's first target, Clark planned to execute an end run around Ohio warriors in order to stage a backdoor attack at Detroit. The strikes on Kentucky's settlers were led primarily by the Ohio country's Shawnees, Mingos, and Delawares, who had looked to Detroit for support since Virginia militias had taken control of Fort Pitt. Conversely, the Illinois natives, as witnessed by a Piankeshaw gift soon to be made to Clark, disliked the British and generally were willing to become Virginia allies because they had experienced very little interaction with settlers. Had a successful 1779 Detroit siege occurred, Clark presumably would have mounted an Ohio attack in conjunction with troops from Fort Pitt, and squeezed the native Ohio Confederacy into capitulation.

When it was all over, Clark would write a long letter to George Mason summarizing the events connected to the Illinois Expedition and, in the flush of victory, remember the circumstances of the expedition's beginnings somewhat differently than he would recall a dozen years later. "I immediately Resolved to encourage an Expedition to the Illinois. However, to make it publick was a certain loss of it. I propos'd the plan to a few Gentlemen, they communicated it to the Governour. It was immediately determined on . . . though but a few in the House knew the real intent of it." Mason, Virginia's strongest charter advocate, would have been among the few who knew, as his position within the government was prominent and his relationship with Clark close. "Continue to favor me with your valuable Lessons," Clark wrote him. "Continue your Reprimands as though I was your Son. . . . Think not that any promotion or confer'd Honour will occation any unnecessary pride in me."[28]

Jefferson later corroborated Clark's role in the plan. "It was an idea of his own, & he came down from his native county to propose to Govr Henry to raise volunteers himself and undertake the reduction of the Illinois post." Clark accepted command of the newly created Illinois Regiment after a committee appointed by Henry and composed of George Wythe, Mason, and Jefferson promised Virginia's compensation. He was commissioned a lieutenant colonel in the Virginia militia and,

> After being engaged, I was then as Determined to prosecute it with Vigour, as I was before indifferent about the Command. I had since the begining of the War taken pains to make myself acquainted with the true situation of the British posts on the Fronteers; and since find that I was not mistaken in my judgment. I was ordered to attact the Illinois, in case of Success to carry my Arms to any Quarter I pleased. I was certain that with five hundred Men I could take the Illinois, and by my treating the Inhabitants as fellow Citizens, and shew them that I ment to protect rather than treat them as a Conquered People. Engageing the Indians to our Interest &c, It might probably have so great an effect on their Countrymen at Detroyet, (they already disliked their Master) that it would be an easy prey for me.[29]

Ironically, the financial fates of George Croghan, the French and Indian War traders, and everyone who had purchased or received land as payment from Croghan hung in the balance when George Rogers Clark first approached the Virginia Executive Council. The Indiana Company's leaders had given up hope of the enormous Vandalia colony, so they employed Trent, Morgan, Smallman, and John Gibson as commissioners to carry out the company's original grant distributions and hoped to begin selling land for fifty dollars per 100 acres as early as 1777. Patrick Henry had recognized the Indiana Company shortly after he became governor and approved its sale of land south of Fort Pitt, but Virginia's assembly overrode the governor and banned the company's distribution of the "back lands of Virginia on both sides of the Ohio." When the commissioners received word of the decision and understood Virginia's western designs, they again appealed to the assembly in October 1776 for approval of the original land grant. With their futures now in their own hands, Virginia's legislators opted not to give up control of the West, and denied the company's land grant.[30]

Had the assembly chosen to recognize the Indiana Company, Virginia would have relinquished responsibility for the Kentucky settlers who lived within and beyond the grant land, and Kentuckians would have been free to create an independent government or attach themselves to any other government that sought the connection, as Clark warned. With Virginia's recognition of Kentucky as its territory came the abolition of colonial land companies within its (royal) charter and the financial ruin of Pennsylvania traders who had been teased with the possibility of reparations for more than a decade.

4

William Croghan

Immigrant

> Victory or Death.
> —George Washington, 25 December 1776

George Croghan's nephew would have a war unlike Clark's in nearly every way. William Croghan's Revolution was the one of schoolbooks, populated with the famous names and places known to every student of American history. Unlike George Rogers Clark, William Croghan knew early on what a soldier's life was and, for reasons that remain obscure, chose independence in North America rather than a career as a British officer.

Born in Ireland in the year of Clark's birth, he probably was the son of Nicholas Croghan, a Dublin merchant, and his wife, Ann, whose maiden name was likely to have been Heron. The Croghans originally hailed from County Roscommon, and had been landowners and members of the Irish Anglican Church for generations. The family began to appear in the records of Dublin's St. Nicholas Without Parish early in the eighteenth century, along with those of relatives, Smallman, Heron, and Clarke.[1]

The British Sixteenth Regiment of Foot was stationed in Dublin in the 1740s until it embarked for New York in 1767. Once there, a portion of the unit traveled to Albany, where the unit staffed forts in the lakes Champlain and George area for two years before it rejoined the full regiment in British West Florida, on the lower Mississippi River. There is no conclusive proof of William Croghan's association with the regiment, but the army's departure from New York coincides with his employment by Albany merchants who were well-known to George Croghan and supports William Croghan Jr.'s later declaration that his father had been in

William Croghan miniature. Unknown artist.

service to the British army before the Revolution. Croghan's presence in New York by this time is further confirmed through George Croghan's brother, Nicholas, who concluded a 1769 letter to George, expressing gratitude "for the many feavours you have Conferid on my Son Wm. Your goodness in Setling him wth. Messrs. Thos. & John Shipboy Merchants in New York to Learn trade & Commerce." However it came about, William Croghan arrived in North America educated well enough to manage correspondences and keep regular books for his employers at a young age. He became a man who was successful by every measure and who would die in his roomy home near Louisville, far from Dublin, surrounded by a large family. But first, he had to survive the American Revolution as an officer under the command of George Washington.[2]

Young Croghan purchased a large tract of land on the Ohio River, just beyond Fort Pitt, from his uncle in February 1776. He lived there only a short time, making modest improvements before the Revolution began, and left for war with the assumption that his future lay in the fine parcel. He had been in the Fort Pitt area a few years, and, for a portion of that time at least, he lived with and worked for a farmer named James Innes.

Innes would administer George Croghan's 1782 will, and when he drafted his own will in 1791, he used the opportunity to settle old scores with William, who apparently left an unpaid loan when he started for war. "Whereas a William Croghan whom in the year 1771 I rescued from beggary, drunkenness, and contempt and took under my protection and patronage and in the 1776 presented a captaincy in the 8th Virginia Regiment, and who if anything is solely indebted to me for it has by every fraudful artifice, base insidious practice and circumventive plausibility, obtained from me a bond."[3]

Unlike his colorful uncle, William Croghan's character is laudable in every other known document. Innes lived in that part of Pennsylvania claimed by Virginia, and after Dunmore appointed George Croghan and various family members to the West Augusta Virginia Court, it is difficult to understand the circumstances in which Innes's influence would have been greater than George Croghan's in securing a Virginia captaincy for William. Regardless of its origin, William Croghan's company initially was composed of 147 Fort Pitt–area men who primarily were Irish Protestants, despite their designation as the Tenth Company of the Eighth Virginia, known as the German Regiment of the state's Continental Line. He received his officer's commission on 19 April 1776, but his company temporarily was reassigned to the First Virginia Regiment and left Williamsburg on 17 August to begin a march north to Fort Lee, New Jersey. The company crossed the Hudson River to newly constructed Fort Washington about 15 September, just as Washington's army, nineteen thousand men strong, was digging in to form a defense against the Hessian forces British general William Howe had sent as an advance unit.[4]

The battle for New York had begun nearly three weeks earlier, in Brooklyn, where Howe's land troops trapped Washington's army, their backs pushed to the East River. An American survivor later wrote that "dread and awful expectation" failed to capture the horror of the rebels' experience in the struggle for Long Island, much of it sensed even before the fighting began. Howe's twenty-five thousand soldiers, many of whom were Hessians and Highlanders, were experienced professionals who were, on average, five years older than were the farmers and storekeepers who constituted the Continental Army, and the rebel forces were keenly aware of their odds. Howe had additional support from his brother, Admiral Richard Howe, anchored in New York harbor with twelve hundred guns and ten thousand seamen. By day's end on 27 August, the Americans had absorbed an appalling defeat and survived complete collapse only with help from the weather and Washington's unwavering nerve. Described by some who experienced it as the worst of their memories, a thunderstorm began the day after the battle and continued into the night. Washington, who knew Howe would have nothing to gain by exposing his troops to the inclement weather, engineered an escape by confiscating moored East River boats to evacuate his army in the dead of night. By dawn on 29 August, his army was in Manhattan, falling into their first sleep in at least three days.

Congress had decided to change the name of its fledgling government from that of the United Colonies to the United States on 9 September, but its military commander was too busy to register the modification immediately. Howe left Long Island to invade Manhattan on 13 September, sending a Hessian force to the cliffs of the Hudson River to soften the enemy with an attack on Fort Washington, while he marched his troops from Kip's Bay to a Broadway camp. Washington had ordered his army north, from his Battery headquarters to the Heights, days earlier, and, although the Hessians temporarily fell back 16 September, he understood the next attack would come from the full British force.

Captain William Croghan's American Revolution began the day his company joined the Continental Army at Fort Washington, and his first orders were to put his men to work to create defenses in preparation for Howe's attack. The tenth company remained in place only long enough to appear on one hectically gathered muster on 30 September as the Virginians were among the two thousand Americans who rode north with Washington on 14 October to escape Manhattan, leaving Nathanael Greene to hold the fort "as long as possible." After a fight at White Plains that was effective only because it succeeded in convincing Washington to give up New York City, Howe returned Hessian commander Wilhelm von Knyphausen south to capture the fort and take three thousand prisoners on 16 November. By choosing to capture the fort, Howe again allowed Washington to escape, this time to Fort Lee, which Washington found recently abandoned; indeed, breakfasts remained on the fires. With a British company close behind them, William Croghan and the Continental Army crawled into Newark on the twenty-second in miserable weather and desperately short of food and supplies,. "The sufferings we endured are beyond description," one soldier later recalled. "No tent to cover us at night—exposed to cold and rains day and night." Acutely aware that their campaign to date was one of retreat, Washington aide Samuel Webb wrote, "I can only say that no lads ever showed greater activity in retreating than we have." New Virginia recruit James Monroe first saw Washington during this twenty-five-mile, rain-drenched retreat. "I saw him . . . at the head of a small band, or rather in its rear, for he was always near the enemy, and his countenance and manner made an impression on me which I can never efface." Washington's ill-advised Long Island offensive resulted in the loss of New York City for the rest of the American Revolution, which ensured the safe transportation of British supplies and secured the Crown's colonial headquarters through 1783.[5]

The Earl Charles Cornwallis, an aristocratic general whose love for his army equaled that which his soldiers held for him, was in North America as Howe's second-in-command. Ironically, Lord Cornwallis had voted against Parliament's implementation of the 1765 Stamp Act, but his lifelong training as an officer now placed him at odds with the colonists he once defended. It was Cornwallis who watched Washington steal deeper into New Jersey, toward Brunswick, and who shadowed him across the frozen November fields, hoping to trap the Continentals into surrender. The two generals, one trained to be a land surveyor, would confront one another regularly for the next five years, before the bitter struggle was concluded in one of the most unanticipated military outcomes of the eighteenth century.[6]

The Americans reached Brunswick on 29 November, where Washington had to decide where to winter his army without advice from his own second-in-command, Charles Lee, who remained absent and uncommunicative in Vermont. The commander was cheered by the arrival of William Alexander, Lord Stirling, who providentially brought a thousand new recruits along with him, but with Cornwallis just two hours away, two thousand Maryland and New Jersey militiamen walked away from the war, their terms of enlistment expired and their commitment to revolution exhausted. Howe issued a clemency order for the area's inhabitants on 30 November, reflecting the Crown's aim to protect the peace while Congress and Parliament reached some sort of détente through winter negotiations, and with every indication that the rebellion was about to collapse, he joined Cornwallis at Brunswick, eager to end the thing before Christmas. It was at Brunswick, though, that widespread British plundering, destruction, and rape caused the formerly Loyalist population to reject Howe's clemency and persuaded Washington to make a last stand.[7]

With Howe and Cornwallis at his heels, Washington reached Trenton on 7 December and spent the night moving his army across the Delaware River and into Pennsylvania. Artist Charles Willson Peale, a Pennsylvania volunteer, witnessed the "grand but dreadful" spectacle, and wrote, "The hallooing of hundreds of men in their difficulties getting horses and artillery out of the boats, made it rather the appearance of Hell than any earthly scene." William Croghan had been sent to scout the Elizabethtown area, but rejoined the main body of the army as it crossed the river into Pennsylvania. Once there, his company joined one of the camps spread along a twenty-five-mile stretch on either side of Washington's McKonkey's Ferry headquarters. Howe watched the army cross the river and, satisfied the rebels would stay put until spring, returned to his own comfortable headquarters in Manhattan. He announced the winter pause in fighting on 13 December, the day after Congress and much of Philadelphia had bolted to the comparative safety of Baltimore; but Cornwallis, the better officer, remained uneasy and successfully pressed for Hessian forces to be quartered as far west as Trenton.[8]

Washington was now reduced to a full force, ill and well, of only thirty-four hundred troops, with more than half the army due to return home at year's end. In this forbidding setting, the small camps shrank rapidly, diminished by smallpox, yellow fever, and desertion. A desperate call for recruits was issued, which resulted in a strong show from New England and new support from Pennsylvania and New Jersey militias, and the commander offered ten dollars to every volunteer who would stay beyond his initial commitment. "My brave fellows, you have done all I asked you to do. . . . If you will consent to stay one month longer, you will render that service to the cause of liberty, and to your country, which you can probably never do under any other circumstances."[9]

The additional month Washington begged from his soldiers was the last chance the Americans had to achieve a military victory before Congress surely would have been forced to negotiate a defeated peace, so there was little to lose with a bold plan. Huddled in shivering knots along the river on 23 and 24 December 1776, the soldiers listened as Thomas Paine's newly printed *The American Crisis* was read aloud by the literate among them. "These are the times that try men's souls," they heard. "The summer soldier and the sunshine patriot will, in this crisis, shrink from the service of his Country, but he that stands it now deserves the love and thanks of man and woman."[10]

Settled on the passwords "Victory or Death," Washington began what he knew could be the last military campaign of his life around two in the afternoon on 25 December. In an operation that continued until daybreak the next morning, twenty-four hundred Americans pushed through the ice and crossed the Delaware to march through a snowstorm to Trenton. Two more units with three thousand men were to cross the river at different locations to divert and block the Hessians, but one failed to cross and the other arrived too late to participate in the battle. The weather degenerated all night as rain turned to sleet, and sleet to snow. Two men, maybe three, would freeze to death before their Durham boats returned to Pennsylvania, but the desperate surprise attack gave life to the dying Revolution, and although James Monroe and Washington's nephew were badly wounded, no American perished in the fight. One hundred and six Hessians were killed or wounded, including their commander, Col. Johann Rall, and 918 became prisoners of war.[11]

In reaction, Cornwallis was ordered out of Manhattan and into New Jersey, in order to restaff Trenton and boost troop numbers at Princeton. Croghan's company was among the scouts who trailed him, and it was they who provided Washington with the information he needed to mount one last campaign surprise. Five hundred Americans were left in camp as decoys on the evening of 2 January 1777 while the rest of the army quietly walked away from their smoldering fires to roll through the New Jersey night to stage a dawn attack at Princeton. Popular Brigadier General Hugh Mercer was cut down in the advance guard after being mistaken by the Hessians for Washington, who then rushed to the center of the action as the armies fought head-on. The Americans left the field as victors and quickly retreated to a new camp at Morristown, New Jersey, where Croghan and the rest of the ragged army were inoculated with the smallpox vaccine to stem illness in the ranks. When the Eighth Virginia Regiment returned from Charleston in January, Croghan's company was reassigned to its original regiment under Col. Abraham Bowman, and the captain spent much of the winter and spring scouting the New Jersey countryside. In a welcomed change from the previous year, he received leave to visit friends in Philadelphia during an unexpectedly quiet season of war.[12]

George Washington by C. W. Peale. Courtesy of Yale University Art Gallery.

The Crown grew weary of the prolonged manner in which Howe approached what London considered an isolated rebellion and, in the summer of 1777, ordered two major offensives designed to end the American Revolution. With the assumption that New England was the driving force behind the uprising, "Gentleman Johnny" Burgoyne was to march south from Canada, past Fort Ticonderoga, around Lake George, and onto the Hudson, where Albany would be taken. From Albany, Burgoyne's army would move on to Manhattan, effectively severing the "head" of the rebellion from the remaining colonies. Simultaneously, the largest military flotilla seen in North America set sail in August from Sandy Hook, New Jersey, with the Chesapeake Bay as its destination. When Howe, Cornwallis, and fifteen thousand British and Hessian soldiers came ashore near Elkton, Maryland, universal opinion dictated they would move over the Baltimore-Philadelphia road, cross Brandywine Creek at Chadds Ford, and go on to capture the American Congress, which had returned to Philadelphia. If the British plan worked, Howe would defeat Washington near Philadelphia; failing that, he would push the Americans back to New York, where Burgoyne would attack from the north and squeeze Washington into submission.

Washington was fully aware of Howe's location, so, after he threatened any soldier who marched out of step with thirty-nine lashes, and with Hamilton and Lafayette riding on either side, he paraded his army straight through Philadelphia on 24 August to meet the British commander. His troops, now swollen to twelve thousand men, sported green sprigs to symbolize victory, and were smartened up in fresh uniforms provided by France. William Croghan, who was saddled with his fellow Virginians, understood that the purpose of the occasion was to sway uncommitted onlookers, no matter the outcome of the looming battle.[13]

The foggy dawn of 11 September found Washington and Lafayette pacing the American line, encouraging their men as Anthony Wayne fought hand to hand with von Knyphausen's Hessians. Washington had stretched his troops along Brandywine Creek's eastern bank the evening before, when he massed the largest defense at Chadds Ford, and protected the several natural fords that he assumed Howe might select for smaller crossings. Knyphausen had left camp at 5 a.m. with five thousand men to cross the creek exactly where Washington anticipated, but the American general nevertheless worried that British forces were only partially engaged. As the morning wore on, contradictory scouting information began to flood field headquarters and confuse the commanding officers, who were unaware that Howe and Cornwallis and eighty-two hundred soldiers were at that moment marching north of the American line, approaching the army's right flank from the rear.

Washington finally received word shortly after noon that Howe had been spotted to the north, but, not yet grasping the British battle plan, he repositioned the divisions of Lord Stirling and Adam Stephen, including Croghan's company, to form a northern blockade should the reports prove true. Jonathan Clark, an experienced soldier, and his younger brother, John, who had joined the Continental ranks a month earlier, were among the Virginian officers who fought with Croghan that day. Stirling and Stephen rushed the men to a point beyond Jeffries' Ford, covering three miles in thirty minutes, but after new intelligence indicated Howe was approaching from behind Knyphausen, Washington rescinded the orders. As the American divisions retraced their steps from Jeffries' Ford, Washington realized the latest reports of Howe's presence were false and countermanded his instructions, returning Stirling and Stephen north, this time with John Sullivan's division. The army again raced to defensive positions, but by then there was no question of Howe's location. As they found themselves directly in the path of the British army, the American generals rapidly formed a defensive line, with Stephen's fifteen hundred Virginians holding the right flank, Stirling's division at the center, and Sullivan at the left. Howe, having forced his artillery over seventeen hilly miles through an eight- to nine-hour march, sat down for tea and watched as the equally exhausted American troops fell into position.

The British army broke Sullivan first, followed by Stirling. The Virginians held Sandy Hollow hill and fought Cornwallis's men into the afternoon, when Washington, still on the Brandywine, heard the fire. Now fully focused, he forced a local Quaker farmer at the end of his sword to show him the way to the fight, leading Nathanael Greene's division in a mad, four-mile run through harvest fields to the battle site. Stephen's men were abandoning the hill as Greene's arrived just before 6 p.m., and although Greene was said to have maintained a "noble" rearguard action, the whole Continental force ended the day in a retreat led by the wounded Lafayette and covered by Casimir Pulaski, straggling into Chester after dark, badly shaken and decisively defeated. Or, as Jonathan Clark's compact journal entry summarized, "an action about 5 OClock, our army obliged to give way, and retreated to Chester." The carnage was so great that Howe sent a messenger to American headquarters to remind Washington that dying and wounded soldiers left on the battlefield should be attended to immediately. Greene estimated American losses at twelve to thirteen hundred men; Howe would claim 577 killed and wounded. The Battle of Brandywine Creek was the bloodiest of Washington's command, and when his biographer wrote, "Washington conducted the Brandywine operation as if he had been in a daze," few people could contradict him.[14]

The general's reputation as a leader was about to undergo savage criticism, which led to a season of renewed Loyalist sentiment, but Philadelphia's Dr. Benjamin Rush reserved his harshest comments for Washington's staff. "[Green is] a sycophant to the general, speculative without enterprise. [Sullivan is] weak, vain, without dignity, fond of scribbling, in the field a mad-man. [Stirling is] a proud, vain, lazy, ignorant drunkard. [Stephen] a sordid, boasting, cowardly sot."[15]

Howe's army headed toward Philadelphia, but British major general Charles Grey detoured on 20 September to make an uncharacteristically bloody night raid on Anthony Wayne's troops. Camped near Paoli's Tavern (Malvern, Pennsylvania), the weary men were asleep when Grey's unit charged shortly after 10 p.m. It was over by midnight. Wayne lost 201 men and had 71 captured; Grey reported 4 dead. Wayne traveled with fifteen hundred regulars in his division and another thousand militia troops attached to his unit, so, while his losses were not devastating by the standards of eighteenth-century warfare, the conditions of many of the bodies led both military and civilian witnesses to label the fight a "massacre." The Continental soldiers would remember the events at Paoli's long after the Revolution concluded.[16]

Congress again deserted Philadelphia, this time for York, before the victorious British army descended on the city on 26 September. Cornwallis and a detachment of officers remained in the city through the winter, but the greatest part of the British army camped six miles out of town, at Germantown. From this vantage point, the army provided a buffer between Philadelphia and Washington, whose troops were at loose ends in the fields beyond the city, and created fewer problems among the citizenry.

Largely with Scott's encouragement, Washington and his resilient officers voted to mount a last, year-end attack to "remind the English that an American army still existed," and, as were most of Washington's battle plans, it was a cheeky one. In an attempt to reenact the successful Trenton siege, his army assembled west of Germantown at dusk on 3 October to form four parallel columns that were to march approximately fifteen miles, over four separate roads, to strike the still sleeping British army before dawn. Unlike the attack at Trenton, the flanking militia divisions were seven miles from one another, which made communication impossible. Assigned to Greene's column, Charles Scott's brigade, including the Eighth Virginia Regiment, joined those of George Weedon, Peter Muhlenberg, and William Woodford as they rode in Stephen's division to form Washington's left wing.[17]

The organization took longer than it should have, and the march was stalled at different stages by uneven terrain and darkness. As the sun began to rise across the Delaware River, Washington heard John Sullivan's column fire at Mount Airy, ahead of the targeted attack. Sullivan was successful in creating a British retreat to Benjamin Chew's nearby house, but the fight alerted the British army that an attack had begun. Consequently, when Washington, Knox, and Stirling neared Chew's large home, they fell under heavy attack by the British soldiers who had commandeered it. The response wasted valuable time and cost the lives of fifty-seven soldiers before Washington finally pulled away an hour later to conduct his planned attack.

Now behind schedule, three columns engaged the nine thousand British soldiers at their Germantown camp. The force of the attack lay with Sullivan because the flanking militias had difficulty finding position in the thick wheat fields, and Greene had not yet arrived. When Greene grasped the situation, he suddenly moved so quickly that one regiment lost him, and those who stayed with him were blinded by smoke when they finally reached the fight. Inexplicably, Stephen veered from the column to inspect the commotion at the Chew House and, in a clumsy attempt to reassemble, collided with Wayne's division and initiated a friendly fire skirmish. If the battle plan had not yet fallen apart, the outcome was decided when the entire Ninth Virginia Regiment, which included John Clark, separated from Greene in the confusion and walked into British hands, or as Jonathan Clark characteristically understated, "Something unfortunate happening [our army] was obligated to retreat."

Howe reported 70 killed, 450 wounded, and 15 soldiers captured at the end of the day; Washington, 150 killed, including those at the Chew House, 520 wounded, and 437 captured, nearly all of whom were members of the Ninth Virginia. Stephen afterward was court-martialed and, having been found guilty of intoxication during the battle at Germantown, was dismissed from the service.[18]

It was a loss for the Americans, of course, but a self-inflicted one that could have been avoided, and rather than mourn the setback, the army was elated by elements of its success. Most importantly, French authorities invited American envoys into a small room off the Palace of Versailles' Hall of Mirrors on 17 December 1777, and within its blue-damasked walls, announced that France would recognize America's independence from Britain. The United States had been working since 1775 to convince the king of France to join them, but because of the timing of the announcement, the battles at Brandywine and Germantown are often cited as the proofs France required of American skill. In fact, they *were* Washington's strongest shows of force to date, but if a victory convinced the French, it was Burgoyne's Saratoga defeat at the hands of Horatio Gates and Benedict Arnold that secured the alliance. And so, while William Croghan did not realize it, as he slept in the cold Pennsylvania night in the weeks following Germantown, the Revolution had just turned in America's favor.

5

The Illinois

> The Enemy could not suppose that we should be so mad as to attempt to march 80 Leagues through a Drowned Cuntrey in the Debth of wintor.
> —George Rogers Clark, *Memoir*

Patrick Henry did not yet know about the French alliance when he created "the largest and most complex unit raised by Virginia during the Revolution" for George Rogers Clark. He assigned the unit special militia status for the defense of the Western Department, and issued Clark two sets of instructions on 2 January 1778. The first instructions were meant for public consumption and directed Clark to raise seven militia companies to spend three months in Kentucky for the defense of the district's settlers.[1]

The second instructions were meant for Clark's eyes only, and defined the scope of his authority in the Illinois Territory and Virginia's ambitions as well. He was authorized to raise seven companies of fifty men each for the "Enterprize & with this Force attack the British post at Kaskasky. . . . It is earnestly desired that you shew Humanity to such British Subjects and other persons as fall in your hands. If the white Inhabitants at that Post & the neighbourhood will give undoubted Evidence of their attachment to this State . . . Let them be treated as fellow Citizens & their Persons & property duly secured. . . . But if these people do not accede to these reasonable Demands, they must feel the miseries of War."[2]

Days later, Clark received word from Henry that David Rogers was on a mission to New Orleans to secure gunpowder and was reminded of the governor's eagerness to see the Illinois Regiment push on to Detroit or Vincennes. Clark appointed captains Leonard Helm and Joseph Bowman, each an old friend and Kentucky pioneer, to raise companies for the expedition. William B. Smith was advanced £150 to recruit troops on the Holston River, and former West Augusta neighbors, William Harrod and John Montgomery, were sent to Redstone Old Fort. It was at Redstone that the continuing Virginia–Pennsylvania boundary dispute first impacted the plan. Henry's public orders allowed him to enlist men for the defense of Kentucky, but did not present a compelling case for the removal of soldiers already in place for the defense of the Pittsburgh area. Clark's *Memoir* later recorded, "Many Gentn. of Boath parties [Virginians and Pennsylvanians] conceived it to be Injurious to the publick Interest to draw of[f] men at so Critical a moment for the defence of a few detached Inhabitants that had better be removed. . . . Meeting with several disappointments it was late in may before I could leave the Redstone settlement with three companies and a considerable number of Families and private adventurers. Taking in my stores at Pittsburg and weling [Wheeling] I proceeded Down the River with Caution."[3]

Eighteen months after the event, he wrote, "I set out from Red Stone the 12th of may," and after meeting quartermaster James O'Hara's company at the Kanawha, "We . . . had a very pleasant Voyage to the falls of Ohio." O'Hara was on his way to Arkansas to reinforce James Willing's party, dispatched from Pittsburgh to clear the Mississippi River of any British forces and secure supplies for the western war in New Orleans. "I observed the little Island of about seven acres oposite to whare the Town of Lewisville now stands seldom or never was intirly covered by the water." He took possession of what became known as Corn Island on 27 May 1778, "dividing the Island among the Families for Garden."[4]

The value of the civilians who had attached themselves to his entourage would increase in his estimation. "These families that followed me I now found to be of Real service as they ware of little expence, and with the Invalids would keep possession of this Little post until we should be able to Occupy the Main shore which happened in the Fall agreeable to Instructions I sent from the Illinois." The character of many of his initial recruits evoked a dimmer description in July, after more than a month of training. Clark later wrote O'Hara, who apparently remained in New Orleans, as the letter fell into the hands of Spanish officials there and no doubt initiated a wry reaction from the Spaniard who translated it. "You will remember the situation in which you left me at the Falls and the type of people with whom I had to deal. . . . After having killed some and punished or imprisoned others, [the rest] became the best subjects imaginable."[5]

The rowdy band of about 170 militiamen set off on 24 June, "after spending a Day of amusement in parting with our friends of Kentucky they to Return to the defence of their Cuntrey and we in serch of new adventures. . . . We left our Little Island and Run about a mile up the River in order to gain the main Channel and shot the Fall at the very moment of the suns being in a great Eclips which caused Various conjectures among the superstitious." The expedition continued down the Ohio and, on the evening of the fourth day, camped at the site of the old Fort Massac. William Linn arrived the next morning after rowing from the Falls to deliver the electrifying news of the United States' diplomatic agreement with France. Clark must have smiled as he tucked the copies of the announcement away for safekeeping, for he knew he would make good use of the news in the weeks and months ahead.[6]

On the evening of 4 July, thanks to Linn's and Gibson's contacts with Thomas Bentley, Clark found boats moored on the east bank of the Kaskaskia River, across from the town of the same name. Two hours later, the regiment moved silently through the dark night, nearly naked, to surround Fort Gage (a modification of the town's former Jesuit seminary), where a dance for the townspeople was under way. "I immediately divided my little Army into two Divisions ordered one to surround the Town, with the other I broke into the Fort, secured the Governour Mr. Rochblave in 15 minutes had every Street secured, sent Runners through the Town ordering the People on the pane of Death to keep close to their Houses, which they observ'd And before daylight had the whole disarmed; nothing could excel the Confusion these People seemed to be in, being taught to expect nothing but Savage treatment from the Americans."[7]

Fernando de Leyba, the Spanish lieutenant governor at St. Louis who would become a Clark confidant, wrote, "George Rogers Clark arrived in Kaskaskia in hunting shirt and breechcloth, naked of foot and limb and with his bed, food and gun on his shoulder." Clark later explained his appearance at the first meeting he conducted with the town's leaders. "After some time the priest [Pierre Gibault] got permission to wait on me. He came, with five or six elderly gentlemen with him. However shocked they already were from their situation, the addition was obvious and great when they entered the room where I was sitting with other officers a dirty, savage appearance. . . . We had left our clothes at the river . . . torn by the bushes and briars. They were shocked, and it was some time before they could venture to take their seats, and longer before they would speak."[8]

With the group assembled, Clark told them Simon Kenton had placed the fort's commandant in irons and driven his family from its home, but the general population should not be threatened by Philippe de Rastel, Sieur de Rocheblave's imprisonment. "I told them that I was sorry to find that they had been taught to harbour so base an oppinion of the Americans and their Cause: Explain'd the nature of the dispute to them in as clear a light as I was capable of, it was certain that they were a Conquered People, and by the fate of War was at my mercy and that our Principal was to make those we Reduced free instead of enslaving them as they immagined." When Gibault, a priest newly arrived from Canada, asked whether "I would give him liberty to perform his duty in his Church, I told him that I had nothing to do with Churches more than to defend them from Insult. . . . This seem'd to compleat their happiness."[9]

Levi Todd, brother of Clark's captain, rode to St. Louis to inform Spain officially of the Virginians' presence at Kaskaskia. Simultaneously, Joseph Bowman led a party of American troops and French volunteers fifty miles north to Cahokia, where about three hundred French residents were convinced to take the oath of allegiance to the new nation and eighty enslaved Africans were placed under Virginia authority, which ended their comparatively relaxed subjugation under French and British control. Rocheblave would be taken to Williamsburg as a prisoner by John Montgomery, but when informed of the Rocheblave family's plight, Governor Henry ordered Clark to take care of the commandant's relations and return all his wife's household goods as far as it was possible to do so.[10]

Clark then turned his attention to Post St. Vincent, a town known as Vincennes by the French inhabitants who had imprisoned George Croghan thirteen years earlier. After Kenton had been sent to assess the strength of British forces stationed at the town's Fort Sackville, Clark described the town as being about the size of Williamsburg and concluded that he "was by no means able to march against it. . . . I was resolved if possible to win their affection which I thought myself in a fair way of doing." He proceeded with mediation rather than force in his communication with the townspeople, and placed Gibault and Dr. Jean Laffont at the head of a French–American delegation sent to Vincennes, where on 20 July the citizens swore oaths of allegiance to the Americans. Leonard Helm then entered the town, raised a flag over the fort, and announced the stockade henceforth would be known as Fort Patrick Henry.

"I now found myself in possession of the whole, in a Country where I found I could do more real service than expected; which occationed my situation to be the more disagreable as I wanted Men." With his limited resources never out of mind, Clark called a conference of the Miami Confederacy at Cahokia to introduce the Virginians' presence on the Mississippi, and hoped for the best. His skill in negotiating with the Illinois nations and their tribal settlements remains an essential component in Clark's status as a military leader. He was a consummate planner, and although the vagaries of luck and bluff influenced the formulation of his American Indian policy, just as they enhanced his reputation in Kentucky, Clark's approach to native negotiations was deliberate and was influenced more by men such as George Croghan and Sir William Johnson than Dunmore. His traditional British playbook, expressed in the patronizing, diplomatic language employed for decades, shaped Clark's initial communications with Illinois' native leaders, but his contacts with Spanish and French diplomats quickly enhanced his early success with the regional population.

As he explained to George Mason,

> It may appear otherwise to You, but [I] always thought we took the wrong method of treating with Indians, and strove as soon as possible to make myself acquainted with the French and Spanish mode which must be prefferable to ours, otherwise they could not possibly have such great influence among them. . . . It was with astonishment that [we] viewed the Amazeing number of Savages that soon flocked into the Town of Cohos to treat for peace, and to hear what the Big Knives had to say. . . . I told them that I had Instruction from the Great Man of the Big Knives not to ask Peace from any People but to offer Peace and War, and let them take their Choice. . . . I presented them with a Peace and War Belt. . . . They, with a great deal of seeming Joy took the Belt of Peace.[11]

Soon after the successful negotiations were completed, Clark received a warning from James Willing in New Orleans. "I am pleased to hear of the Indians coming in to make peace, beware of them they are Treacherous

People and when you least expect will fall on you. I am well acquainted with the Kaskaskia Gentry. They are damn'd Rogues as well as their ancient Leader RocheBlave. God send him a sight of Williamsburgh, Govr Henry won't be displeased to see one of these *Hair Buyers.*" Clark nevertheless appeared confident when he returned to Kaskaskia from the conference, and he spent much of the remaining season securing supplies from Spanish governor Bernardo de Galvez through Pollock. He also ordered household goods—china plates, a demijohn of "Taffea," salt cellars, a "Large Walnut Chest wt Drars [and] one Iron Coffe Morter"—and, with his enslaved servants, settled into a temporary home.[12]

Henry, too, was pleased with the outcome and informed Virginia's legislature that "by dispatches which I have just received from Col. Clark it appears that his success has equaled the most sanguine expectations. He has not only reduced Fort Chartres and its dependencies, but has struck such a terror into the Indian tribes between that settlement & the Lakes . . . [that they] have submitted to our arms all their English presents, and bound themselves by treaties and promises to be peaceable in future."[13]

In a quick move designed to claim the Illinois Territory before Congress could do so, the Virginia Executive Council created Illinois County, which comprised the "several posts in the Country of Illinois and on the Wabash." John Todd, a lawyer before he was named Clark's captain, was recommended by his commander and soon appointed as head of the county's civil government, relieving Clark of that responsibility. Five additional companies were to be raised and placed under Clark, who was addressed as commander-in-chief of the Virginia troops in the county of Illinois. In his *Memoir,* Clark noted he was able to reenlist the "greatest part" of his troops and sent Linn to the Falls with orders to move the civilian settlement from Corn Island to the southern bank of the Ohio.[14]

When Clark took possession of the Falls, he inadvertently had appropriated Maj. John Connolly's colonial land grant, at that time legally owned in partnership with Col. John Campbell. Connolly had been arrested in Maryland in 1776, carrying a message from his benefactor, Dunmore; and, with Campbell traveling to New Orleans with David Rogers in search of gunpowder, Virginia wasted little time in the consideration of prewar land claims approved by a British governor. Clark generally is acknowledged as the founder of Louisville as he directed civil and martial

Henry Hamilton. The Filson Historical Society, Louisville, KY.

law there even after the settlers moved to the shore in the autumn of 1778, and he spent that year regularly traveling from Kaskaskia to the Falls to supervise matters at the settlement.[15]

British commanders at Fort Detroit used their native allies as spies and reacted swiftly to the threat Clark's success posed to their position in the West. The Detroit River settlement, founded by French officer Cadillac in 1701, had fallen into British hands when French Montreal was captured in 1760. British officials used the post much as their French predecessors had, and rewarded regional Native Americans for making raids against their enemies. Henry Hamilton, the artistic son of a member of the Irish parliament, who had been appointed lieutenant governor of Quebec at the outset of the Revolution, received an express from the Illinois on 8 August that disclosed that "a party of Rebels" had surprised Kaskaskia and probably subdued Vincennes. In response, the new governor of Quebec, Frederick Haldimand, suggested some of the tribes supported by Detroit's officers might "be induced to undertake expeditiously to clear all the Illinois of these Invaders." Consequently, on 7 October, Hamilton made ready to vacate Detroit for Vincennes with a well-supplied force of 162 men reinforced by 70 native warriors.[16]

The expedition began unpropitiously; the field cannons fired in celebration from one of the thirteen bateaux caused an explosion that sank the boat. Hamilton's little army then floated and dragged its supplies across 450 miles of alternately drought-stricken and frozen terrain before it approached Vincennes on 17 December. Along the way, his intellectual interests led him to spend many evenings in the several Indian settlements the army encountered, absorbing the mystical practices he witnessed. "The deepest silence and most serious attention was observable during the prayer, no such thing as laughing or whispering so common in our places of Worship. . . . I was affected by the humble and reverential worship." Along the way, Hamilton passed the time with his books and drew excellent images of the French and native peoples he encountered.[17]

Congress had ordered Fort Pitt commander, General Lachlan McIntosh, to organize an attack on Detroit in June 1778. McIntosh had tarried into the fall, which prompted Henry to post new orders to Clark in December, apparently without concern for possible conflicts with federal strategies. "With your whole force you are to protect the Inhabitants of the Country & as occasions may serve, annoy the Enemy." He then identified two objectives for Clark's next summer's operation. "These are 1, an expedition against Detroit, or 2, against those tribes of Indians between the Ohio and Illinois rivers which have harassed us with eternal hostilities." In his desire to protect and expand Virginia's interests, Henry had argued that Clark was in a better position than the Georgian, McIntosh, to reach Detroit, but Clark demurred, answering, "A small army from Pittsburgh conducted with spirit may easily take Detroit and put an end to the Indian war."[18]

Clark instead focused his attention on Henry's second objective and dismissed rumors of a British approach, guessing, "It was preparation to give the Army from Ft. Pitt as warm a Reception as possible &c." He faced a myriad of obstacles connected to Virginia's occupation of Kaskaskia while he waited for the return of Todd, and central to his problems were the nearly worthless Virginia currency with which he was to pay for supplies, and his slave policy.

When Britain replaced France as proprietor of the Illinois Territory, the French Black Code that permitted enslaved men and women to remain together as families was wisely maintained; the code also limited daily hours of labor and created days of relaxation on Sunday. After a series of events that ended in disruption between the enslaved townspeople and Clark's men, he issued a proclamation on 24 December aimed at the "too great liberty enjoyed by the red and black slaves . . . causing the ruin of the colony." Clark banned the sale of alcohol to enslaved men and limited their freedom after dark without written permission. And although he permitted the Virginia traditions of Sunday slave dances and religious holidays to continue, proclamation offenders were whipped publicly. At the least, four of Clark's enslaved Africans and Cato Watts, the Corn Island veteran attached to Major John Donne, would participate in the difficult establishment of Fort Jefferson two years later, and commissary records that prove Clark requisitioned clothing for the enslaved people about to accompany him "to the Falls of the Ohio to make an Expedition against the Indian towns" suggest his household traveled with him into British and native conflicts. Kaskaskia, with a racial ratio of one enslaved person to every two free inhabitants, was Clark's first command outside the Virginia plantation culture in which he was reared, and it presented challenges that tried the experiences of John Clark's second son, leaving him wanting by most meaningful standards.[19]

While Clark sorted through administrative responsibilities at Kaskaskia, Leonard Helm jotted a quick note to him from Vincennes on 17 December 1778. "Theer is an army within three miles of this place." Later, "The army is in three hundred yd of the village. You must think how I feel, not four men that I can really depend on but am determined to act brave. . . . I know its out of my power to defend the town as not one of the militia will take arms thoug before sight of the army no braver men. There is a flag at a small distance. I must conclud." Within hours, Helm stood with three remaining Americans to face Henry Hamilton, who understood the situation and treated the men amicably. Fort Patrick Henry immediately reverted to Fort Sackville, and Helm's letter was seized before it reached a messenger.[20]

A week before he was informed otherwise, Clark had assumed Helm was safe within the Vincennes stockade and that Detroit might already be in the hands of McIntosh. "All this Information gave us at first Some pleasure until we learned that the army from Pittsburgh instead of marching into DeTroit had spent their time in Perade and Building a new post to facilitate their future designs." Clark, with a handful of officers, was enjoying a Prairie du Rocher ball in January when he received word British scouts were in the area. Feigning lightheartedness, the Virginians quietly left the dance and rode hard through the night to Kaskaskia, where they carefully assessed the situation before they entered the town. Once there, a message from Francis Vigo, an Italian trader and former Spanish soldier who was friendly to the American cause, confirmed that Hamilton had taken Vincennes. Clark remembered in 1790 that when they received Vigo's 29 January report, "We now Viewed our selves in a very critical Situation." He anticipated Hamilton would organize an Indian force in the spring and "that nothing in this Quarter could withstand his arms. . . . We saw but one alternative, which was to attack the Enemy in their Quarters. . . . If we ware fortunate it would save the whole if otherways it would be nothing more than what would Certainly be the consequence if we should not make the attempt."[21]

Clark knew Hamilton's standing with the largely French population at Vincennes would be weakened by the townspeople's knowledge of the new Franco-American alliance, and because British forces normally were unwilling to travel in off-weather, he decided the element of surprise would be on his side if he left immediately for Vincennes. "The Season of the year being also favourable as the Enemy . . . would be of[f] their Guard and probably would not think it worth while to keep out Spies."[22]

Patrick Henry probably was heartened by a 3 February letter from Clark that assured the governor of his resolve to strike Fort Sackville. "Being sensible that without a Reinforcement which at present I have hardly a right to Expect that I shall be obliged to give up this Cuntrey to Mr. Hamilton without a turn of Fortune in my favour, I am Resolved to take the advantage of his present Situation and Risque the whole on a Single Battle." The letter continued, "Great things have been affected by a few Men well Conducted. Perhaps we may be fortunate. We have this Consolation that our Cause is Just and that our Cuntrey will be greatful and not condemn our conduct in case we fall through. If so this Country as well as Kentucky I believe is lost."[23]

As he prepared for the attack, Clark had the "large Mississippi Boat" James Willing used in New Orleans retrofitted as a row galley and christened the *Willing*. Brought upriver for Clark's use, the warship was the first armed boat on the Ohio River. Among its crew was Caesar, an enslaved artificer who had been among Willing's men and who would stay with Clark's regiment through the war. Although it broke Virginia law, Clark would see that Caesar soon was issued a rifle and considered an enlisted man.[24]

John Rogers left Kaskaskia as captain of the *Willing* on 4 February with forty-six men and instructions to guard the mouth of the Wabash River against a British approach before turning up the Wabash to support the Vincennes attack. The Virginians and their French volunteers were then "Conducted out of the Town [Kaskaskia] by the Inhabitants and Mr. Jeboth [Pierre Gibault] the Priest, who after a very suitable Discourse to the purpose, gave us all Absolution. And we set out on a Forlorn hope indeed; for our whole Party with the Boats Crew consisted of only a little upwards of two hundred." In one of his last precampaign acts, Clark gave Gibault permission to cross the Mississippi because the priest feared for his life with Hamilton in the country.[25]

Major Joseph Bowman's journal recorded the daily events and hardships of the Illinois Regiment's epic march to Vincennes. Discounting crewmembers in the *Willing,* Bowman counted Clark's force at 170 men, a number that included two local French volunteer companies recruited in Illinois. In "rainy and drisly weather" that would continue to impede progress, the small army began the 180-mile trek to Vincennes in the middle of the day on 5 February. The sweep of terrain that lay between Kaskaskia and Vincennes was low and devoid of most natural features save a few creeks that man or horse normally could cross easily, but that month, the plain alternately was soggy and frozen, and the creeks and rivers swollen far beyond their banks. Clark soon would have occasion to talk about "some particulars of his march" with Henry Hamilton, who described them in his own journal as "very extraordinary. He [Clark] had left the Illinois when the Waters were out & had marched for 15 days successively, his people being exposed all that time to the inconveniences of marching thro a flooded Country. They set out without provision trusting entirely on the Buffaloe or other game they might chance to fall in with on their route."[26]

After twelve days of infrequent meals and hard rest, the regiment reached the Embarrass River, then called the Little Wabash, on 17 February. As he gazed across what appeared to be a lake, Clark might fully have understood his odds for the first time, and sent scouts in search of the *Willing*. The men spent a full day building rafts and ferrying their supplies through the freezing water, but Bowman reported on the eighteenth they were close enough to Vincennes to hear "Govr Hamiltons morning Gun."[27]

The Wabash River that runs beside Vincennes was five miles wide in February 1779, and presented obstacles greater than the numbing hunger the soldiers had endured for most of the march. Not once, but three times, men, supplies, and a dozen horses had to move through the freezing, shoulder-high waters, as they swam and crawled from one bit of emerged land to another. When they realized yet one last watercourse had to be crossed, some men balked; others collapsed midway through the crossing, begging to be left. Clark's place in American history was born in the icy waters of the Wabash, as he pushed his men, encouraged their flagging spirits, and led by example.[28]

The Illinois Regiment finally arrived within sight of Vincennes on 23 February, when Clark sent word ahead to residents. "Being now within two miles of your village with an army determined to take your fort tonight, and not being willing to surprise you, I am taking the measure of requesting such of you as are true citizens and desirous of enjoying the liberty I bring you to remain quietly in your houses" and "those (if any there be) that are friends to the King of England, I desire them instantly to repair to the fort and join the hair Buyer Genl and fight like Men."[29]

Meanwhile, he organized an approach deliberately staged to impress the town's residents. The scant hills near Fort Sackville, none higher than eight feet, offered just enough coverage for the men to crisscross one another, flying their colors and any other cloth that would answer the need, to suggest that the army was many times larger than it actually was. Bowman wrote, "We advanced slowly in full view of the town but as it was a matter of some consequences to make ourselves appear as formidable as possible, on leaving our place of concealment we marched and countermarched in a fashion calculated to magnify our numbers." After they eagerly accepted food from citizens and received a diplomatic call from the son of Piankeshaw chief Tobacco, Clark and his army scattered to make camps from which they peppered the fort through the night. Vincennes shuttered its homes at dusk and prepared for the next day's attack, but, familiar with regular nightly fire from friendly Indians, the officers inside the fort carried on with a celebration to mark the completion of recent improvements.

Prisoner Leonard Helm and Governor Henry Hamilton sat together enjoying hot toddies and piquet, unaware of the Virginians' arrival.

Hamilton received word of Clark's presence sometime during the night. "The fort began to play her small Arms" at dawn on the twenty-fourth. "One of our Men slightly wounded," Bowman recorded. Clark sent Hamilton a message ordering an immediate surrender "to save yourself from the Impending Storm that now Threatens you," to which Hamilton responded that "he and his Garrison are not disposed to be awed into any action Unworthy of British subjects." Indeed, Hamilton wrote that when his men were read Clark's demands, they "declared they would stand to the last for the honor of their Country, and as they expressed it, would stick to me as the shirt to my back."[30]

After the firing became "very hot on both sides," Hamilton's men began to waver. Helm emerged as hostage messenger to offer Hamilton's surrender with the honors of war should he and his men be allowed to return to Detroit. Clark countered, saying he would accept an unconditional surrender within thirty minutes. "I expect you shall immediately surrender yourself with your Garrison prisoners at discretion. If any of the stores be destroyed or any letters or papers burned, you may expect no mercy, for by Heavens you shall be treated as a murtherer." Helm soon returned with the counter: "Lieutenant Governor Hamilton acquaints Colonel Clarke, that neither he or his garrison are to be prevailed on by threats to act in a manner unbecoming the character of British Subjects," but invited Clark into the fort. Clark refused outright, but agreed to meet Hamilton at the gate.[31]

According to Bowman, as the messenger returned with Hamilton's reply, "there came a party of Indians down the hills behind the Town, who had been sent by Govr Hamilton to get some Scalps and Prisoners from the falls of Ohio. Our Men having got news of it pursued them kill'd two on the Spot wounded three took 6 Prisoners Brought them into Town two of them proving to be White men That they took Prisoners, we releas'd them and brought the Indians to the Main Street before the Fort Gate there tomahawked them and threw them into the River."[32]

Hamilton recorded a bitter description of the incident in more detail.

> About two in the afternoon the party of Indians which had gone towards the falls of Ohio returnd, and advancing over the common to the fort, seeing the English flag flying and not knowing that

> we were attacked, discharged their pieces—tis usual with them to fire three vollies on their approach to a fort or a town, as a salute, this is practiced also among themselves. . . . Colol. Clarke being informed of their arrival, sent off 70 men to attack them, who fired on these people unprepared for such a salute, killed one wounded two and made 5 of the rest prisoners taking them to the Village.
>
> On their arrival, they were placed in the street opposite the Fort Gate, where these poor wretches were to be sacrificed—one of them a young Indian about 18 Years of age the son of Pontiach, was saved at the intercession of one Macarty a Captain of Colol. Clarkes Banditti, who said he was formerly owed his life to the Indian's father. One of the others was tomahawked either by Clarke or one of his Officers, the other three foreseeing their fate, began to sing their Death song, and were butcherd in succession, tho at the very time a flag of Truce was hanging out at the fort and the firing had ceased on both sides. . . . The Blood of the victims was still visible for days afterwards, a testimony of the courage and Humanity of Colonel Clarke.[33]

Bowman and Hamilton each offered fair, but subjective interpretations of the killings at Vincennes on 24 February 1779. Clark had responded both strategically and viscerally when the war party arrived at the fort, because Hamilton's reputation in Kentucky as the "Hair Buyer" was not unwarranted. The British governor had continued the frontier tradition established by each European nation during the French and Indian War because scalps were as easy to acquire as hostages, and he preferred not to feed and clothe captives. During his time as Detroit's commander, 8,640 scalping knives had been distributed to his Indian allies, and during the first eight months of 1778, he accepted 110 scalps and 55 prisoners from the frontier. Hamilton, nevertheless, had not witnessed the brutality that created his scalps, and the shock of Clark's reaction to seeing them remained with him long after his surrender.[34]

The events of 24 February occurred more or less as follows: Clark's men rode out to greet the party and shot and killed several of the warriors on the spot. The others immediately surrendered and, realizing their error, prepared for death. Clark's Cahokia commander was Captain Richard McCarty, a British army deserter who interceded on behalf of one young man recognized as Pontiac's son. Pontiac had once spared McCarty's life, and the captain wished to return the favor; Clark assented. Incredibly, one of McCarty's men then recognized his own son among the remaining captives, taken prisoner years earlier. Again, Clark released the boy. Hamilton and his army watched from 100 yards away as the remaining six warriors knelt, and one by one, had their skulls crushed by a tomahawk. The last, party leader Macutte Mong, received three blows from the executioner before he was thrown into the Wabash.[35]

Clark later recorded the reason for his orders, which were based in his Kentucky experience during the bloody summer of 1777. "I wanted an excuse to put them to Death or other ways treat them as I thought proper that the Cries of the Widows and Fatherless on the Frontiers that they had Occationed now Required their Blood from my Hands." He indicated to Mason that his intention was to drive a wedge between the Indians and the British force. "I had now a fair oppertunity of making an impression on the Indians that I could have wished for; that of convincing them that Governour Hamilton could not give them that protection that he had made them believe he could. . . . It had the effect that I expected: instead of making their friends inviterate against us, they upbraided the English Parties in not trying to save their friends and gave them to understand that they believed them to be liers and no Warriers."[36]

Clark fully understood the effect of the slaughter upon everyone present, and in the stunned silence, calmly asked Hamilton to discuss terms of surrender. Hamilton recorded the meeting. "In consequence I met him on the parade outside the Fort, he had just come from his Indian tryumph all bloody and sweating. [He] seated himself on the edge of one of the batteaus, that had some rainwater in it, & while he washed his hands and face still reeking from the human sacrifice in which he had acted as chief priest, he told me with great exultation how he had been employed." Clark's show of "so little mercy" pressured Hamilton into producing another set of conditions for capitulation. Clark again rejected them, and as the day neared its violent end, Hamilton ruefully accepted Clark's demands for surrender and agreed to the document that ended with the traditional, but to Hamilton's mind, gratuitous phrase, owing to "The Hon'ble Terms allw'd and lastly confidence in a Generous Enemy."[37]

Hamilton later would record that his reasons for surrender were based upon the behavior of Clark's "unprincipled motley Bandetti," and that the "poltronnerie and treachery of our French Volunteers who made half our number . . . with the certainty of the St. Vincennes men having joined Colol. Clark and the miserable state of our wounded men, all conspired to make me adopt the disagreeable terms of capitulation." The British officer nevertheless participated in the formal surrender of Fort Sackville the next morning, 25 February 1779. "At ten o'Clock we marched out with fixed Bayonettes and our Knapsacks," Hamilton noted. "The Colors were not hoisted this morning that we might be spared the mortification of hawling them down but the Rebels had them presently hoisted with their 13 Stripes over them." Fort Sackville again was known as Fort Patrick Henry.[38]

In the celebration that followed Hamilton's surrender, several cannons were fired in the evening, which accidently ignited a store of gunpowder that exploded and caused scattered injuries. The expedition's careful diarist, Joseph Bowman, received the worst of the damage and would die in August, never having recovered from his wounds. Hamilton, along with twenty-six other prisoners, left Vincennes on 8 March, dispatched in a boat to the Falls of the Ohio, from where they would be marched overland to Williamsburg.[39]

Clark intended to initiate the Detroit campaign when he returned to Kaskaskia, but when anticipated reinforcements were directed elsewhere, he abandoned his plans and cemented relations with regional Indians. Hamilton's successor, Col. Arent De Peyster, wrote that he feared if the Illinois Regiment were "not routed by some means that the whole Mississippi Trade is knocked up," but he remained at Detroit, deprived of the post's usual number of native allies. Clark's recapture of Vincennes quashed the only successful western Revolutionary offensive executed by Britain. Hamilton had meant to follow the victory with conquests at Kaskaskia and Cahokia before making a sweep through Kentucky that would conclude with the capture of Fort Pitt. His defeat deflated French and Indian support in the Illinois and neutralized Ohio Valley natives and their tribes. Detroit remained elusive, but ultimately, unnecessary, as the United States' ability to maintain Kentucky and the Illinois country through the conclusion of the 1783 Treaty of Paris negotiations became the most important outcome of the Revolution in the West.[40]

Clark's *Memoir* noted the members of the Illinois Regiment were substantially rewarded for their "hardship and endeavor," and Bowman wrote Isaac Hite, "At the surrender of the Garrison we got" in addition to artillery pieces, "a Large quantity of Militery stores and Indian goods to the amount of Twenty Thousand Pounds," most of which had been ransacked from a British boat captured by Helm. Clark recalled, "The Provitions was taken for the Publick and the Goods Divided among the whole except about 800£ worth of cloath the Troops," but a letter penned to his father shortly after he and brother, Richard, returned to Kaskaskia suggests otherwise.

> No person Commanding on this Continent is in a more Critical Situation than I am. Surrounded on all sides by Numerous Nations of Indians with English officers among them Incouraging them to war. . . . I don't doubt but you have before this time had a full account of my late Attact on post St Vincents. After an Ingagement of Eighteen Hours the famous Governour Hamilton and his Murdering Band fell into my hands, Expences in this Cuntrey is amasingly high. It has Cost me [not] less than twelve or thirteen Hundred pounds since I have been in it. . . . I instructed one Mr Randolph that does business for me to give you Ten Thousand Pounds to keep for me. . . . If Dicky and myself should be both lost . . . this Cuntrey will be worth Seven years Trouble of my Brothers to Seek after my Fortune which at this time Cant be less than Twenty Pounds Sterling as my success in Trade has been Equal to that of war.

Remembering the lessons of his childhood, he closed in acknowledgment that some things yet lay beyond his control, and that his "greatest glory is to adore the Suppreme director of all things."[41]

Many years later, Clark said of his military career that he had "adopted a plan, & that Genl. Washington, the Governor of Virginia & Pennsylvania; all approved it, & appeared anctious to aid the plan & Carry it into affect." When asked if the expedition had been intended for the particular benefit of the State of Virginia or the general benefit of the United States, Clark responded: "I did not look upon it as a local thing. . . . The first Object was the Reduction of Detroit, after that was affected & possession had of Lake Erie . . . [to] make head quarters on the Lake at some advantageous Spot . . . thereby cuting off the communication between the eastern

& western Indians, & preventing further British Supplys to the western Indians and affect the British Interest about Niagara." As he contemplated the events of 1779 in future dark days, when his willingness to fight for and live within Spanish or French territory was public knowledge, George Rogers Clark remembered he had captured Vincennes for his country.[42]

6

Washington's Soldier

> I was very sorry to Receive such Orders Being in Great Doubt of my ever Having it in my Power if Once Returned to [Charles] Town, I could ever again Leave it Except as a Prisoner.
> —William Croghan, April 1780

After the battle at Germantown, the Continental Army limped into a little settlement that lay twenty miles northwest of Philadelphia. The winter was not the worst Revolutionary armies would endure, but the conditions in which the Americans lived at Valley Forge, particularly when compared to their British counterparts in Philadelphia, were stark. Camp physicians estimated that of the ten thousand or so men who arrived in December, nearly one-quarter did not survive until June. Very few were lost because of exposure; rather, the majority died of bronchial illnesses brought on by relentless smoke, which, coupled with pneumonia, typhoid, dysentery, typhus, and malnutrition, proved deadly. With twelve soldiers assigned to a hut sometimes shared with visiting wives and children, the Valley Forge camp was the fourth-largest population center in British North America in the spring of 1778. In addition, Valley Forge was home to a significant number of servants, enslaved, indentured, and hired. Washington set the standard with the employment of Elizabeth Thompson and the use of two enslaved couples—Willie Lee, his manservant, and Lee's wife, Margaret Thomas, who acted as laundress, and Hannah Till, his cook, and her husband, Isaac. Thompson, an Irish immigrant, traveled ahead of the general to most of the field headquarters he established during the war to supervise the unpacking of his personal belongings and oversee the domestic activities of his many temporary homes.[1]

The Eighth Virginia Regiment, still under the command of Abraham

Bowman, had been assigned with the Fourth and Twelfth Regiments to Brigadier General Charles Scott's brigade in May 1777, as part of Lafayette's Division. The Virginians moved into the southern section of the Valley Forge encampment in December, shortly before the Eighth Regiment reported eighty-six men, fifty-three of whom were considered fit for duty. William Croghan was present and able at every Valley Forge muster from December through the camp's last roll call in June 1778, and like most of the army's young officers, he shared his hut with three other men. Beyond his quarters, Croghan endured the winter in part with Nathanael Greene, Baron Friedrich von Steuben, Henry Knox, John Peter Gabriel Muhlenberg, Casimir Pulaski, Anthony Wayne, Alexander Hamilton, John Marshall, and James Monroe. Jonathan Clark, now a major serving as Bowman's field officer, returned to Virginia for the winter but was back at Valley Forge on 13 April. Despite appalling camp conditions—Washington rode among the huts with a kerchief held to his face—Valley Forge's survivors benefited from the arrival of Steuben, who, with Lafayette, had brought a professional style of military training to the Continental Army and prepared it for the final stage of the Revolution. Scott, who would command the army's elite American Light Infantry after August, was named Washington's chief intelligence officer that spring, and William Croghan was commissioned his brigade major. As such, Scott led men who were exceptional marksmen, intelligent and agile equestrians, and veteran soldiers who could function independently in and out of battle. None of these talents would be wasted in the ferocious battle that lay ahead.[2]

While Washington used the months at Valley Forge to organize and train his army, the British government took advantage of the winter to remove Howe as its North American military commander and replace him with Lieutenant General Sir Henry Clinton. Acutely aware of the French agreement, Clinton opted to remove his army from Philadelphia and return to New York, where he could better defend his position against the presumed arrival of the French navy. After the heavy artillery and three thousand Loyalist residents were placed on boats bound for New York, the arduous task of transporting ten thousand men, another thousand camp followers, and fifteen hundred baggage and supply wagons across the Delaware River and into New Jersey was completed on 18 June.[3]

Washington, who shared Clinton's belief that the French navy would enter North America at New York, was right behind him. Lighter and faster than the British army, the new Continental Army, now 13,503 men strong, was rested, reclothed, and better trained than at any earlier stage of the war. With the two armies marching roughly in parallel lines, it was clear a substantial battle could take place if either general wished it to happen. Clinton certainly did not, but Washington's young officers eagerly argued for the opportunity to meet the new British commander on the field. Charles Lee, who inexplicably continued as Washington's second-in-command, favored harassment rather than a fight, saying it would be "criminal" to put the Continental Army's "amateurs" on the battlefield against professional British soldiers. Wayne, Greene, Steuben, and Lafayette continued to lobby for an attack, but Lee's motion carried, prompting Alexander Hamilton to respond that Lee's plan "would have done honor to the most honorable body of midwives and to them only."[4]

After it became obvious the British army was lumbering toward Monmouth Court House, Washington offered command of the harassment unit to Lee, who refused and suggested that the task could better be performed by a "young, volunteering general" rather than the army's second-in-command. Washington then assigned command to Lafayette, who left immediately with four thousand men. When he realized the task force was large enough to win attention should it succeed, Lee rescinded his refusal. Torn between his friendship with Lafayette and his awe of Lee, Washington chose to send Lee after the young French officer with orders to take command after Lafayette initiated action, which set the stage for confusion and near catastrophe.[5]

Clinton reached Monmouth on the afternoon of 26 June, having experienced his first casualties after traveling less than twenty miles through unusually humid weather and sandy, difficult countryside. Washington's army had covered essentially the same distance, but did so in the cool of the night on 25–26 June. Both armies rested on the twenty-seventh, as Washington spent most of the day fuming over conflicting scouting intelligence while Lee moved toward Lafayette's position with an additional thousand men. At the end of the day, Lee retired without ordering scouts to watch the British movement after he informed his officers he would play the next day's events "by ear."

Clinton moved out of Monmouth at 4 a.m. on the twenty-eighth; Lee and Lafayette, with Anthony Wayne's and Charles Scott's brigades among the five-thousand-man unit, pulled away at 7 a.m., five miles behind. Washington and the main army trailed behind. Lee was to attack Cornwallis's rear guard as soon as the bulky British convoy left camp, but Cornwallis, seeing him, assessed the size of Lee's force and turned his guard to meet the Americans head-on. Lee fired one volley and retreated: rather than attacking Cornwallis, Lee realized that the British rear guard, made up of five infantry brigades, Grenadiers, and the Queen's Rangers, was about to attack *him.* Lafayette attempted to move Lee's army back into position, but the action confused the field officers, who assumed they were in retreat. Scott later would claim he was ordered back by Lee, and in full retreat, he ran into Washington, riding hard for the front. A series of commands and countermands followed, and all present were led to conclude that Lee, if he had a plan at all, was incapable of executing it. As the Americans stood in confusion and anger on the field of battle, Clinton turned his full army around, and, with Cornwallis in the lead, drove into Nathanael Greene's wing with furious force. Washington took the middle of the field, barking orders to Lafayette, who assumed command. Cornwallis's unit savaged Washington's right while Anthony Wayne held Henry Monckton for three consecutive charges that ended only when Monckton, shot dead from his horse, fell into the arms of one of Wayne's men.

The Battle of Monmouth Court House was fought on a blistering day that created as many heat-related casualties as battle wounds. It was reported that many of Washington's, but none of His Majesty's soldiers, removed their jackets and fought bare-chested. Officers, soldiers, and animals rode wildly until exhaustion and dehydration brought them to the ground. Aaron Burr never again was fit for active duty, and dozens died of sunstroke. The battle ended in a virtual draw with each army claiming the day, but it was a statistical victory for Washington. British losses were put at 358 killed or wounded with no fewer than 60 dead of heat. Six hundred British soldiers, including 440 Hessians, made their ways back to Philadelphia as deserters. Washington is thought to have buried 249. Lee was arrested, tried for insubordination, and dismissed from the army. Major William Croghan joined other Monmouth officers who voiced extreme criticism of Lee's battlefield behavior, and his commander, Scott, would write that Washington "swore that day til the leaves shook on the trees. Charming! Delightful! Never have I enjoyed such swearing before or since!"[6]

Monmouth was the last significant northern engagement of the Revolution. The American army remained no match for the career soldiers who fought for Britain, but it now was led by battle-tested veterans who knew the terrain and were gaining national support. The battle was the longest single action of the Revolution, and the only one in which Washington's army remained on the field throughout the conflict.

After Monmouth, the wife of a British officer offered the use of her nearby home as Washington's temporary headquarters. The general accepted, and he and his officers lingered at Theodosia Prevost's Hermitage through the summer, a stay that resulted in James Monroe's and Aaron Burr's infatuations with their sophisticated hostess. Mrs. Prevost continued correspondences with the two young officers after the army moved on to White Plains (her letters to Monroe were written in English; the better-educated Burr frequently received and sent missives in French). Burr would remain in New Jersey throughout most of the remaining Revolution, and although the luckless Lt. Col. Prevost would die in Jamaica of yellow fever in December 1781, his wife clearly and publicly appeared to be in love with Burr before the end of 1780.[7]

Washington reorganized the Continental Army through a statement released 14 September 1778 that consolidated his depleted regiments. The Fourth Virginia Regiment absorbed the Eighth, and with Scott's temporary withdrawal from active service, Col. John Neville commanded the newly organized regiment, with William Croghan commissioned the regiment's major. The Fourth was reassigned to General William Woodford's brigade, and although he maintained a significant army at White Plains, Washington sent a slightly larger force, including Woodford's brigade, to Middlebrook, New Jersey, at the end of November. With major war activity limited to the sea, Croghan spent 1779 leading scouting parties across the northern New Jersey countryside, maintaining supply lines through the lawless Ramapo Mountains into the Jersey plains, and reporting regularly to White Plains, seeing little action. He was so much at his leisure he was given a furlough in January and February to visit Philadelphia, and subsequently forwarded a chatty, tongue-in-cheek letter to his friend Barnard Gratz. "We spend our time very Sociable here, Are never disturbed by the Enemy, have planty of Provisions, & no want of Whiskey Grog. We sometimes get good Spirits; Punch, &C, and have Madeira Sometimes. We have a Variety of Amusements. Last Evening the Tragedy of Cato was performed at Brunswick by the officers of the Army."[8]

The decision by the British army to sit out most of the 1779 northern land campaign was a consequence of something more than the officers' reluctance to abandon the comforts they knew in New York City. As he again scouted British activity from Smith's Clove, near White Plains, Croghan informed Gratz on 7 August that the main body of the British army was hunkered at Fort Washington in northern Manhattan, but that "all their ships of force [had] gone out of the [Sandy] Hook and that the enemy is in much confusion at New York; . . . Count D'Estaing and Admiral Byron have had an engagement in which the latter was worsted, having lost five ships, and several much damaged." The French navy had arrived in North America, and the British were distracted.[9]

The Continental Army decamped from its base in New York in November 1779 and, because the roads and rivers already were frozen over, spent nearly a month making its way again to Morristown, New Jersey. The first Morristown Camp had been a slipshod operation, but in late 1779, the huts were built to such specifications that Governor William Livingston scornfully wrote, "Perhaps in the final result . . . the Neighbourhood will [not] regret that a disproportionate quantity of their wood was sacrificed in such a cause." The assault made upon New Jersey's trees proved fortunate; the coming months would live in memory as "the hard winter," and starvation and weather conditions proved far worse than those experienced at Valley Forge. Morristown's soldiers sometimes went without meat for a week at a time, but Washington's officers managed a series of dances and fetes (French officers had arrived) that buoyed them through the miserable conditions. Alexander Hamilton even managed to win the hand of one of Philip Schuyler's lively daughters in the midst of the otherwise frozen encampment. Sadly, Morristown's Virginia regiments would not have Hamilton's opportunities, as neither soldier nor officer would hear wedding bells that spring.[10]

In London, the Crown, unnerved by France's new role in the war, moved to conclude the rebellion through a new southern offensive. Clinton sailed from New York a day after he enjoyed Christmas celebrations in Manhattan, and Cornwallis followed with most of the army. Washington understood the next British offensive would take place as far from the French fleet as possible, and on 8 December, shortly after the Virginia regiments had completed their new Morristown huts, he ordered the First and Second Virginia brigades to Philadelphia to begin a march to Georgia or South Carolina. Croghan mustered Woodford's brigade on 9 December and started for Pennsylvania.[11]

Before he had left for the Revolution, Croghan had rented a room and left his clothes with a Mr. Taylor in New Germantown, which lay in the foothills beyond Harrisburg and Carlisle. He reached Taylor's in a freezing rain on the night of 12 December and, after resting, inspected his clothing, which he left to his "boy" to prepare and pack for the trip south. The roads and streams between Philadelphia and Lancaster were so treacherous "the horses could not stand" and the snow stood "three feet deep," so the major enjoyed a short visit with George Croghan (20–22 December) while he waited for improved weather conditions. He rode through "extream cold" on the twenty-third to reach Philadelphia, where he dined with Woodford the next day, and on 12 January he left with Major Charles Pelham to join Neville's regiment. Neville was moving slowly—his was the last unit in Woodford's brigade and was hampered by the conveyance of six 6-pounders and the quartermaster's supplies. The journey was appalling, "several troops have their Hands, feet and Other parts of their Bodys Frozen," but gratefully was broken in Frederick Town, Maryland, where Croghan was reunited with the regiment in time to enjoy a ball hosted by the townspeople.[12]

To General Benjamin Lincoln, who anxiously awaited in Charleston, Woodford's brigade must have appeared to travel at a casual, almost indifferent pace through Maryland and Virginia. The army rested at Fredericksburg in early February, where Croghan reported that snow and icy roads did not prevent the officers' attendance at a birthday party on 11 February with Washington's family. Although Woodford received word from Lincoln on 15 February that the British had arrived in Charleston, the army participated in a second birthday celebration for Washington in Richmond and enjoyed another ten-day rest near Petersburg.[13]

With the roads free of ice, Woodford moved more vigorously, but gruelingly, through the flooded Carolina backcountry, and by the time he reached the outskirts of the city on 30 March, thousands of British troops were amassed in Charleston's harbor. The Americans saw immediately that Lincoln's fortifications were inadequate for the battle that lay ahead. Scott later described the situation to Barnard Gratz, "I assure you dear Sir . . . we had the most disagrreable journey to this place that I ever experienced. We arrived in the evening before the siege commenced, during which,—not having the most distant hope of success,—you may easily figure to yourself my feelings." Scott argued for an immediate evacuation, but Lincoln, encouraged by South Carolina's lieutenant governor, resisted.[14]

Croghan spent most of April camped at Lampries Point, participating in strategy sessions that ultimately would lead to surrender. Sent across the Cooper River to scout British positions, he was ordered back to Charleston on 8 April, but he obeyed reluctantly. Still, he assessed the situation optimistically on the day that would end with the Americans' last evacuation route being closed. "The army and citizens are in high spirits and have no doubt of their ability to defend the city and make Sir Henry [Clinton] again give up thought of taking it."[15]

Croghan attended the officers' meeting on 19 April, where local officials pleaded with the army to stay in Charleston until the last extremity. Croghan's journal recorded the officers' determination that the "last extremity" had been reached the following day. Terms of an honorable surrender were presented to Clinton, who rejected them, and fighting continued for three more weeks, with the American army surviving on a diet of rice, bad meat, and coffee until the attack ended on 4 May. Benjamin Lincoln officially surrendered Charleston at 11 a.m. on 12 May 1780 as 12,700 British land troops and another 4,500 naval troops looked on. Croghan joined 244 other officers and about 3,000 soldiers in grounding their arms to the tune of "The Turk's March" as the largest American defeat of the Revolution was accomplished.[16]

Croghan informed Michael Gratz of the surrender on 18 May. "We had a pretty constant fire from our side six weeks, and from the enemy twenty-nine days; not many lives lost on our side. The second day after the enemy took the town, their magazine blew up by accident which destroyed all the arms they received from us and near a hundred lives." Bleak as the situation was, his connection to the commanding Prevost family placed him in enviable standing among Charleston's prisoners. Prior to the American campaign in Georgia, General Augustin Prevost had moved from Jacksonville to Savannah and placed his son, Major Augustin Prevost Jr., and brother, Lt. Colonel Jacques Marcus Prevost (husband of Theodosia, who remained in New Jersey), in key positions within his command. Susanna Croghan Prevost, William Croghan's cousin, traveled with her husband to Savannah and Charleston.[17]

The American officers held at Haddrell's Point were permitted by Cornwallis to move within a six-mile radius of camp, and to trade and correspond with whomever they pleased, so William Croghan wrote his uncle George soon after his capture. "Major Prevost Settout from this place for Savannah yesterday. . . . [He] is to be stationed here & has now gone for Mrs. Prevost [Croghan's cousin] & Expects to be here with her about two Weeks hence. I am on Parole at a place called Haddrell's Point near this Town, but got permission to Come see the Major, who has been Exceedingly kind in Endeavoring to get me a Parole to go to the Northward & in every respect Serve me."[18]

In addition to Scott and Jonathan Clark, Croghan was imprisoned through the muggy Charleston summer with fellow officers Col. Richard Clough (Cluff) Anderson of the Fifth Virginia Regiment and Clark's younger brother, Edmund, formerly an ensign with Decrome de la Porte's French company, but now a lieutenant in Nathaniel Gist's Third Virginia Regiment. Croghan, the Clark brothers, and other Virginia officers were placed on a "flag schooner with a fair Wind" on 7 February 1781, after providing a "Sloop on Chas'Town bar with a flag necessary for the prisoners." The sloop carried rank-and-file American soldiers to New York Harbor, where they would join the seven-thousand-man prison population that roughly equaled the number of American casualties sustained from 1775 to 1783, but Croghan and other officers were released on parole until each was exchanged for a British prisoner. Soon foundered "on the Frying Pan" of North Carolina's Outer Banks, where "many rye Faces & Dreadful apprehension" were detected, "a Negro pilate came on board to take us to Edenton where we arrived on the 17th."[19]

Unceremoniously dropped at Edenton, the men spent some time and an extravagant amount of money to buy horses and carts for their baggage, but the Clarks were able to reach their father's Caroline County home on 2 March 1781. William Croghan appeared with Jonathan Clark in Caroline that March, but whether he was a guest of the Clarks is not known. He and Jonathan rode together through the rain on 25 March "near Capt Marshalls & returned lay my fathers," which meant that he, and possibly Croghan, spent the night at John and Ann Clark's home. Soon after this entry, Croghan returned to Philadelphia and New Germantown until he received a commission as army inspector, after which he was ordered to Fort Pitt to wait out his parole. His appearance at the fort coincided with that of George Rogers Clark, who was working frantically to put together an expedition against Detroit; but in that critical summer, all the world looked to the eastern shore of North America where at last, the United States of America would win or lose its revolution.[20]

Increased frustration with Clinton, who had returned to New York, triggered the Crown's decision to give Cornwallis the autonomy to conduct Britain's southern campaign as he wished. After a spectacular victory at Camden, Cornwallis left South Carolina and marched through North Carolina and into Virginia in pursuit of Lafayette, who had been joined by Anthony Wayne and Steuben in May. Lafayette returned the favor and paced Virginia until Cornwallis was driven onto the state's peninsula, while Greene, having replaced Horatio Gates as southern commander after the Camden campaign, made camp in the Carolinas to dissuade Cornwallis from escaping to Charleston.[21]

French general Jean Baptiste Donatien de Vimeur, comte de Rochambeau, had arrived in Rhode Island with 450 officers and 5,300 soldiers in July 1780, and for a year, he corresponded from Newport with Washington, who remained on the Hudson at Newburgh with nearly 4,000 men. Washington pushed for a joint Franco–American attack on New York City, and unwilling to give up his New York obsession, convinced Rochambeau to join him north of Manhattan early in July 1781. Fifteen French brigades, transported with the aid of fourteen hundred horses and six hundred oxen, met Washington near today's Scarsdale on 6 July, at which time each commander offered compliments to the other's army. Washington's expressions were sincere; the well-rested French army surpassed even the British troops, whose appearance had begun to reveal the grind of a five-year war. But French officer Baron von Closen provided an honest description of Washington's troops. "I had a chance to see the American army, man for man. It was painful to see these brave men, almost naked with only some trousers and little linen jackets, most of them without stockings, but would you believe it? Very cheerful and healthy."[22]

After a tour of British defenses, Rochambeau concluded that a victory would not be possible at New York, but appealed to his navy for help elsewhere. Washington had no choice but to accept the situation, and his 1 August journal entry recorded the conclusion that he must now look to the South. The journal did not record an equally important turn of events: the sudden presence of Rochambeau's fleet had panicked Clinton, and unaware of Washington's decision to move south, the general hunkered down in Manhattan with more than ten thousand soldiers and ordered many of Cornwallis's troops back from Yorktown.

As Lafayette's troops steadily tightened the noose surrounding his army, Cornwallis began the work of trenching on 2 August in preparation for the inevitable battle. Aware of his increasingly tenuous position, he appealed to Clinton for more men and material, but Clinton's personal fear was greater than his concern for Cornwallis's army. He responded to his general, advising shelter. "I beg leave to recommend it to you . . . to take a defensive station in any healthy situation you choose, be it at Williamsburg or Yorktown." The letter went on to request several battalions and additional artillery for the defense of his New York army, and so, depleted of men and stranded at Yorktown, Cornwallis fretted.[23]

Washington received confirmation on 14 August that the commander of the French Caribbean fleet, Francois Joseph Paul, comte de Grasse, had set sail with thirty-two warships from the West Indies, en route to the Chesapeake Bay. With this news, however, Rochambeau issued a caveat: de Grasse's navy would be available only until 15 October, at which time it would return to the Caribbean. The French government was offering its final support to Washington, who would have to coordinate and execute the Revolution's decisive battle within eight weeks, 450 miles south of New York. The combined Franco-American army immediately prepared to evacuate, leaving Philipsburg, New York, by 18 August.

Clinton easily could have destroyed Washington's northern army before Rochambeau's arrival triggered the beginning of the Yorktown campaign, but he instead chose to plan a defensive operation aimed at an anticipated French naval attack. When he received word that Washington and Rochambeau had reached Philadelphia on 31 August, he at last understood the armies were moving south and sent word to Cornwallis that reinforcements were on the way. The relief was limited to a navy fleet commanded by Sir Thomas Graves, who quickly returned to New York after he encountered de Grasse's far superior force on 5 September; and afraid to weaken his own defenses, Clinton disregarded his message and sent nothing more to Yorktown.[24]

Washington lingered with Rochambeau in Philadelphia for a few days, and in nearby Chester County for another, as he waited for news and the arrival of additional men. In Chester, they learned de Grasse had reached the Chesapeake and was in position to make a swift move to Yorktown.

Washington and Rochambeau bolted from Pennsylvania with their aides, stopping for three days at Mount Vernon to draw battle plans and visit the home Washington had not seen for six years; from there, they went to the bay, where they were transported to de Grasse's magnificent flagship, the *Ville de Paris.* Lafayette joined them at Williamsburg on 22 September, and six days later, the largest military force yet assembled by the fledgling United States, nearly twenty-thousand-men strong, began the twelve-mile march to Yorktown.[25]

As the Franco–American units established camps near the British army, French engineers and officers knew they would take control of the attack and provide Britain with its first and only European-style battle of the Revolution, and although Washington rode out each morning with Rochambeau to inspect the trenches, he ceded command on the field to his French counterpart. Cornwallis must have been stunned to see the French army, at once professional and threatening, digging in beyond his redoubts. Wayne recalled their appearance in stark contrast to the shabby American army, describing the French soldiers as "being very tall men, their uniform is white coats turned up with blue, their underclothes are white." Rochambeau later would somewhat generously summarize the roles of the respective French and American armies at Yorktown. "I must render the Americans the justice to say that they conducted themselves with that zeal, courage, and emulation, with which they were never backward," although they were "totally ignorant of the operations of a siege."[26]

Each day, Cornwallis found himself in a more critical situation, cut off from supplies for weeks and able to eke little sustenance from the marshy ground. American scout St. George Tucker reported that four hundred horse carcasses choked the river after the British had been forced to destroy the animals they no longer could feed. A deserter told American officers that of nine thousand soldiers at Yorktown, two thousand lay ill. Cornwallis had written Clinton on 17 September, warning, "If you cannot relieve me very soon, you must be prepared to hear the worst," but Clinton procrastinated. After Cornwallis received word on 29 September that a fleet would leave New York about 5 October for his relief, he pulled his defenses back to tighten his line and ordered round-the-clock fire at the enemy. American artillery was not in place until 9 October, when the French engineers who had built the fortification allowed Washington the honor of the first shot. An American officer reported the ball ricocheted from several town houses before it landed in one and destroyed the tableware of several British officers who were dining, leaving one officer wounded or dead.[27]

The allied army was within three hundred yards of British lines by 12 October, which prompted Cornwallis to send a desperate message to Clinton. "Nothing but a direct move to York River—which includes a successful naval action—*can save me.* . . . We cannot hope to make a long resistance." By the fifteenth, Cornwallis had lost all hope. He sent final word to Clinton, writing that the situation was then so "precarious that I cannot recommend that the fleet and army should run great risk in endeavoring to save us." Shortly after 9 a.m. on the seventeenth, a British drummer and officer, one beating a parley and the other waving a white handkerchief, appeared on the British works and cannon fire stopped for the first time in two weeks. Blindfolded, the officer was brought behind American lines with a message from Cornwallis: "Sir, I propose a cessation of hostilities for twenty-four hours and that two officers may be appointed to meet . . . to settle terms for the surrender of the posts at York and Gloucester." Washington gave him two hours; Cornwallis responded at four thirty. All parties met the following morning and Washington, who did not attend the negotiations, returned Lt. Colonel John Laurens and the Marquis de Noailles with word that Cornwallis's army would be treated under the same terms afforded the American army at Charleston the year before. Cornwallis would not be allowed to concede with honors.[28]

The articles of surrender were signed at 11 a.m., 19 October 1781. At 2 p.m., the French army, dressed in white uniforms and sporting well-polished boots, formed a long column opposite the Americans, "clad in small jackets of white cloth, dirty and ragged, almost bare footed." British and Hessian troops marched between the columns, each head turned only in the direction of the Frenchmen. After arms were surrendered and colors transferred, the troops returned to formation and Brig. General Charles O'Hara appeared, carrying Cornwallis's sword. Cornwallis, he declared, was unable to attend the ceremony and offered the sword to Rochambeau, who deferred to Washington. The commander-in-chief of the Continental Army refused to accept it and indicated Benjamin Lincoln would receive the honor in recognition of his treatment at Charleston. Washington threw up a tent that evening, large enough to accommodate forty diners, and invited French, British, and American officers to join him. Lord Corn-

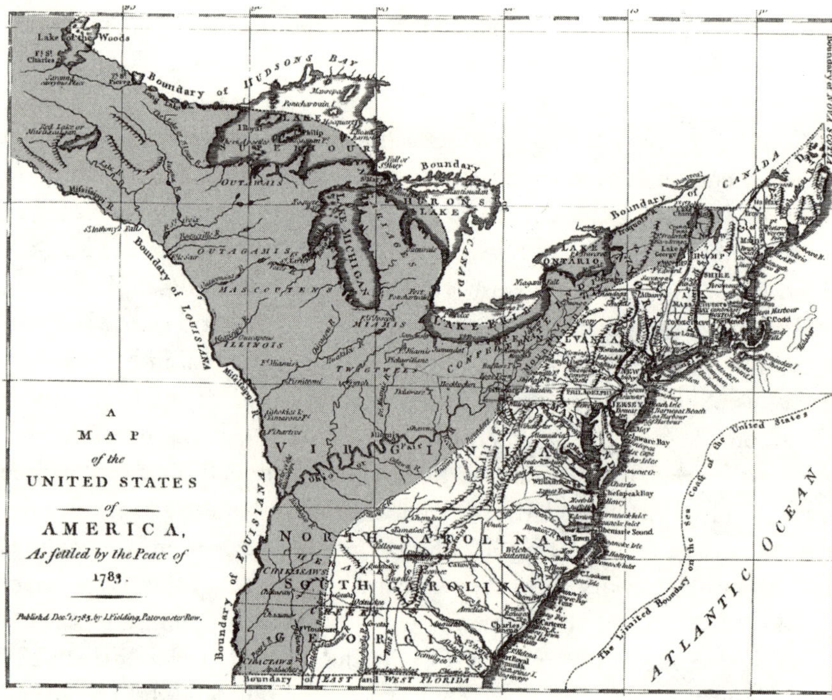

Map of the United States at 1783 peace. London, 1785. Library of Congress.

wallis declined. The British fleet sent to save Cornwallis arrived off the coast of Virginia five days later. With eight thousand British soldiers now prisoners of war, there was nothing for the ships to do but transport the few area Loyalists to the safety of New York.[29]

Major William Croghan had ridden quickly from Fort Pitt to participate in the definitive Revolutionary War battle, intending to shoulder a substantial role in the fighting. Croghan believed he had been exchanged for a British officer and joined his regiment at Yorktown only to learn he would not be permitted to fight. He nonetheless was put to work behind the lines throughout the battle, and proudly joined the Continental officers when the British army surrendered. "The first of October, flattering myself I was Exchanged Settout to Join the Army at the Seige of York, but finding I was not, came to this city [Philadelphia] Immediately after seeing Lord Cornwallis' army lay down their arms."[30]

In the end, the combination of Clinton's utter lack of sea or land support and the arrival of the superior French force doomed Cornwallis at Yorktown. Surrounded by de Grasse's navy and Rochambeau's land troops, and unaware that Yorktown would be the last French commitment in the Revolution, he had no option but to surrender. This was the last major battle of the American Revolution; the loss to the hated French, coupled with mounting expenses required to fight a war an ocean away, swayed many in Parliament, if not to support the Americans, to abandon the effort to oppose them. The victory would lead directly to the signature of the Treaty of Paris, which formally severed the United States of America's colonial ties with London, but the conclusion of the Continental Congress's war had little impact on the fighting that continued in the American West.

7

Detroit

My very soul was wrapt in the expedition.
—George Rogers Clark, 1779

With the fort at Vincennes secure, Detroit became George Rogers Clark's single objective during the final months of the Revolution. Even as Henry Hamilton made his way to Williamsburg as a prisoner of war, Clark had begun to tease Detroit's new commander, Captain Richard Lernoult, with a deliberately provocative introduction of himself. "I learn by your letter to Gov. Hamilton that you were very busy making new works, I am glad to hear it, as it saves Americans some expenses in building. The Officers of Fort Pat. Henry solicit Captain Lernoult to present their compliments to the Officers of his garrison." Clark's enthusiasm for his next task was genuine, but Patrick Henry had other promises to keep in 1779, and redirected his western commander away from Detroit.[1]

Henry had outlined the advantages of an American rather than British presence in West Florida when he succeeded in creating a pact with the Spanish governor of New Orleans at the beginning of the Revolution. Among the carrots he offered Spain were control of the lower Mississippi and a promise to build a fort for use by both Spain and Virginia. Jefferson was not an admirer of Henry, but when he succeeded him as governor in 1779, he honored Virginia's pact with Spain and ordered the creation of "a fort at the mouth of Ohio which together with other posts meant to be established on the Ohio may form a chain of defence for our Western frontier and at ye same time protect our Trade with New Orleans."[2]

Clark sent men to New Orleans to confirm Virginia's mercantile relationships with Oliver Pollock and others, and following Jefferson's orders, announced the decision to give up the posts at Kaskaskia, Cahokia, and Vincennes. "The one probable Method of Maintaining our Authority in the Illinois," he wrote John Todd, "is by Amediately Evacuating our present posts and let our whole force Center at or near the Mouth of the Ohio." Clark was, and would remain, Jefferson's man.

He arrived at the confluence of the Ohio and Mississippi rivers on 19 April 1780 with about 250 militiamen and settlers from the Falls area. Jefferson's assumption that civilian pioneers would want to surround the fort and provide food and services for the garrison soon was proven wrong. Chickasaw opposition pinned the few settlers within the walls at Fort Jefferson, where the tense atmosphere was further irritated by infrequent arrivals of excessively inflated supplies from New Orleans. It soon was obvious the three hundred land warrants of 560 acres each, sent to Clark by Jefferson as incentives for military and civil participation, were hardly enticing to the few who considered living near the new fort. Hundreds of miles beyond the edge of civilization and described by its commander as "this remote hole," the fort and its tiny adjacent settlement, optimistically known as Clarksville, stood little chance of becoming a viable community. Under regular attack and deprived of almost every material necessity, the outpost withered without support from Virginia.[3]

Fort Jefferson struggled to survive for reasons that proved true throughout the commonwealth's "backwoods" territory: as an independent government, Virginia could neither manage nor afford its western land claims. Clark, whom Virginia's leaders sent nearly everywhere west of the mountains to accomplish nearly everything during the Revolution, had left the fledgling Clarksville less than a month after his arrival for the defense of Spain, at war with Great Britain for nearly a year. As a Spanish lieutenant governor, Fernando de Leyba had established a home at St. Louis with his wife, Marie, and daughters, Rita and Pepita, in June 1778, less than a month before the Virginians' arrival on the Mississippi. He and Clark had initiated a friendship that extended beyond their mutual interests in securing the support of one another's governments, and Clark arrived in time to participate in the defense of the 26 May British assault on St. Louis.[4]

A traditional, but unconvincing story has continued over the centuries that suggests that Clark had a romance with one of the women in de Leyba's household. An October 1779 letter from John Todd to Clark that was among the documents collected in the mid-nineteenth century led historian Lyman Draper to conclude that de Leyba's sister was the object of Clark's affections. "Your Br [Dickie] is well, Madame Leyba is dead, Madamlle Terese still a Maid &c&c&c. If I could get an Opp[ortunit]y of sending you some thing good to Toast your Sweet Heart in I would." Three extant letters from Clark to de Leyba include references to the Spaniard's "ladies," but neither Terese nor a sister was mentioned. In one, de Leyba's daughters were offered compliments as "my two favorites the little Misses," which marked the most intimate communication known between the men.[5]

Marie de Leyba had died in September 1779 and her widower's will was recorded by Francis Vigo shortly before the governor's own death. It provided for his daughters, mentioned his mother, and made arrangements for the disposal of his wife's belongings, but it did not acknowledge a sister. If Todd's letter can be taken at face value, Clark apparently developed a romantic link with someone on the frontier in the summer of 1779, and although his family never was told the details, seventy years later, some among them concluded that postwar financial and legal entanglements left him without the means to support a wife and doomed the relationship. Clark was not associated with a woman to whom he was not related during the remainder of his life, and the meaning behind Todd's comment remains obscure, its significance lying primarily in an attempt to understand the several probable causes of Clark's post-Revolution depression.[6]

Captain Robert George begged Clark to return to the Mississippi on 28 October, citing starvation among the troops and settlers at Clarksville. "Our present distress puts me under the necessity of informing you by Express the absolute necessity of your presence at this place," but his commander was detained elsewhere by his superiors. Jefferson was at ease with the thought that his Mississippi fort thwarted an anticipated British action there, and so, he directed Clark to Virginia's northwestern territory and ordered him to push the Indians north of the Great Lakes and beyond the "Illinois River," as "the same world will scarcely do for them and us." Clark followed orders, but continued to promote the Detroit expedition, which Jefferson kept in play for various reasons, although he privately thought it had little chance of success.[7]

Jefferson's reaction to Indian activity beyond the Ohio River was not a new concern for Virginia's governors. James Alton James believed the Frontier War began with the 10 November 1777 murder of Cornstalk and

Daniel Boone after Chester Harding.

his son at Fort Randolph, built on the site of the Shawnee chief's 1774 Point Pleasant defeat. Held at the fort as a negotiating pawn with area Shawnees, the peaceful Cornstalk and his party were victims of frontier revenge after two hunters were found nearby, murdered by native men. Paradoxically, at the moment of her brother's murder, Nonhelema—known by settlers as the Grenadier Squaw because of her striking physicality—had left the fort on a mission to deliver deliberately misleading intelligence to Loyalist, Alexander McKee. Patrick Henry ordered the arrest and trial of Cornstalk's assassins, but as no other Fort Randolph soldier would testify against the men, they were acquitted. James's theory overlooks the bloody spring and summer that western settlers had just endured, but does offer a definitive marker by which the next violent eighteen years can be measured.

Two months after Cornstalk's death, Daniel Boone and twenty-six other men left the comparative warmth and security of Fort Boonesborough for the Lower Blue Lick Springs, where they carried out the difficult job of making salt. They were captured by more than a hundred Shawnee warriors led by Blackfish, who was making war in retaliation for Cornstalk's assassination. The prisoners arrived at [Old] Chillicothe on 18 February, where some of the captives were adopted by native families; Boone's adoptive sponsors apparently were Blackfish and his squaw. The village, called Chalahgawtha by its residents, was the traditional center of Shawnee culture in southern Ohio, and had been established on the Little Miami in 1774 after Dunmore's War had driven its people from the Ohio River. The Shawnee Confederacy, always nomadic, was more so during the years between the French and Indian War and Tecumseh's 1813 death, and Chillicothe would be rebuilt again after Clark destroyed it.[8]

Near starvation, the Shawnees marched the hostages on to Detroit, where they hoped Governor Henry Hamilton would exchange them for food and other provisions. After he was treated "with great humanity" by Hamilton, Boone was not allowed by Blackfish to be exchanged and consequently was returned to Chillicothe. He later would say his ransom was refused because of Blackfish's great affection for him, but Hamilton wrote that the Indians meant to "effect something" from Boone's continued presence with them.

Given an unusual amount of freedom, Boone made his escape on 16 June and rode until his horse gave way. He then ran the rest of the way down the Bullskin Trail to the Ohio, and on to Boonesborough, some 160 miles. When Blackfish and Boone next met days before the September siege of Boonesborough, the chief was said by Boone (an inveterate teller of tall tales) to have asked, "My son, what made you run away from me?" Boone responded he had wanted to see his wife and children. "Well, if you had asked me," Blackfish replied, "I'd have let you come." Negotiations toward a failed peace continued for several days before the Shawnees launched an eleven-day attack that ended 17 September 1778 with the Indians' withdrawal.[9]

As the Boonesborough attack raged on, Simon Kenton rode from the fort for Ohio to capture the ponies left behind by the warriors. He was captured on 13 September and taken to Chillicothe, where, unlike Boone's relatively mild captivity, Kenton was targeted for death before he was rescued and delivered to Detroit by renegade Simon Girty, whom he had met first at Fort Pitt. Before his exchange, Kenton, whose survival instincts were extraordinary, reconnoitered the topography associated with the Shawnee capital and later recalled it all.

In retaliation for the Boonesborough siege, Col. John Bowman organized a Chillicothe raid in the spring of 1779 and succeeded in stealing three hundred horses and mortally wounding Blackfish. New Detroit commander Arent De Peyster consequently sent captains Henry Bird and Alexander McKee to Kentucky on 1 June 1780 with a force of 850 British regulars and warriors to avenge the militia's activity of a year earlier.[10]

McKee had remained in the Fort Pitt area for more than a year after the Revolution began, as a neutral observer of British and American activity. After growing disgusted by militia brutality against peaceful Delaware Indians in the area, he abandoned his home and reported to Detroit as a British sympathizer. It was apparent as he and Bird moved with their troops toward Kentucky that commander Bird, more engineer than officer, was not in control of his men. Bird knew Clark was on the Mississippi and hoped to strike Louisville in the colonel's absence; but convinced otherwise by fellow officers who feared Clark's retribution, the rangers agreed to travel east, along the Ohio. They entered Kentucky at the Licking River, where, within days, they attacked Ruddle's and Martin's stations and captured 350 prisoners.

Clark learned almost immediately of the presence of the Detroit army and left Fort Jefferson "with what men we could spare." With one unit sent by boat to the Falls, Clark took two companies with him in a rough tear through Kentucky to warn the settlers. He arrived near Harrodsburg just after the Ruddle raid, where he received notification from Jefferson that the Detroit expedition again was tabled in favor of a retaliatory attack against the Ohio Shawnees. Bird returned to Detroit on 4 August with little inclination to see Kentucky again, and Clark, disappointed with Jefferson's orders, continued to believe a Shawnee raid would be pointless without a victory at Detroit. He had written William Fleming earlier in the spring to reject a proposed Ohio expedition, saying he "was hartily sorry for the great loss of Blood and property sustained by Kentuckians [but an Ohio expedition] would be so far from giving us Peace that it would only Agravate the war by destroying an [Detroit] Expedition already planned."[11]

The latest bloodshed had not changed his opinion, but resigned, he cast about for a means of fulfilling his orders. Jefferson would reimburse him for expenses connected to the expedition, he understood, but with no advance payment to organize the campaign, he appealed for help. Fort Pitt's commander, Daniel Brodhead, refused any role in the campaign, but in recognition of Clark's role as military commander in the West, he wished him well. "I don't know how far it may be in your Power to make an attack upon the Shawanese & their allies but if it can be done with a probability of success I hope you will attempt it, because I am persuaded that they are the most hostile of any Savage Tribe and could they receive a severe chastisement it would probably put an end to the Indian war."[12]

Finally, to ensure adequate participation in the 1780 campaign, four of every five men in Kentucky were conscripted, and those remaining were ordered to form a home guard. In all, a thousand buckskinned men rode to the Falls in July with the destruction of the Shawnee villages at Chillicothe and Piqua as their target. John Floyd, whom Clark would describe as "a soldier, Gentleman, and a Scholar," and frontier friends William Harrod and William Linn led the Kentucky units, supplemented with fifty Virginia regulars and twenty-six Illinois Regiment veterans. A brass six-pounder, liberated from Fort Sackville the year before, also went along.[13]

Clark traveled up the Ohio in a flotilla of barges, keelboats, and pirogues, while hunters under the command of Hugh McGary moved by foot along the northwestern bank. After they confiscated most of the food cargo from a boat bound for Louisville, the army built a small stockade to house supplies and casualties at the mouth of the Licking River, as McGary's unit had been attacked with several injuries. George Rogers Clark began Kentucky's 1780 Shawnee Expedition with Simon Kenton and Benjamin Logan at his side. Logan's deputy, Daniel Boone, protected the militia's rear. Boone and Kenton were experienced, which was indispensable to Clark, but every man in the 1780 campaign was a hardened pioneer who, by then, knew something of the American Indian and everything about the rifle slung over his own shoulder.

John Clairy, one of Logan's recruits, had been turned by Bird's army and, after he crossed the Ohio, deserted the militia and quickly moved north, ahead of Clark. Aware of Clairy's intentions, Clark pushed his men to their limits, disgruntling both volunteers and draftees to ensure the possibility of a surprise attack at Chillicothe. Although little more than a hundred people lived in the village during the winter, the population soared to more than a thousand during the growing seasons, and the militia expected a strong resistance.

The men moved in four columns, roughly forty yards apart, with Clark riding ahead of artillery wagons. After they cut and bridged nearly seventy miles of road, they were denied rest and were forced to march through the night of 5–6 August; it was near midnight when the Shawnee scouts spotted them and began the evacuation of Chillicothe. Clark was alerted to the activity at dawn, at which point the army broke into "a good smart trot" to cover the few miles that separated them from the village. Chillicothe's women, children, and invalids had been moved to safety and the warriors were out of sight when the Kentucky militia arrived. The hungry troops feasted into the night on acres of vegetables left ripe in the fields and food yet cooking in warm pots. The town was destroyed the next day before Clark started for the Piqua settlements, twelve miles ahead, but a sudden storm stopped their progress and the sodden militia again spent the night on alert, this time in a hollow square formation.[14]

Clark had them on the march at dawn, attesting to reports made by Detroit's informers, who were impressed with the manner in which he drove his men and controlled the famously independent Kentuckians. The Piqua villages came into sight at two thirty on the afternoon of 8 August, and from his position near the Mad River, Clark easily could see his opposition. Three hundred Shawnee, Mingo, Wyandot, and Delaware warriors stood ready, their families and hostages protected under a limestone shelf near the river.[15]

Kenton and Logan led three hundred men to the rear of the villages to prevent an Indian retreat while Linn, Harrod, and Floyd took their men west, into the treed periphery of the large cornfield that separated the militia from the Indians. The Shawnees opened fire as William Oldham's advance company sprinted across the open prairie, and the battle began before either side was prepared. Clark was at the center of the militia, and his men negotiated both the river and open fields under fierce attack. The exchanges continued until about 5 p.m., when many of the native fighters disappeared—some into their cabins and others into the woods. Clark called a halt to the shooting just long enough to reposition his guns before he destroyed most of the stockade that surrounded the cabins. Warriors streamed forward, and, in response, the militia reverted to its hollow square formation and fought in hand-to-hand combat.

By nightfall, the natives had repositioned themselves to protect their families, but the militia had had enough and camped in what was left of the stockade. They buried their dead within the remains of the structure the next morning before they burned it to the ground in hope that the ashes would discourage the Indians from disturbing the graves. Clark's cousin, Joseph Rogers, who had been captured near Blue Licks on 28 December 1776 and had lived since then at the Piqua villages, was among the bodies. Shot in native dress as he ran toward the militia the day before, Rogers lived long enough to tell Clark the warriors' plan of defense had been interrupted when the troops reached them a day earlier than they had thought possible.[16]

Both armies spent the next days in depredation: the Indians unearthed the Kentuckians' bodies and scalped the corpses, and the militia needlessly killed two unarmed Shawnee men at Chillicothe and murdered a woman before they burned the food supplies meant to feed the Shawnee people through the coming winter. After the native party tracking the militia's withdrawal saw the woman's body, they burned their American hostages at the stake.[17]

Without enough food to continue the raids, and satisfied Jefferson's orders had been met, Clark turned for home. He composed a full campaign report for the governor on 22 August, and informed his father of Joseph Rogers's death the following day. In the letter to John Clark, he also warned of a developing political tension that would consume Kentucky for more than a decade. "The Shawnees have at last got Defeated and their Cuntrey laid waiste. . . . The partizans in these Cuntries are again Soliciting me to head them as [their] Governor General as all those from foreign States are for a new Government but my duty obliging me to Suppress all such proceedings I shall loose the Interest of that party." He was a Virginian, and continued to conceive of Kentucky's future only within the commonwealth. The Shawnees and their allies were not defeated, and in 1780, could not dream of defeat, but having done as requested, Clark now looked again toward the source of Kentucky's turmoil: Detroit.[18]

After months of further violence and neglect, John Montgomery was sent to Fort Jefferson in 1781 to evacuate the settlement's surviving inhabitants, which effectively ended the short, brutal history of Jefferson's outpost, but by that time, the governor was in thrall to other crises. Virginia's legislature had agreed to abandon its claim of jurisdictional autonomy in the West on 20 December 1780 after the Continental Congress asked all the colonies to facilitate the creation of an American Union under the Articles of Confederation. Faced with bankruptcy, in part because of the expenses associated with administering its western territories, Virginia agreed to accept the secession if the new federal government assumed all the costs associated with Clark's western expeditions. In reality, Thomas Jefferson had little choice but to agree to the new Articles on 2 January 1781 because Benedict Arnold, now a British officer, was on the James River and Virginia was in desperate need of federal troops.[19]

The British fleet had appeared at the mouth of the river on 31 December, and by 3 January 1781, eighteen hundred men under Arnold's command were advancing toward the new state capital at Richmond with the objective to destroy southern supply lines and draw Nathanael Greene's army away from Cornwallis. The diversion worked. Washington ordered Greene up from the Carolinas and sent Steuben to Richmond to gather supplies.

Clark was in Richmond at the time to confer with Jefferson. With the governor's western goals accomplished, Clark had received a Christmas Day letter from Jefferson that outlined his and Washington's plans for the Detroit campaign and optimistically reported the possibility of the loan of Continental troops for the expedition. "We have . . . determined that an expedition shall be undertaken under your command in a very early season of the approaching year into the hostile country beyond the Ohio, the principle of which is to be the reduction of the British post at Detroit." Now in Richmond to finalize the expedition's plans, Clark again was sidetracked by business he had not wished for when Steuben, who quickly organized the defense of Virginia, pressed him into service. With Jonathan and Edmund yet prisoners in Charleston, and Johnny held in New York since the Germantown battle, Clark accepted the opportunity to render some harm to British troops along the Atlantic Coast.[20]

Arnold ransacked Richmond on 5 and 6 January before he withdrew down the James River, but some of his most intense fighting on the way to the capital had been at the river's narrows near John Hood's farm, about thirty miles southeast of the city. Steuben earlier had encouraged Jefferson to place a small fort at the location, but the governor, unable to believe British forces would reach Richmond, declined. The defensive action had failed, but Steuben sent Clark with about three hundred infantry to disrupt Arnold's departure. Hessian captain Johann Ewald wrote on 10 January of their retreat to Hood's, where the waiting British boats already were heavy with Richmond's plunder. "Despite a sudden gale and thunderstorm, General Arnold ordered me to get into the boats with fifty Jagers [elite German light infantry units], along with Colonel Simcoe with two hundred rangers, Colonel Dundas with two hundred of the 80th Regiment, and Major Robinson with two hundred men of his corps." Ewald described the encounter he and several Jagers had with a mounted American advance party, probably Clark and his officers, along the sandy road that cut into the area's dense woods.

> We had hardly marched a half an hour, when some twenty musket shots were fired at the head. . . . Instead of halting and searching . . . everybody kept on marching. After a lapse of about half an hour, [at a crossroads] we heard two extraordinarily loud voices. . . . At that instant, a terrible fire fell out of the woods from the front and left among Robinson's honorable [Loyal] Americans. Weeping, wailing, and gnashing of teeth arose, and one captain, two officers, and some forty men were either killed or seriously wounded. . . . General Arnold himself came to the head, which was in the greatest confusion. . . . The general requested me, with the most courteous expression, to take command of the advanced guard.[21]

Jefferson later informed the Virginia legislators that "Colo. Clarke (of Kaskaskias) had been sent on with 240 men by Baron Steuben, and having properly disposed of them in ambuscade gave them a deliberate fire which killed 17 on the spot and wounded 13. They returned it in confusion by which we had 3 or 4 wounded, and our party being so small and without bayonets, were obliged to retire on the enemy's charging with bayonets." Arnold had left the James the morning after the scrimmage. Later in the day Steuben ordered Clark to Cabbin Point, but with Arnold's withdrawal, Jefferson no longer needed Clark to dally on the James. He forwarded the go-ahead for the Detroit campaign, and Clark responded immediately. "I have examined your proposed Instructions. . . . I dont Recollect of anything more that is Necessary Except the Mode of paying the Expences of the Garison at Du Troit, in Case of Success."[22]

Washington had sent instructions to Daniel Brodhead at Fort Pitt on 29 December to alert him to the Detroit Expedition. "The State of Virginia have determined to undertake an expedition [for] the reduction of Detroit. Colonel Clark, who is to command the expedition, will probably be the bearer of this himself." Washington ordered Brodhead to supply artillery and men and select a detachment led by a Continental officer of "inferior rank to Colonel Clark" to accompany the expedition. "I do not think the charge of the enterprise could have been committed to better hands than Colonel Clark's. . . . The unbounded confidence which I am told the western people repose in him is a matter of vast importance; as I imagine a considerable part of his force will consist of volunteers and militia, who are not to be governed by military laws, but must be held by the ties of confidence and affection to their leader."[23]

With no means to end the ongoing frontier war other than to attack the reinforced Detroit stockade, now called Fort Lernoult by the British command stationed there, Clark accepted his orders and began the work with determination. Promoted to the rank of brigadier general by Jefferson on 22 January, but still unsure of his authority to raise an army in Virginia's rapidly changing political environment, Clark traveled to the Youghiogheny River home of Washington's closest assistant, William Crawford, to ask for advice. The bitter Pennsylvania–Virginia border conflict again undermined his attempt to recruit two thousand men near Fort Pitt, and as the Revolution wore on, the dispute widened to embrace a fundamental question that divided Congress: Who administered the land west of the mountains?

Divisiveness and jealousy between the states and between Continental Army and Virginia militia officers left Clark with few options. He advised Washington and Jefferson that Steuben had given him permission to name an old comrade as the expedition's second-in-command, but Brodhead, a Pennsylvanian, refused to allow John Gibson's detachment to leave the fort. "Col. Broadhead would not agree to suffer Col. Gibson's Regt to go on the Expedition as he said he could not answer for it. . . . We are taking every step in our power to Raise Volunteers." Without money for recruitment incentives, he was reduced to enforcing an illegal draft, which further incited old divisions.[24]

Clark wrote directly to Jefferson and Washington from Fort Pitt on 20 May 1781 to prepare the men for his worst fears. "I hope your Excellency will Excuse me in taking the liberty of troubling you with this Request," he addressed Washington.

> The Invasion in Virg[ini]a put it out of the power of the governor to furnish me with the number of men proposed for the Enterprise to the west. . . . From your Excellencies letters to Colo

> Broadhead I conceived him to be at liberty to furnish what men he pleased, Convinc'd he did not think as I do or other ways he would have had no objection. . . . The hopes of obtaining a grant of those troops has Enducd me to address your Excellency myself as it is too late to consult Governor Jefferson farther on the subject. . . . Should we fall through in our present plans and no Expedition take place it is to be feard that the consequences will be fatal to the whole frontiers as Every Exertion will be made by the british party to Harrass them as much as possible and disable them from giving any succours to our Eastern or Southern forces.[25]

As he readied his available troops, Clark publicly maintained some optimism the Detroit expedition could be successful, but privately he feared the campaign was lost before he left Pitt. He expressed his discouragement to Jefferson in early August. "I do not yet Condemn myself for undertaking the Expedition against Dutroit, I yet think had I near the number of men first proposed [I] should have carried it. I may yet make some stroke among the Indians before the Close of the Campayn, but at present Realy to be doubted. I have been at so much pains to Enable us to prosecute the first plan that the Disapointment is doubly mortifying to me and I felt for the dreadfull Consequences that will Ensue throughout the frontier if nothing is done."[26]

With what must have been a sense of foreboding, the company pushed away from Fort Pitt in mid-August without Gibson, who had been named interim commander after Brodhead's recall. Gibson had begun to represent the Gratz brothers' mercantile operations at the fort before he was named commander, and he would rue the day he became involved in the expedition at all. With Washington distracted in New York, Clark purchased most of the expedition's supplies from Gibson with a Virginia promissory note that would not be honored by the commonwealth despite Clark's pleas, and as a consequence, the fort commander later would spend time in Lancaster's debtors' prison.[27]

Local Fort Pitt militia leader, Archibald Lochry, had agreed reluctantly to follow Clark with a hundred Pennsylvania volunteers and most of the expedition's supplies. Major William Croghan, parolled at Fort Pitt, aptly summarized the situation in a letter written on 18 August, the day Washington and Rochambeau left New York for Yorktown.

> A few days ago General Clarke settout from this Country by Water, with about four Hundred Men, Including Officers & Colonel Crockets Regiment, flattering himself he would be Join'd by some more from Kentuckey, & the Falls of the Ohio, about half way between this & the Falls. The General Expected 1500 Men from this part of the Country & is much Shagreen'd at his disappointment having provisions, Amunition, Artillery, Quarter Masters Stores, Boats, &c Sufficient for upwards of 2,000 Men. Had the Country people turn'd out & went with him I have no doubt the people of this Side of the Mountain in particular would be Sencible of the advantage they must reap, by being able to live at their plantations without the dread of being Scalp'd, which is far from being the case at present. . . . I much fear the General will be disapointed in Getting Men down the river from Kentuckey & the Falls, if so the State is thrown into an Infinity of Expence, without any advantage, as the few Men the General Now has, is not More than Might be Necessary to Guard the Great Number of Boats, Stores, &c he has with him. From every Account we have the Indians Are prepairing to receive him And if they Should Attack him in his present Situation, either by land or Water, I dread the Consequences. The Reason so few went with him from this place, is Owing to the dispute that Subsists here between the Virginians & Pennsylvanians Respecting the true bounds of the Latter, And the General being a Virginian was oppos'd by the Most Noted Men here in the Pennsylvania Party.[28]

As usual, George Rogers Clark and his advance militia floated down the Ohio River in the dark of night, while British captains Alexander McKee and Joseph Brant, George Croghan's new son-in-law, waited near the mouth of the Great Miami River with a band of warriors from Detroit. In the dim moonlight, Brant, who had married Catherine Croghan eighteen months earlier, judged Clark's entourage to be too large to attack and, along with McKee, remained mounted, as they watched the opportunity to capture their target disappear into the night. Unfortunately for the Pennsylvania militia unit, Brant's party stumbled into an unexpected victory the next day when Lochry made a midday camp within sight of the warriors. The Pennsylvanians surrendered before Lochry and thirty-six other men were murdered, most of them tomahawked after having been forced into kneeling positions of submission; the survivors were marched to Detroit. All supplies were lost, ending any hope Clark may have held for the Detroit march. When news of the disaster reached Clark, he returned to the Falls with the men who chose to move to the newly constructed Fort Nelson and dismissed the others. George Washington found time to write Clark. "I feel not only for the public disappointment, but for your own, as I doubt not you had the affair much at heart."[29]

At Detroit, Brant's actions were described in a letter from a British officer to Daniel Claus, Sir William Johnson's son-in-law and a former deputy superintendent in service with George Croghan.

> We have the agreeable news of Captain Brant's having on the 20th ultimo, with about 100 whites and Indians, taken fourteen Boats with Troops, provisions, etc., part of Colonel Clark's Army on their march from Fort Pitt to St. Duskey, the whol amounting to one hundred & one. He [Brant] on the occasion as usual, behaved with so-much good Generalship, that not one of the whol party escaped without the loss of a man on his side. Colonel Lochry, Commandant of the party, six officers, & thirty privates were killed in action. . . . Eleven other officers of diferent ranks & fifty-two privates prisoners. He [Brant] is so particular in his return that he mentions the name & style of every person. When the Express left the camps, McKee and Tompson were pushing forward to join Brant with about seven hundred, who was then not more than three miles from the rear of Clark's Army, which the prisoners said will not exceed five hundred.[30]

Flushed with victory, the British rangers and Indian company separated into parties to spread havoc as far as the Falls of the Ohio. The settlers at Squire Boone's Painted Stone, Kentucky, station already had survived several Indian skirmishes, and as Brant and McKee moved closer, prepared to take shelter nearer Louisville under Clark's protection. On 13 September, as most of the evacuees approached Long Run Creek en route to Linn's station, some fifty Miami warriors from Brant's party attacked, killing about fifteen settlers. The following morning, Colonel John Floyd set out from Linn's with twenty-seven mounted militiamen to bury the dead and rescue the remaining Painted Stone occupants. The renegades, now reunited with Brant to form an army of two hundred warriors, anticipated the rescue. In an ambush along Boone's wagon road (US 60), seventeen militiamen were killed or captured. Although Brant urged his men to destroy Boone's station before they left the area, the Hurons in the party turned back to the Ohio River, and Brant and McKee followed. Clark dispatched three hundred men from Fort Nelson to bury the victims at the massacre sites and rescue the settlers stranded at Painted Stone.[31]

Brant's 1781 raids concluded a summer that had begun for Clark in preparation for a march on Detroit, and ended with scores of deaths on the Ohio, and as many again in Kentucky. Sixty-three Americans had reached Detroit, not as conquerors, but as prisoners of war.

Part 3

Boundaries

8

Frontier Wars

> I have been very uneasy since we heard the News of the Shawanese Misfortune who fell into the hands of the white Savage Virginians.
> —Joseph Brant to Sir John Johnson, 25 December 1782

After Lochry's defeat, native alliances north of the Ohio were encouraged by British officers at Detroit to renew pressure on Kentucky, where settlers now feared attack from every direction. "This country calls aloud for an Expedition wishing me to put it into Execution but so strangely Infatuated that all the methods I have been able to persue will not draw them into the field," Clark lamented to Jefferson. "Too few I doubt will turn out afraid I believe that they will be led on something too desperate for their Delicate stomacks."[1]

His sense of things was confirmed when a council of Kentucky officers met in Louisville to determine it was impractical to begin an expedition across the river at that time. The council instead recommended that the West's military commander protect the Bluegrass region and build a strong fort on the Ohio at the mouth of the Kentucky River and, if possible, another at the Licking River. "The Sentiments of General Clark were different from ours in this Respect," Todd wrote Thomas Nelson, who served briefly as Virginia's governor in 1781. "He imagined the Falls to be a post of the first Importance, as he always expressed it, the Key of the Country." The situation was further complicated in December 1781 when Benjamin Harrison V became governor and immediately directed Clark to call up the militia to man four posts along the Ohio and build three or four gunboats. "You will very probably ask how the Business required to be done can be carried on without Money. The answer indeed is difficult."[2]

Virginia's war debt was such that Harrison created a board of Western

Commissioners to "assist in the settlement of the accounts in the back Country," and in late January 1782, he dispatched Col. William Fleming to direct the daunting task of assembling expense records from all those who had served or supplied goods during the Revolution. Clark, who continued to consider his Kentucky residency to be a professional obligation, expressed his frustration with the commissioners and their growing criticism in a February 1782 letter to Thomas Jefferson. "I hope that you think me worthy of a Correspondence and favour me as such during my stay in the back Cuntry which I am determined shall be as short as possible. I cant with propriety leave it at present. Nor can I be easy until I see some of those my cuntry men that speak so loudly of what they are pleased to call Quixotic scheams. I shall recommend it to them to learn a little more of the geografy of their own Cuntry and its true Interests before they presume to speak so frely for the future."[3]

Without any funds to construct the forts, and against the advice of settlers who perceived no benefit from the governor's orders, Clark proceeded to build a gunboat to patrol the Ohio and Kentucky rivers. John Floyd, instructed by Clark to supervise the construction, was required to enlist every man in the Jefferson County militia to complete the work at the Falls. He reported their progress to Harrison on 2 May. "We have . . . a Galley on the stocks that will be furnished in about twenty days, that I think will do business: She is seventy-three feet Keel, calculated for Navigation of the Ohio, to have forty-six oars one hundred and ten men. One six, six fours, and a two pounder is her proposed metal . . . on the galley, gunnels . . . play on hinges and raise her side so high that she can lay within pistol shot of the shore without the lease danger." The galley would not succeed as Harrison hoped; rather than protect settlers, its appearance on the Ohio would rouse the Miami Confederacy to increased action. The gunboat proved to be more a symbolic gesture than a defensive tactic, but as each side continued the Frontier War, it was an order that would scar Clark rather than Harrison.[4]

As frontier tensions escalated, Pennsylvania militia leader David Williamson led a band of Fort Pitt–area men across the Ohio River in March 1782, and after they ate and slept in their hosts' quarters for some days, Williamson and his men massacred ninety-six of the Christian Delawares (Lenni Lenapes) who had welcomed them. The twenty-eight men, twenty-nine women, and thirty-nine children who were murdered had taken shelter in the Moravian missionary village of Gnadenhutten (Ohio) to live as passive observers who refused to participate in the war. The sudden appearance of Williamson's unit, while not particularly wanted, probably had not been a cause of alarm, and the overwhelmingly pragmatic decision to entertain the frontiersmen far outweighed any tribesman's personal contempt for the obligation. After the slaughter, the bodies were set afire while eighty horses were loaded with plunder and taken back to Pennsylvania.[5]

So great was the shock and anger resulting from the massacre that knowledge of its details was passed for generations between both native and settler communities. In the coming century, shortly before his death, Tecumseh reminded William Henry Harrison, "You recall the time when the Jesus Indians of the Delaware lived near the Americans, and had confidence in their promises of friendship, and thought they were secure yet the Americans murdered all the men, women and children, even as they prayed to Jesus?"[6]

Major William Croghan had returned to Fort Pitt a few weeks after the Gnadenhutten massacre and found the fort in worse condition, if possible, than when he had left for Yorktown. William Irvine had inherited dismal conditions from John Gibson, who had been undermined by local militia leaders and backwoodsmen who mistrusted the new commander because he had once taken a Mingo woman as his wife. To Gibson's relief, Irvine arrived as his replacement within weeks of Lochry's defeat, but the soldiers of the Seventh Virginia Regiment who were left behind made their continued discontent known. Fort Pitt's noncommissioned officers and soldiers had not been paid or furnished with supplies for more than two years, and their attitudes regarding civil and military authority were as contemptuous as those of the surrounding community. Croghan was second in command under Irvine when he indicated his concern about the fort's state of affairs on 20 April. "Having been but a few days at Fort Pitt on my first arrival [since Yorktown] on this side of the mountains, I know but little of the politics. . . . The country talks of nothing but killing Indians and taking possession of their lands, *and* disputes in jurisdiction between Pennsylvania and Virginia, for a more particular account of which I shall refer you to Colonel Croghan, whom I gave a long account of the proceedings of the people of this country."[7]

Outraged by the murders of the peaceful Delawares, native Ohio-area parties mounted counterattacks throughout the Ohio River valley. Anxious, Irvine ordered William Crawford, who had retired from the army in 1781, to respond. The forty-nine-year-old colonel had not participated in the Ohio raid, but became the object of the Delawares' fury when he and a portion of his militia unit were captured near Sandusky in May. The chilling details of the terror that followed were recorded by Croghan in one of American history's most graphic accounts of frontier war.[8]

> The pennsylvania Militia form'd an Expedition against the Indians about three Months ago, but Instead of going against the Enemys of the Country, they turn'd their thoughts on a Robing plundering Murdering Scame, on our well known friends the Moravian Indians. All whom they mett, they in the Most Cool and Deliberate Manner (after living with them apperently in a friendly Manner for three days) Men Women & Children in All Ninety three Tomahawk'd Scalp'd & burn'd, Except One boy who after being Scalp'd made his Escape to the Delaware Indians . . . who have ever Since been Exceedingly Cruel to All prisoners they have taken. About Six Weeks ago 500 Voluntiers of this Country Commanded by Colonel William Crawford, went on an Expadition against the Indian towns. The Men behaved amiss, no More than about 100 having faught the Indians who came out from their towns to Meet them. The firing Continued at long Shots with Rifles for near two days. . . . The Second Evening our party broke off & Retreated in the Most disorderly Manner. Colonel Crawford and a few of the others finding the Men would pay no attention to Orders were going on . . . when a body of Indians . . . took them prisoners. We had no Certanty of this unhappy affair untill yesterday when Doctor Knight who was taken with Crawford came into the Garrison in the Most Deplorable Condition Man could be in and be alive. He Says that the Second day after they were taken they were Carry'd to an Indian town strip'd and then Blacked, and Made to March through the Indians who, Men, Woman & Children, beat them with Clubs, Sticks, fists &c in the Most Cruel Manner. Col. Crawford and the Doctor were confined together all night. The Next Day they were taken out, Black'd again & their hands tied behind their backs, when Col. Crawford was lead by a long rope to a high Stake to the top of which the rope about the Colonel

> was tied, all round the Stake a great quantity of red hot Coals were laid, on which the poor Colonel was Obliged to walk barefoot, and at the Sametime the Indians firing Squibs of powder at him while Others pock'd burning Sticks into Every part of his body, thus they Continued torturing him for about two hours, when he begg'd of Simon Girty a whild renegade, who was standing by to shute him, when the fellow Say'd "don't you see I have no gun." Some little time after they Scalp'd him & struck him on the bear Scul Several times with Sticks. Being now utterly Exhausted he lay down on the Burning Embers when the Squaws put Shovelfuls of Coals on his body which dying as he was made him move & Creep a little, the Doctor was obliged to stand by to See this Cruelty performed. When the Colonel was Scalp'd they Slap'd the Scalp over the Doctors face, saying this is your great Captains Scalp, tomorrow we will Serve you so.[9]

The war now carried out in North America's West no longer concerned itself with government or diplomacy. Staggered by the execution of Crawford, western settlers sought revenge for the friend who had been known on the frontier since the French and Indian War. The hideous death suggested no man was secure and no woman safe from the atrocities associated with this warfare, a realization reached by Native Americans no later than Gnadenhutten.

The Delaware and Crawford murders proved to be only the beginning of another long season of killing. At Detroit, Alexander McKee and William Caldwell organized a force of "eleven hundred Indians on the ground and three hundred within a days march" to attack Fort Fincastle (Wheeling), the first significant settlement south of Fort Pitt. But, when McKee spotted Clark's galley on the Ohio, he decided to drive his army into Kentucky to discourage further activity by settlers south of the river.[10]

The rangers managed to keep a band of three hundred Hurons, Delawares, Shawnees, and Mingos together long enough to stage a major late summer campaign that remains alive in the annals of Kentucky's pioneer history. Combined British and Indian forces struck Bryan's Station, the largest frontier post in Kentucky, on 16 August 1782, but by the time reinforcements arrived from Lexington, Boonesborough, and other stations, the remnant of the Detroit army had retreated across the Licking River to the Lower Blue Lick Springs. One hundred eighty-two frontiersmen assembled the next day to decide whether they should attack McKee and Caldwell immediately or wait for the anticipated arrival of Benjamin Logan, who was thought to be bringing several hundred men. The Fayette County militia, under the command of John Todd, and the Lincoln County men, led by Stephen Trigg, decided to track the natives.[11]

The warriors had left an obvious trail, easily guiding the Kentuckians to the southern bank of the Licking early on the morning of Monday, 19 August. McKee, Caldwell, and Simon Girty saw them coming and ordered the Indians to dig in near the top of the adjacent hill before the militia approached a U-shaped bend in the river, where the officers paused for a last conversation. Boone, the most experienced Indian fighter in the party, correctly approximated the size of the enemy and advised the men to wait for Logan, but the talk dissolved into taunts that tested bravery and manhood, and ended when Hugh McGary mounted and challenged the others to follow. Todd and Trigg joined the riders in an attempt to bring order, and years later, it still was said that Boone reluctantly followed, shouting, "Come on, we are all slaughtered men."[12]

Once across the river, the militia split into three groups led by Todd, Trigg, and Boone. McGary charged up the hill first and lost most of his unit when the Indians poured from their positions to fire down on the climbing men. Trigg was killed in the first minute, as were most of his men. Todd was shot in the chest, causing his horse to rear wildly and break, neither to be seen again. Surrounded, Daniel Boone pushed his men into the woods for safety, but not before his son, Israel, was killed next to him. The Battle of Blue Licks was a slaughter. A burial party returned to the site on 24 August to find most of the bodies scalped and mutilated. Unable to identify their friends and family members, the men buried the dead in a mass grave near the water and returned to the mothers, widows, and daughters left behind.[13]

Clark, compromised by a lack of funds and an unwilling army, accused McGary of creating the Blue Licks tragedy, but he was blamed by many for his failure to build forts along the upper Ohio River. Governor Harrison, too, worked quickly from Richmond to shift responsibility from himself, ignoring the impossible position in which he had placed Clark. "If he had obey'd the Orders," he wrote Fleming in October, "it is probable the late Misfortune would not have happen'd. . . . A report much to his prejudice prevails here of his being so addicted to liquor as to be incapable of Attending to his Duty, by which the public Interest suffers much. I must beg the favor of you Gentlemen to inquire into this in a private Way and let me know your Sentiments, his being a Military Man makes it improper to have a public inquiry by those who are not so."[14]

A bereft Daniel Boone, and others interested in protecting central Kentucky, complained bitterly. "Military Operations that for 18 Months past have been carried on in Consequence of Orders from the Executive [governor], have rather been detrimental than Beneficial. . . . Our Militia are called on to do Duty in a manner that has a tendency to protect Jefferson County, or Rather Louisville, a Town without Inhabitants, a Fort situated in such a Manner that the Enemy coming with a design to Lay waste our Countrey would scarcely come within one Hundred miles of it, & our own Frontiers, open & unguarded."[15]

Willing to take advantage of the militia's desire to extract revenge, and accepting responsibility for reestablishing his authority with Kentucky's settlers, Clark organized a counterattack. He forwarded a message to Irvine that expressed his hope for an Ohio rendezvous with troops from Fort Pitt, and marched out of Louisville's Fort Nelson in November 1782 with eleven Jefferson County companies. They met the Lincoln and Fayette men at the mouth of the Licking River, the rendezvous point for the 1780 Ohio expedition. When the full eleven-hundred-man army crossed the Ohio on its way to New Chillicothe, pioneer icons Floyd, Boone, and Logan led the county battalions, but the ghosts of their recently dead companions were in mind.

The Kentuckians made a sweep through the lower Shawnee towns and found most of them recently deserted, but "in a few Hours two thirds of their Towns was laid in ashes and everything they ware possess'd of destroy'd except such articles most usefull to the Troops." Clark lingered in Ohio for a counterattack or word from Irvine, unaware the expedition from Fort Pitt had not been organized. Only when he returned to Louisville would he learn Washington had been assured by the British that all "Savages" had been called in from the Ohio River valley, which rendered Irvine's campaign unnecessary.[16]

Brant and McKee had waited at Upper Sandusky until the end of

October for the arrival of the enemy, but eventually returned to winter quarters disappointed in their failure again to capture Clark. Brant urged Sir John Johnson to retaliate. "[W]ee the Indians wish to have the Blow return'd on the Enemy as early as possible. . . . We think the Rebels will ruin us at last if we go on as we do one year after another, Doing nothing only Destroying the Government goods & they Crying all the while for the great Expenses so we are in as it were between two Hells."[17]

Back at the Falls, Clark's exhaustion with the interminable political and societal quagmire in which he functioned began to surface. "Every Exertion in my power have been made for many years for the Defence of this Department, knowing the safety of all our Frontiers depended on it," he explained to Harrison before he added that he had taken steps to keep great numbers of Indians "in our Interest," while "attempting to destroy the Interest of that Numerous Clan of Partizans or pretended Proprietors residing in Philadelphia That was endeavouring to Divide the Counsels of the People here." His reference, of course, was to Congress.[18]

In addition to the necessity of defending his actions as military commander, Clark was faced with mounting bills that resulted from the purchase of provisions for the 1780 and 1782 campaigns, even as the 1779 Illinois expedition accounts were not yet reimbursed. Fleming's western commissioners' journal noted on 27 March 1783 that "General Clark laid before the Board sundry accounts of Goods received & Issued by him, with accounts against the Officers of the Illinois Regiment, without which the Commissioners could not Settle their Accounts." The western accounts finally were closed in June with a summary report that must temporarily have pleased Clark: "It appears to the Commissioners that there is due to General George Rogers Clark, for flour &c furnished the garrison at Fort Nelson. £1204.6.5½ Specie, as p. account & vouchers, for his pay &c as colonel from 2nd January 1778 till 22 January 1781. £1101; for his pay &c as Brigadier General from 22 January 1781 till 26th June 1783 £1092.10; in all £3397.16.5. as pr. account Bundle M. No. 37."[19]

The Virginia state government decided the commonwealth's unstable financial position was so aggravated by Kentucky's ongoing need for a military presence that it had no choice but to follow the lead of other states and reduce its militia. Clark understood Kentucky was to be left to defend itself and that he was about to become unemployed. Harrison confirmed his suspicions in July 1783.

> The conclusion of the War and the distressed situation of the state with respect to its finances call on us to adopt the most prudent economy. It is for this reason alone I have come to a determination to give over all thoughts for the present of carrying on an offensive War against the Indians, which you will easily perceive will render the services of a General officer in that quarter unnecessary, and will therefore consider yourself as out of Command, but before I take leave of you I feel myself called on in the most forcible manner to return you my thanks and those of my Council for the very great and singular services you have rendered your Country in wresting so great and valuable a territory out of the hands of the british enemy, repelling the attacks of their Savage allies and carrying on successful war in the heart of their Country, this tribute of praise and thanks so justly due.[20]

9

End of Glory

> That you have enemies you must not doubt, when you reflect that you have made yourself eminent. If you meant to escape malice you should have confined yourself within the sleepy line of regular duty.
> —Thomas Jefferson to George Rogers Clark, 26 November 1782

As an officer, Croghan's existence at Fort Pitt was measurably more comfortable than the soldiers' lives, but he nevertheless used the waning months of the war to prepare for a future that did not include the military. It fell to him to call the last muster of the Seventh Virginia on 1 January 1783 and to dismiss its soldiers from service in the American Revolution. He then rode to Philadelphia and on to Virginia, where he spent two weeks before he returned to Fort Pitt to await his own dismissal from the army. Croghan had been working since 1778 to have his Fort Pitt–area deed recognized by Virginia, who claimed the territory. He had bought the 6,424-acre tract for £702.12 on 20 February 1776, eleven days after he organized the Tenth Company of the Eighth Virginia Regiment. Although George Croghan had given his creditors large parcels of land as payment for debts he could not pay, it is likely his nephew paid Croghan outright for his portion of the grant, located on the Ohio at Raccoon Creek.[1]

William had written Barnard and Michael Gratz throughout the Revolution, to keep the brothers abreast of war activity and exchange news of mutual interest. Barnard, in particular, enjoyed a close relationship with both Croghans—George bequeathed large tracts of land to him and his daughter, Rachel, by way of his 1782 will—and William appealed to Barnard and his brother for wartime income and assistance with his land grant application. "By letter from Colonel Grayson, I am sorry to learn the Indiana claim will not be allowed by the state of Virginia and that Colonel

Croghan's and some other similar grants must share the same fate. Pray let me know what is done," and "Did Colonel Neville or any other person witness my deed?"[2]

Croghan returned to Fort Pitt for the last time on 31 January 1783 and immediately wrote Barnard Gratz.

> Pray, what has Congress said about Colonel Croghan's lands? I have been told that a committee of Congress reported that the Indiana Company were at great losses, expenses, etc., but that the land should belong to the States. . . . Pray . . . was Croghan's lands mentioned? The agreed boundary between Pennsylvania and Virginia is run, by which the whole of Colonel Croghan's grants are taken into Pennsylvania. How are we to get them again from Pennsylvania? I believe we must petition for such parts as would have been out of Pennsylvania had the line been agreeable to Charter. . . . Pray let me hear from you if you think Virginia will be allowed all the Back Country they claim.[3]

The results of the final survey marking the Pennsylvania–Virginia boundary would not be announced until 1784, but the outcome of the survey south of Pittsburgh generally was known by 1783. William Croghan's 1776 Virginia purchase lay in Pennsylvania, and after 1784 would disappear from history. Croghan's only wealth now was connected to the land he would receive from Virginia as a seven-year officer in the state's Revolutionary continental line, and that land would fall within Virginia's "back country."

Relieved of his military responsibilities in March, Croghan attended the Society of the Cincinnati's first meeting at the Verplanck House in Fishkill, New York, in May 1783 as an original member of the exclusive officers' organization. Alexander Hamilton, who would become the second president of the society, chaired the meeting that selected George Washington as its first president, a position the general would hold until his death in 1799. Thirty-one years old, without family or connections, and resigned to the loss of his Pittsburgh-area tract, Major William Croghan looked to a place that allowed self-made men to achieve all that his missing pedigree would prohibit on the Atlantic Coast, and moved to Kentucky with a job ensured by Virginia.[4]

George Rogers Clark's commission as brigadier general expired in

George Rogers Clark by Matthew Harris Jouett. The Filson Historical Society, Louisville, KY.

1783, and he spent much of the summer and fall of that year in Richmond, organizing old campaign receipts and considering his future. His friend Thomas Jefferson did his best to interest him in various projects, many of which were based in the science of natural history, for which both men shared a passion. Jefferson reminded Clark he could send scientific material east at no expense, and Clark responded in October 1783 with a large package and long letter sent from his parents' home in Caroline County.

> With this you will receive those shells &c that I mentioned in the last Letr I did my self the Honour of writing to you. . . . You will also Receive a few seads of what the Kentuckyns. call sd Coffee Tree. It makes a beautiful shade and I believe will flourish with

> you. As I expect to spend the Insuing winter and spring in the western Cuntry free from all public consern, of which I have had too much Experience to think of dabling again, it will give me pleasure to Transmit to you any kind of information in my [possession] that you could wish for.[5]

Late in the year, Jefferson wrote to inform Clark of his concern that a large sum of money had been subscribed in England "for exploring the country from the Missisipi to California. They pretend it is only to promote knolege. I am afraid they have thoughts of colonizing into that quarter." Although he had doubts about raising the necessary money, Jefferson wanted Americans to explore the expanse to California before the English company arrived. "How would you like to lead such a party?" Clark answered from Richmond, and told Jefferson he could no longer work for the public but needed instead to place himself on safe financial footing. "Your proposition respecting a tour to the west and North west of the Continent would be Extreamly agreeable to me could I afford it. . . . Should Congress risolve to have the western Country Explored I should take pleasure in lending all the aid in my power as an Individual. It is what I think we ought to do. . . . I have late discovered that I knew nothing of the lucrative policy of the world supposing my duty required every attention and sacrifice to the Publick Interest but must now look forward for future Support." Like Croghan, Clark needed a job, but in the meantime, he worked to secure payment for the men of his regiment. Just as they would do for their continental line soldiers, Virginia's legislators opted to pay the debt owed the Illinois Regiment and its other state line militias with land rather than currency.[6]

A 150,000-acre tract that lay northwest of the Falls of the Ohio River had been reserved specifically for the Illinois Regiment when Virginia ceded its Northwest Territory to the federal government, but not without pressure from Virginia's secession negotiator, George Mason. Clark had been granted thirty-six thousand acres "with a great deal of Ceremony" on 16 June 1779 by "the Tobacos Son Grand Chief of all the Peankeshaw Nations & of all the Tribes." The Piankeshaw gift, in turn, lay within the boundaries of Virginia's grant to the Illinois Regiment. With regard to the Piankeshaw gift in 1779, Clark had told Mason, "I had no idea of having Property in the Lands myself, knowing the Laws of my Country

Justly against it. . . . I chose it at the falls of Ohio suspecting that I might hereafter find it necessary to fortify that Place for conveniency of free Intercourse." Within the year of receiving Clark's notification of the Piankeshaw gift, however, Mason made the argument for its inclusion within the Illinois Regiment grant, "As Col. George Rogers Clarke planned and executed the secret expedition, by which the British posts were reduced, and was promised, if the enterprise succeeded, a liberal gratuity in lands in that country for the officers and soldiers."[7]

Mason's petition also referred to Virginia's pre-expedition promise of 300 acres for each soldier, but the final division of land was made otherwise. After 1,000 acres were set aside for the town of Clarksville (Indiana), 236 soldiers received grants of 108 acres each, and 64 officers received a total of 123,512 acres, 8,049 of which were reserved for George Rogers Clark. Mason's proposal to include a separate tract to Clark that would represent the 36,000-acre grant from Tobacco's Son was not approved. Clark, instead, was to receive "seven miles and a half square at the great falls of the Ohio . . . upon the northwest side thereof, which hath been given to him by the Wabache Indians for his services, and as a testimony of their friendship to him, and of their attachment to the commonwealth of Virginia and the cause of America."[8]

Clark understood where his future would lie, yet hoped to remain clear of political or military involvement in Kentucky. He was appointed and certified principal surveyor of bounty lands for the Virginia State Line troops on 17 December 1783 by the College of William and Mary, which maintained its monopoly on surveyors' licenses after the Revolution. William Croghan had formulated his own postwar plan during one or more of his many trips to Virginia, and he joined Clark as his deputy in the business of surveying Kentucky and Ohio for the benefit of Virginia's Revolutionary militia veterans. He and Clark posted bond on 20 December 1783 as "Principal Surveyors of Public lands" for the Virginia State Line (Virginia's Revolutionary militias) and navy, which entitled them to "one half dollar for each thousand acres as Surveyor's fee."[9]

Within weeks, the Virginia governor appointed Croghan's old friend Colonel Richard Clough Anderson as principal surveyor for the Virginia Continental Line, the state's Continental Army veterans. Croghan and Anderson remained in Richmond with the Washingtons and other members of the Society of the Cincinnati for a 19 February celebration of Washington's birthday and left the next day for Kentucky. There, they joined Clark to secure office spaces and, in July 1784, opened their Louisville, Virginia, land offices. The three men would live and work together for the remainder of their lives.[10]

Despite Croghan's apparent status as a novice surveyor, he began his work for Virginia's state line veterans using the position in the time-honored manner—he speculated in unclaimed land. The Clark and Croghan entry, survey, and account books still exist, and Croghan's name appears in the first entry of state line surveys, with the registration of his purchase of four thousand acres on the Mississippi "on the Iron Banks," near the abandoned Fort Jefferson. The purchase was made with partners (and longtime Clark connections) Mayo Carrington, John Montgomery, and John Rogers. Croghan would acquire more than fifty thousand acres during his lifetime, most of it within the Virginia Military District, and although Clark would work as the state line's surveyor for a shorter period, he, too, invested in the unclaimed land of western Kentucky.[11]

Clark hired his cousin to lay out a tiny commercial center within the grant designated for the Illinois Regiment, and notified his men the land was available. Governor Harrison objected to the grant settlement and told Clark what he already knew. "It is a very fair conclusion to suppose that the Legislature never meant that the Lands should be possessed or entered on till Congress should have obtained them from the Indians either by treaty or purchases. . . . [As you] must well know it would involve us in a most bloody & expensive war which we are at this time not in any degree able to support or are prepared for."[12]

The occupation of Clark's grant by the members of his regiment did not result in an Indian war or the development of a settlement that inconvenienced anyone, and Clark never profited from the grant's location or his residence there. The Clark family invested heavily in the grant lots, but eventually sold them with little or no profit. Harrison's concern nevertheless was a legitimate one, fueled by a report made by General Peter Muhlenberg, who had made an exploration of the Ohio River in 1784 and afterward advised Congress the Shawnees had given his party "repeated hints, that if we meant to take any of their lands on the [North and] West side of the Ohio, it would not be given up without a contest." If a general or partial treaty were not made with "the Shawanese before the fall," Muhlenberg was convinced, "a War is unavoidable. The frontier Inhabitants show as much inclination for it as the Indians, expecting that troops from every quarter will be sent to their assistance."[13]

As a result of the Muhlenberg report, Clark was chosen by the United States Congress to serve as one of five "Commissioners for holding Treaties with Indians" shortly after he returned to the Falls to begin his work as surveyor. Reluctant to accept the federal appointment, he was urged on by Jefferson, who wrote, "It will bring you forward on the Continental stage." When he agreed to the duty, Clark abdicated most of his responsibility in the surveyor's office to Croghan, as he "was never at one moment out of the imploy of Congress from the 20th Day of October 1784 . . . untell the End of the treaty of Miami including the three months I was at New york."[14]

The federal commission urged upon Clark was tasked with the serious intention to settle Indian conflicts in the South and West, and he spent the spring and early summer of 1785 in New York and Philadelphia involved in establishing the commission's strategies. The United States had concluded a permanent peace treaty with the Six Nations in October 1784, two days after Clark began his work for Congress and, with Clark present, made a temporary peace with the Delaware, Wyandot, Chippewa, and Ottawa nations in January 1785; but these treaties had no impact on the determined Shawnees.[15]

Clark received new orders from commission chairman General Richard Butler in July. "Late accounts from Fort Pitt gives reason to think that matters are going wrong in the Indian department. . . . As you have the care of collecting the Indians of the most westernly district it will not be inconvenient to you to attend to these matters on your way down the river." He dutifully arranged for a treaty conference to begin at the mouth of the Great Miami River in the autumn of 1785 and sent notifications to the Indians of the Western District. "In order to accommodate the different Nations of Indians as much as possible, we have determined to meet them & you at the mouth of the said Miami River on the first day of October next and expect that you will be punctual in attending and that your hearts will be disposed to wipe away past errors. . . . We expect that you will collect and bring with you all the Prisoners, white and black which were take by you, or Persons who reside among you through the late war."[16]

When Clark and Butler arrived at the Great Miami River, they decided to hold the conference about a mile above the mouth of the river; Fort Finney, therefore, was established near the site of the Lochry massacre.

The natives responded slowly to the invitation. "I am Sorry to hear there is so little prospect of the Indians coming to the Treaty," William Croghan wrote Clark from Louisville. "I fair they are more inclined for War. . . . Last Friday there was a Man killed on Floyds fork, & Saturday & Sunday two Others in the Neighborhood of Boons. . . . There is not a Sheet of Writing paper to be had at this place."[17]

At last, representatives of the Wyandot and Delaware nations arrived, but the Shawnees, who continued to claim the land north of the Ohio, and "the fellows the present treaty was intended for . . . seem to hang back." Ebenezer Denny, a veteran of Cornwallis's defeat, recorded the details connected to most of the country's major western military events through the end of the eighteenth century and was a particular favorite of Clark's at Fort Finney. He often spent evenings in the general's company to hear stories of the Revolutionary West, and noted in his conference journal that, "When he [Clark] was present, the great warriors never noticed any other General."

As the commissioners waited for the tardy Shawnees, the entire conference came together each evening for entertainment normally provided by the natives. Denny's journal recorded the arrival of Delaware chief Bohengeehalus, "one of the greatest warriors," who realized George Rogers Clark was seated near him. The chief went to Clark, and, "instead of taking hold of each other's hands, they gripped nearly at the shoulder, and shook the left hand underneath the right arm," expressing mutual respect.[18]

Nearly three months elapsed before key Shawnee figures arrived, during which a strained tedium grew among the commissioners and Clark became uncharacteristically solemn and withdrawn. Butler recorded the change in personality: "A mysterious something in his conduct, which I cannot comprehend, or am I certain he can comprehend in himself, as I cannot remember a single proposition of his which has not been [either] agreed to or himself convinced of its being improper, but he is very modest and makes but few."[19]

Denny's journal dated the long-delayed arrival of the Shawnees as 8 January 1786, and it carefully outlined the difficult three-week negotiation that followed. Near the end of the conference, Clark swept his cane across the table to remove a proffered mixed belt, which indicated war as well as peace was possible if the United States did not recognize the Shawnee claim to all lands beyond the Ohio River. The outburst had its desired effect and a treaty was concluded on 1 February with five hostages left behind to guarantee the return of Indian prisoners. The proud Shawnees left dejected, but not before Chief Moluntha asked only that the Americans "have pity on their women and children."[20]

As a result of the Fort Finney conference, Congress would adopt the significant "policy to extinguish Indian land titles through purchase[,] and diplomacy replaced the concept of conquest by virtue of the outcome of the Revolution." Clark held little hope that peace would come to the trans-Appalachian region until the United States could make the British evacuate their western posts, but he acknowledged to Patrick Henry that "Some good Consequences has Already Appeared in the peaceable behavour of Some of those Indians." The conference ended with Clark, Butler, and Samuel Parsons determined to arrange a future conference in a more accessible place to carry on the work of peace negotiations.[21]

George Rogers Clark was thirty-three years old when the darkness set in. He returned to Louisville to hand most of his official correspondence over to William Croghan, but continued to be viewed as the only man who could protect settlers from native attacks. He received regular calls from Vincennes, pleading for support against the ongoing raids ("We are Dayly alarmed by Hostile Savages, whose Barbarities I can hardly Express. . . . Send us Relief to continue at this place or Send up a party to Guard"), as did Ben Logan, who forwarded a memorial to Patrick Henry, re-elected as Virginia's governor. The document, entitled "Aid to Surpress a Body of Indiens who Resides on the Wabash River," made clear Clark was Logan's choice of leader for the needed expedition. Logan also credited the concern Butler had expressed for Clark's health five months earlier and advised Henry that the general "is Recovered from a low State of health & is likely to be Able to serve the Public."[22]

Clark directed his own summary of the situation to Henry, writing in the spring, "I don't think this country, even in its infant state, bore so gloomy an aspect as it does at present. I doubt great part of these beautiful Settlements will be laid Waste without protected by Volunteers penetrating into the Hart of the Enemys Country, Nothing else will do, Scouts and Forts on the Frontiers Answer but little purpose and in the End cost More than an Army that would do the Business Effectualy at Once."[23]

In this interim period between the end of the Revolution and the ratification of the nation's Constitution, Clark notified federal Confederation president Richard Henry Lee that the Illinois natives had declared war against the United States. Westerners sensed that Spain provoked Native Americans against the settlers while Britain did the same from the north, because the new federal government's ineffectiveness invited chaos as far west as the Mississippi. "The Inhabitants of the Different towns in the Illinois are Worthy the attention of Congress . . . but having no law or Government among them, they are in Great Confusion. And without the Authority of Congress is Extended to them, they Must in All probability fall a Sacrafice to the Savages. . . . I have Recommended it to them to Reassume their former Customs, & Appoint Temporary Officers untill the pleasure of Congress is known."[24]

Virginia's executive council ordered a meeting of militia field officers on 15 May 1786 to determine a course of action for the protection of Kentucky, during which the officers agreed to organize an expedition for the relief of Vincennes and chose Clark to command the campaign. Unsure of their authority to wage war and procure supplies, they turned to the district's supreme court for guidance. The decision of George Muter, Caleb Wallace, and Harry Innes was clear. "We are of the opinion that the executive have delegated all their power under the said law and article of confederation, so far as they relate to invasions, insurrections and impressments, to the field officers of that district."[25]

Mindful that the militia's authority to conduct war had ended with the Revolution, surveyor John May informed the Virginia governor of Kentucky's plan, and in his appeal for support of their actions, he, too, alluded to Clark's recent health. "I find it is the unanimous opinion of the inhabitants of this country that General Clark is the properest person to take command here. . . . I have been with him frequently and find him as capable of business as ever, and should an expedition be carried on against the Indians, I think his name alone would be worth half a regiment of men."[26]

Clark recruited 130 frontiersmen to go to the aid of Americans at Vincennes, but remained at the Falls. Without him, the party never reached their destination, but instead attacked a friendly village of Piankeshaws and killed at least six inhabitants. With one of its men lost in the fray, the militia returned to Louisville, where it was apparent they had succeeded only in worsening conditions at Vincennes. Clark continued to express doubt about his authority and sought advice from Capt. Abraham Chapline, who had been on the frontier since 1774. "I have had the perusel of the Militia Law, and Cant find that we have any power to take the Militia out of the State without their Consent. The Sixth Article of Confederation does not prohibit us from Carrying a Campaign against Any Nation of Indians that actually invades our Country or State."[27]

William Croghan represented Clark at the meeting of Kentucky's militia officers in Harrodsburg early in August 1786 and prepared a directive, signed by Logan.

> Resolved, that an Expedition against the Waubauch & Other inimical Indians is at this time Justifiable, Necessary and . . . practicable. . . . That General George Rogers Clark be Appointed to . . . have the Command & Direction of the Army, at this time Ordered on Offensive Operations against our Enemy Indians. . . . Resolved that the Troops meet at Clarksville the 10th of September Officered Armed & Equipped as the Law Directs. . . . Resolved that the Commanding Officers of the Counties procure by Impressment if Necessary a pack horse &c for Every four Men Amunition, & fifty days provision . . . the Whole to be brought to the place of Rendezvouse. Resolved that General Clark be empowered to send Spies if he thinks proper, and that he procure Guides.[28]

Clark reluctantly accepted the call and at the end of the month gathered his army at Clarksville, the heart of the Illinois Regiment's Indiana claim. With the expectation that the expedition would not receive financial or military support from the federal government or Virginia, but fully assuming that his personal outlay would be refunded, he borrowed against the value of the lands he had acquired as surveyor and charged the rest, thereby financing the campaign. May and Christopher Greenup were recruited as commissary and quartermaster officers and ordered to store fifty days of provisions for a twenty-five-hundred-man force, but by 10 September, only twelve hundred volunteers had arrived at Clarksville. Some Kentucky counties sent word they saw their authority limited to Virginia's boundary, and as the commonwealth had surrendered the Northwest Territory, the militias would not cross the Ohio River. Clark sent Logan to round up the recalcitrant militias and to attack the Shawnees on the upper Miami, and by the time he rode from Clarksville on 17 September, only 790 armed men remained with him.[29]

The campaign was a fiasco from the beginning. Clark acceded to the officers who wanted to send supplies up the Wabash rather than carry them overland to Vincennes, as he had planned. It took weeks for the supplies to reach the town, and many of them were ruined by the time they arrived. As they waited, some of the militiamen stole food and other supplies from local residents. May quit in frustration and returned to Louisville. With Logan at work on the Miami River, the Lincoln County militia mutinied without its colonel, and although Clark pleaded for the men to stay, if only for another two days, they turned for Kentucky.

Even with the use of an unauthorized draft of Vincennes-area men, Clark and his remaining officers agreed their force was too small to achieve a victory. He placed Valentine Thomas Dalton in command of the Vincennes fort and assigned John Rice Jones to commissary duties, and, with the understanding that his authority included impressment, his men captured a Spanish merchant ship and confiscated the vessel's goods. Compounding an act that would follow him through the courts for years to come, and with the knowledge that Spain continued to confiscate goods from American boats on the Mississippi, he conducted a military trial that resulted in the conviction of three Spanish citizens accused of illegal trade. The 1786 campaign concluded with its only success attributed to Ben Logan, who killed eleven elderly Shawnee villagers, including Moluntha, husband of Cornstalk's sister. Nonhelema was taken with twenty-eight other women and their children to Danville, Kentucky, where Clark, Boone, and Richard Butler worked for her release and compensation for the losses she incurred as a Patriot American.[30]

The 1786 Shawnee campaign resulted in western tribes' agreement to cease hostilities until a treaty would be implemented the following April, but the lasting consequence was the permanent injury done to Clark's authority in the West.[31]

Within weeks of Clark's return to the Falls, new Virginia governor, Edmund Randolph, received the disturbing news that a Spanish citizen reported Valentine Dalton had stolen some $20,000 in goods from his Vincennes store. This information, coupled with the December 1786 receipt of a damning letter written to Georgia officials by Louisvillian Thomas Green, marked the end of Richmond's patience with its western Revolutionary hero. Green, who would reemerge in Burr's 1806 western flight, suggested Clark's Vincennes officers were preparing an expedition into Spanish Louisiana under his orders, and that hundreds of westerners were going to follow him.

> The Troops stationed at St Vincent by Orders of Gen G R C have seized upon what Spanish property there was at that place. . . . Genl Clark who has fought so gloriously for his Country and whose name strikes all the Western Savages with Terror together with many other Gent: of Merit engages to raise Troops sufficient and go with me to the Natchez to take possession and settle the Lands agreeable to the lines of that State at their own Risk and expense: provided you . . . give us the Lands to settle it agreable to the Laws of your State. Hundreds are now awaiting to join us with their families seeking Asylum for liberty & Religion.[32]

As if to pour fuel on the fire, an unsigned letter from a Kentuckian (almost assuredly James Wilkinson), addressed to a "friend" in Philadelphia, found its circuitous and deliberate route to Richmond. "Clark is playing hell. . . . J. R. Jones, commissary-general, gets a large share of the plunder, and has his family at Opost [Vincennes]. . . . I plan to get the whole sized and secured for the owners, and Bullett and Anderson will execute it. Clark is eternally drunk, and yet full of design. I told him he would be hanged. He laughed and said he could take refuge among the Indians. A stroke is meditated against St. Louis and the Natchez."[33]

The origin of the two philosophies that framed political perspective in the United States for more than two centuries generally is identified in the struggle between Hamilton and Jefferson, and is placed within Washington's small clique of appointees whose disagreement centered upon the extent of federal authority. In the American West, however, the Federalist and Democratic-Republican parties evolved through efforts to block or gain access to the Mississippi River and the territory beyond it. Spain had closed the Mississippi to American boats in 1784, after which John Jay was sent to Madrid to negotiate a reopening. Jay instead signed an agreement with Spanish envoy Don Diego de Gardoqui to close the lower Mississippi for twenty-five years in exchange for the United States' permission to allow commercial Spanish ships to enter the harbors of the Atlantic Coast and Caribbean. An unacknowledged outcome of the treaty would be that farmers and merchants west of the Appalachian Mountains were to be landlocked for the rest of their lives. James Madison, who understood western concerns better than Jay, wrote Jefferson during the debate and predicted that the West might consider "themselves as absolved from every federal tie" and be willing to "court some protection from their betrayed rights" should the treaty become law. He was correct.[34]

Congress's eventual rejection of the administration's treaty could not erase the bitter reaction its terms generated in the West, nor did it open the Mississippi to the American territories. That many westerners were engaged philosophically, if not physically, in support of some effort to force Spain to open the Mississippi and allow port access at New Orleans is indisputable, and Jefferson's Republicans, who did not wish to be bound by any government body larger than a statehouse, found voice in the many proposals to settle Louisiana and the land that lay beyond. Nowhere was the talk louder than in Kentucky.

The "Spanish Campaigns" that resulted from Jay's negotiations were not limited to Kentucky, but those Kentuckians who were prepared to act against Spain initially overwhelmingly favored Clark as their leader. Convinced the eastern men who comprised the federal government had no interest in establishing commercial competition on the Mississippi River, western men generally considered the colonization of American communities along both banks of the lower Mississippi to be the most effective way to convince the Spanish government to open the port at New Orleans; to sweeten the proposition, some among them had received assurances from Prime Minister William Pitt's government that Great Britain would assist in the business. In his communications with Georgia legislators, Green implied that Clark would lead frontiersmen who wished to resettle to Natchez, where they would be able to harass Spanish ships and directly negotiate the river's future without the bonds of the Jay–Gardoqui Treaty. All that was needed, Green wrote, was for Georgia to release that portion of their charter claim to the Mississippi River.

After Randolph was informed of Green's letter, he approved an "enquiry into the Causes of Certain Commotions within the District" to be held by members of the state constitutional convention meeting in Danville. A committee formed by James Wilkinson, John Brown, Harry Innes, and others was appointed "to wait on General Clarke and receive from him such information as he may think proper to make respecting the establishment of the Corps at Post St. Vincents, of the Seizure of Spanish property made at that place and such other matters as they may consider necessary to give satisfaction to the members of the committee." When interviewed, Clark outlined the reasons for raising troops at Vincennes, and denied "any intention of depradating on the Spanish possession or Property at the Illinois." He insisted he had not seen Green's letter, but admitted that by encouraging the Natchez settlement he might receive a small grant of land. With the exception of Green's letter, there was no indication he or his Vincennes officers planned a Spanish campaign, but the inquiry, coupled with growing concerns about Clark's sobriety, seriously undermined his reputation. The degree, if any, to which Clark, Green, or others were prepared to mount a serious attack at Natchez, and whether the goods seized at Vincennes were meant for a Spanish campaign, is not known. Green's role in the commotion should have been questioned, however, as his "confiscated" letter so closely resembled the writings James Wilkinson produced at the close of 1786 that a connection should have been obvious.[35]

The final report generated by Governor Randolph's committee urged "the absolute necessity of Supporting a Military Post at St Vincents and at the mouth of Eagle Creek . . . and [to] carry into effect the Treaty proposed by General Clarke," but a subsequent memorial to the governor, dated 22 December 1786, and signed by the appointed committee, including Richard Taylor and Richard Clough Anderson, went further. The letter contained a preemptive apology should Green's inference concerning the purpose and consequence of the Vincennes bounty be proven true, and agreed that Clark's men, but not the general, probably misappropriated the goods. A second letter, forwarded to Randolph along with the primary one, recommended Wilkinson, Anderson, and Isaac Shelby as Indian commissioners to replace Butler, Parsons, and Clark. Butler and Parsons, the committee opined, were Pennsylvanians who were opposed to any policy beneficial to Virginia. As for Clark, "We lament that the unfortunate habits to which General Clark is addicted, obliges us to observe that we consider him utterly unqualified for business of any kind." This letter was signed again by Marshall, Taylor, Innes, Brown, and others, but not Anderson.[36]

When he learned of the committee's letter, Logan, who was the only Vincennes campaign participant to weigh in on the subject, wrote to defend Clark's actions and mentioned neither an addiction nor misconduct. Randolph's response was to censure Clark's actions in connection to the Spanish merchants at Vincennes, and to placate the Spanish king through the publication of a February 1787 broadside that disavowed Clark's actions and humiliated him. Clark's terse reply, delivered to Randolph by John Filson, mirrored his state of mind. "I Respect the State of Virginia. The Information you have received hath already been stained with the Blood of your Country, things will prove themselves."[37]

Clark's life devolved into misery. Randolph, unable or unwilling to locate the 1786 expedition receipts, demanded immediate payment of all campaign expenses, to which Clark responded, "I can assure you Sir that the whole of the papers belonging to the Dept. (Some Duplicates only Excepted) was Delivered to the Commissioners and I believe by them Lodged in the Auditors office. . . . After Suffering the fateeques that I have undergone bearing So many malignant pens paying and yet have to pay Large Sumes of money for Supplys that the State Could not get credit for [a] person might reasonably Suppose that of course I must [be] unhappy."[38]

10

Wilkinson

> My views in entering the Military Line are "Bread and Fame," uncertain of either I shall deserve both.
> —James Wilkinson, 1791

Thomas Jefferson had not received Clark's February 1782 letter until August, when his wife, Martha, lay dying. His November response, written two months after her death, was uncharacteristically frank, and foretold events Clark may or may not have understood at the time.

> I perceived by your letter you are not unapprised that your services to your country have not made due impression on every mind. . . . When you . . . enterprized deeds which will hand down your name with honour to future times, you made yourself a mark for malace and envy to shoot at. . . . I was not a little surprized however to find one person [James Wilkinson] hostile to you as far as he has personal courage to shew hostility to any man. . . . You may know him by this description as being all tongue without either head or heart. . . . That you may long continue a fit object for his enmity and for that of every person of his complexion in the state, which I know can only be by your continuing to do good to your country and honour to yourself is the earnest prayer of one who subscribes himself with great truth & sincerity.[1]

The association between the beginning of the end of George Rogers Clark's public life and James Wilkinson's arrival in Kentucky is inescapable. Wilkinson had resigned his Revolutionary military rank after the discovery of his participation in the Conway Cabal, but had since managed to make himself indispensable to the struggling federal government.

James Wilkinson. Courtesy of Independence National Historical Park.

Described facetiously by his bitter enemy Humphrey Marshall as "a person not quite tall enough to be perfectly elegant, compensated by symmetry and appearance of health and strength; a countenance open, mild, capacious, and beaming with intelligence; a gait firm, manly, and facile; manners bland, accomodating and popular; and address easy, polite and gracious . . . assured attention, cordiality and ease," Wilkinson appeared at first blush to be a fortunate man. In reality, he was an ebullient, corpulent prevaricator who was used more often by his employers than they by him. He had come to Kentucky to seek land opportunities for Philadelphia investors and soon opened a store in Lexington, where his influence was bolstered by the manners and style of his Philadelphia wife, Ann (Nancy) Biddle, fifteen years his senior. He would remain until he played out all political options in Kentucky, leaving a trail of ruined careers in his wake.

Clark, soon to enter middle age, was portrayed by Ebenezer Denny as "a stout . . . square man with a high forehead, blue eyes and heavy, shaggy eyebrows" who exhibited "personal prowess, hardihood and a capacity for detail" that promoted "wisdom in his plan and purpose." A straight-talking, unequivocal communicator more comfortable in the rough company of men than women, Clark's social skills were far outdistanced by the glib Wilkinson, whose friendships with the Continental officers who now governed the nation were invaluable. Wilkinson joined Kentucky's constitutional convention in August 1785 with a goal to become the leader of the district's Anti-Federalist faction, and for an incomprehensibly long while, he succeeded in balancing that objective with the achievement of celebrity rather than notoriety.[2]

The state constitutional convention referenced by Randolph and nearly commandeered by Wilkinson began as something quite different. Ben Logan had been told in the autumn of 1784 that Chickamauga and Cherokee warriors intended to make raids into Kentucky, which initiated a meeting in Danville of representatives from each of Kentucky's militia companies. Once there, the men decided to meet again in December to consider actions for their common defense, and drafted an explanation to the Virginia governor concerning their need for another Ohio expedition. They also heard a motion from Ebenezer Brooks that died on the floor, asking for consideration of separation from Virginia. An argument could be made that the meetings were in fact designed to build support for separation, but ten state constitutional conventions would meet before Kentucky achieved statehood, and throughout the process, the delegates hotly debated the question of whether or not a sovereign Kentucky should enter the United States. When the group met again on 27 December, after they learned that the rumors of planned attacks were false, membership expanded to include some older men who were not active in any militia company, and the talk turned to the subject of independence from Virginia.[3]

James Wilkinson did not join the group until the third convention. Having concluded two earlier conventions, the delegates already had agreed to their first objective: "That the [Kentucky] district . . . upwards of five hundred miles from the seat of the present government, with the intervention of a mountainous desert of two hundred miles passed only at particular seasons, and never without danger from hostile nations of savages, precludes every idea of a connection on republican principles." The third convention, in unanimous voice, applied to Virginia's General Assembly to separate the District of Kentucky "from the present [Virginia] government forever." Significantly, the petition did not address the possibility or intention of Kentucky's application to the United States.[4]

Wilkinson, who was selected to introduce the convention's actions to Virginia's General Assembly, penned a letter that proved to be a florid and pugnacious approximation of Jefferson's Declaration of Independence. The assembly nevertheless accepted the petition, and consequently established a series of criteria required from Kentucky before independence would be granted. Kentucky failed to meet the measures dictated within the first Enabling Act, largely because Clark's Wabash expedition drew away so many delegates that a convention quorum could not be reached. Virginia later responded with the creation of a second Enabling Act, which further slowed the process.

In the downtime necessitated by the delay, Wilkinson went to New Orleans. He had tried to receive a passport to enter New Orleans in 1786 and, after Virginia refused, tried a new tack. He wrote directly to the Spanish commander at St. Louis to apologize for Clark's behavior at Vincennes and allude to the general's association with "a certain Colonel Green and other desperate adventurers . . . meditating an attack of the posts of his most Catholic Majesty at Natchez." The letter won an audience with new Spanish governor Esteban Miró, and once there, Wilkinson announced that his mission was to represent "the notables" of Kentucky who wished to know if Spain might be interested in opening negotiations "to admit us under its protection as vassals"—to become an independent state under the protection of Spain.[5]

As key Spanish officials already had surmised, Kentucky's decision regarding national affiliation would hinge in part upon Spain's willingness to open the Mississippi, but, as New Orleans authorities could influence rather than initiate Madrid's foreign policies, an arrangement was agreed upon that might sway opinion both in the Spanish capital and Kentucky. Accordingly, Wilkinson provided Spanish officials with a list of Kentuckians whom he attested could be persuaded to vote for a Spanish affiliation in exchange for monetary payments. These men, suggested Wilkinson, could then be counted upon to support Spanish policy in Kentucky. The largest suggested bribe was $1,000, but Spain agreed to pay Wilkinson $12,333 to facilitate the process. The name of George Rogers Clark, whose postwar financial situation was understood by most men in the district, was conspicuously absent from Wilkinson's list of bribable men. Wilkinson later denied any complicity in the Spanish Conspiracy, but the existence of a 22 August 1787 document that transferred his allegiance from the United States to Spain, coupled with the later awareness of his official Spanish code name, Agent 13, leave no doubt.[6]

Clark had been the uncontested leader of westerners who lived on the Spanish–American frontier in 1780, and in recognition of his authority, James Wilkinson had begun a covert campaign against his chief rival even before he arrived in Kentucky, as evidenced by Jefferson's 1782 letter. Wilkinson hoped to become the first governor of an independent Spanish Kentucky, but he had first to eliminate the competition proffered in the forms of the territory's pioneer heroes. The smear campaign he conducted against Clark came in the guise of anonymous letters and well-placed whispers that questioned his adversary's leadership and sobriety. Unfortunately, Clark unwittingly accommodated him and, because he neither sought nor achieved a public role in the determination of Kentucky's political future, left the stage at the close of 1786.[7]

As Wilkinson schemed in New Orleans, the delegates to the United States' Constitutional Convention sweltered in their airtight meeting hall through the Philadelphia summer of 1787 in an attempt to save the republic so recently won. Almost no American could argue that the government created by the Articles of Confederation had been a success, and so the citizens cheered when delegates emerged with a constitutional draft that provided the organizing principles around which the former colonies could form a united government. With the exception of New York, Middle and New England states generally were comfortable with the restrictions and liberties the draft provided (the issue of slavery excepted), but southerners, who controlled the West and resisted any threat to state authority, were less enthusiastic. Spain immediately set about to disrupt the federal ratification process and worked to produce an alliance of western territories through the man they had hired to effect their goal.[8]

Wilkinson returned to Kentucky in September as the district's most outspoken voice in opposition to the proposed federal constitution. In a particular distinction, he arrived as the only citizen with a "right of deposit" on the Mississippi, with permission to ship goods valued as much as $37,000 to New Orleans. Few people knew he had written an expatriation statement in New Orleans, but lawyer Benjamin Sebastian, the aging John Clark's close friend, was among the selectively informed insiders, as were Harry Innes, soon to become Kentucky's district court judge, and Alexander Scott Bullitt, a successful planter whose land abutted that of Richard C. Anderson's new property. What the man who would become Kentucky's first senator knew was suspected, but never fully understood. Wilkinson had written Miró that John Brown was "a young man of respectable talents [he had been educated at Princeton and the College of William and Mary, and studied law under Randolph, Wythe, and Jefferson], but timid, without political experience, and with very little knowledge of the world." Additionally, he was considered an ambivalent, indecisive fellow who might easily be influenced—exactly what Wilkinson was looking for.[9]

These men followed Wilkinson's lead in demanding separation from Virginia, and Brown initially encouraged Kentucky's fourteen federal constitutional convention delegates, who would vote as part of Virginia's block, to reject the proposed constitution, arguing it would subjugate western interests to those of the coastal states. By the time the Virginia convention met in June 1788, Brown had changed his opinion because he considered the possibility of anarchy to be so great that even a flawed constitution was preferable to none. Kentucky's representatives voted 10–3 against approval of the Constitution of the United States, but the full Virginia delegation, shepherded by Madison and Randolph, approved ratification by a vote of 89 to 79.[10]

Virginia's acceptance of federal law did little to ease friction in Kentucky. Repeated postponements in the consideration of Kentucky's request for independence fueled growing unrest and dissension among the district's leaders and opened the door to unexpected communications. As uncertainty grew, Innes summarized the situation for Governor Randolph. "I am of the opinion that this western country will, in a few years, revolt from the union, and endeavor to erect an independent government, for under the present system, we can not exert our strength, neither does Congress seem disposed to protect us."[11]

Clark had appeared to take no interest in the political debates that hovered around him while Wilkinson and the state constitutional delegates worked in Danville. He wrote Jonathan Clark, "As for the Politicks of this Cuntry first suppose a swarm of Hungrey persons gaping for bread. You may conclude that their Ideas are not Genly Virtuous but as I don't Meddle in their affairs I know but little about them. . . . I shall sell out as fast as I can except particular tracts." Stung by both Virginia's and Kentucky's new leaders, Clark admitted he was prepared to sell most of his Kentucky lands, but he did not tell Jonathan that a month earlier, he had composed a letter to Spanish officials, in which he offered to establish a colony.[12]

Clark had continued to believe an American presence on the Mississippi would result in Spain's agreement to open the port at New Orleans, and so, apparently unaware of the sub rosa terms of Wilkinson's 1787 Spanish agreement, he wrote Gardoqui in March 1788, to acknowledge the illegal appropriation of Spanish goods in Vincennes and offer the establishment of a Spanish colony of expatriate Virginians. Without mentioning their names, Wilkinson, Brown, and the others who had ruined him were the subject of much of the letter, but its intent was clear.

> The true motive of my accusers was . . . a wish for trade with New Orleans, [and] they thought by seeming to take the part of the Spanish subjects they might hope to be favored in their commercial project. When you are informed that these same men have conversed with me on the subject of reducing the Spanish establishments on the Mississippi, you will be able to judge of their principles. This and other circumstances naturally . . . has induced me to put in practice what I have for so great a time contemplated, to offer myself to His Majesty the King of Spain with a numerous colony of desirable subjects.[13]

Clark's terms were brief. He would become a Spanish citizen and be granted land lying along the western bank of the Mississippi River. Each head of household whom he settled in the territory would be granted a thousand acres, and just as he had insisted in Kaskaskia, the residents were "not to be disturbed as to their religion." Clark envisioned himself as the governor of the new colony, ruling with an elected council of citizens. Spain declined his offer, and those of Friedrich von Steuben, Daniel Boone, and John Sevier, who made similar ones, because Miró already had agreed to give James Wilkinson the opportunity and, in exchange, would receive much more than a colony.[14]

Clark's reasons for attempting to found a colony in Louisiana were complex: his disillusionment with Virginia was genuine, and no matter the outcome of the decisions under consideration in Danville, he saw little future in Kentucky. Many of the district's first pioneers were prepared to follow him to the Mississippi to live free of the restraints that so vexed them, but Clark's primary reason to consider expatriation was to earn the ability to settle his debts. William Clark later would attempt to recoup payment the family insisted was owed to George Rogers by Virginia, submitting an itemized bill that totaled $20,593.00. "You will perceive," he wrote, "by this account which was rejected in 1790 or /91 Gen. G.R. Clark had paid in specie $7336 and an interest of $3177 . . . and for which he received in depreciated certificates $535.77 in 1790. This blasted all his hopes."[15]

Wilkinson worked within the governing committee through the summer and fall of 1788 to urge the Kentucky convention's adoption of immediate independence from both Virginia and the United States, but in the end he was disappointed. The committee concluded its work somewhat lamely, with a recommendation that a "manly and spirited address be sent to Congress to obtain Navigation of the River Mississippi" and that "a decent and respectable address requesting independence" be forwarded to Virginia. The convention had backed away from a proposal to leave the federal government because fear of native attacks was becoming a thing of the past for most Kentuckians, but the movement to disconnect from Virginia swelled to include all but the most conservative of the district's country faction. The state convention adjourned until August 1789, by which time Kentucky's progress toward statehood, achieved on 1 June 1792, was irrevocable.

The election of George Washington as the first president of the United States, and the celebration that attended his 30 April 1789 New York inauguration, initially did much to unite the nation, even in the West. Wilkinson acknowledged the shift in public opinion and explained Washington's western tactics to his Spanish employer. "On my arrival here, [Kentucky,]" he wrote Miró in 1790,

> I discovered a great change in those who had been our warmest friends. Many who loudly repudiated all connection with the Union now remain silent. . . . Washington has begun to operate on the chief heads of this district. Innis has been appointed a federal judge; George Nicholas, district attorney; Samuel McDowell and Marshall have been appointed to offices; and Payton Short, brother of our charge d'affaires at Versailles, is made a custom-house officer. . . . I know that Harry Innis is friendly to Spain and hostile to Congress, and I am authorized to say he would much prefer receiving a pension from New Orleans than from New York. . . . I know that Colonel Morgan . . . is as badly treated as I am by the friends of General Washington and by the friends of Congress.[16]

With his opportunities in Kentucky exhausted, Wilkinson reentered the army in 1791 with the same resolute goals he had applied to his mission in the district's politics. Although Washington was well aware of past betrayals, the president opted to keep his enemies close, and Wilkinson rose in rank. When the president named Anthony Wayne over him to be Arthur St. Clair's successor as army commander, Wayne knew what Wilkinson was and prepared himself for the inevitable attack. Informed by Henry Knox that Wilkinson alleged he was incompetent, Wayne quickly responded that his second-in-command was a "vile invidious man," and spoke publicly of Wilkinson's illegal connection to Spain. Undisturbed by the public's awareness of Wayne's opinion of him, Wilkinson remained bold enough to write Louisiana's Spanish governor, Francisco Luis Hector, Baron de Carondelet, of his military goals "to keep down the military establishment, to disgrace my commander, and to secure myself commandant of the army." John Brown later said Washington considered the appointment of Clark as St. Clair's successor "& would have selected him but for the fact that he was not the man he once was," a characterization borne of Wilkinson's input. James Wilkinson would succeed in his objective in 1796, becoming the army's commander upon Wayne's death.[17]

Harry Innes had been a fellow Robertson schoolmate with George Rogers Clark, and was related to him through his mother's family. He wrote Thomas Jefferson in 1791 to provide an update concerning their mutual friend. "I have seen General Clark and find he is writing the history of his expeditions and will complete the work in the course of this summer. I entertain the same ideas of his greatness that you do and consider him as a singular loss to the Western Country. I took the liberty of showing him your letter from a hope that it might cause him to reflect upon his present folly. He was perfectly sober, was greatly agitated by the contents, observed it was friendly and shed tears."[18]

Most of Virginia and Kentucky knew Clark was at sea. He surrendered his title as principal surveyor and lived out of sight at his parents' Louisville home, where he read and wrote. With Madison's and Jefferson's encouragement, and with the knowledge he had abetted Randolph in concluding Clark's career, John Brown had challenged him to take on a new project in 1789. "I have a request to make of you . . . urged to it by some of the most important Characters in the Union. It is that you will favor the World with a Naration of your Campaigns in the Western Country. . . . All wish to know & you alone are in possession of this information. . . . Should you decline to communicate it Posterity will regret the loss of what would constitute the most interesting Pages in the Annals of the Western World & would be an ornament to the History of the American Revolution."[19]

Clark's initial response was indignant, and he warmed to the task only grudgingly. "The requisition you make, sir, is such, that a compliance will be . . . destroying a resolution that I have long concluded on, that of burying the rise and progress of the War in this quarter in oblivion, which is in my power, as all light cast on it by any other person must be faint indeed. Great part of the most material papers are either lost, or made use of as waste paper. . . . It would require time and recollection to collect materials necessary to compose a true narrative of this department."[20]

Quite possibly pleased at last to be asked, and harboring a hope for prosperity that Brown could facilitate, Clark began a noteworthy and wide-ranging correspondence with Brown, who had been elected to the House of Representatives that year. He began the conversation with the description of a mechanism he had invented to pull sets of oars, and asked Brown to help with a patent request. "I doubt Sir, you will smile at the contents of this letter, as it may appear to border a little on the marvellous, when I inform you of an invention that will give a new turn to the face of things throughout the Western country. . . . What I wish you would do for me, is to get a resolution of Congress in my favor, granting me the sole use of those vessels for fourteen years, throughout the Continent. . . . The request, if granted, may perhaps make me some amends for my public losses." James Rumsey already had applied for patent rights to a machinery-propelled boat from the states bordering the Ohio River, and although Clark's invention would have been superior to Rumsey's in the West, it could not be patented in his lifetime.[21]

About the same time, a national conversation began concerning the origin of the mounds in the Ohio and Mississippi river valleys. Triggered by a question posed by the president of Yale University to the *American Museum*'s Noah Webster, who initially suggested the mounds were the work of a twelfth-century Welsh explorer called Madoc, the subject had excited the curiosity of many who thought the mounds must have been built by Ferdinand DeSoto. Ever keen to learn more of nature and history, Clark followed the discussion and, having already begun to relive his memories of western explorations, soon fired a letter to Matthew Carey, editor of the

Museum, expressing his deep understanding of trans-Appalachia's native populations and his impatience with uninformed published opinion.[22]

> Sir: I have some whare in your Museum read a long account of the march of deSoto through these Cuntreys. He is brought to Lexington, taken to the Mouth [of the] Muskinggum, Cross to the Mississury [Missouri], & Fortifying the Cuntrey he passed through and all those emence works are ascribed to him. I think the world ought to be undeceived in this point. So great a stranger to the western Cuntrey as Mr. Webster appears to be, ought to have informed himself better before he ventured to have palmed his conjectures on the World. I dont suppose their is a person living that know the Geography and Natural History of the back Cuntrey better, if so well, as I do myself. It hath been my study for many years. I have made the calculation and venture to inform you that if their was paved Roads from each of those fortifications to the other through out the western Cuntrey, that DeSoto could not have Visited the whole of those works with his army in four years [1538–1542] allowing him the common season for marching. . . . There is not a place on the Ohio that we have attempted to fortify from Pitt down, but we find antient works. Soto might have been on the Ohio but no vestiges remain to prove it.[23]

Clark soon realized the writing process was cathartic, and not wishing to forget his promise to Brown and Jefferson, he returned to the subject of his reminiscences in July 1790. "As to the Narrative," he wrote Brown, "I have been at a great trouble in attempting to recover several copies. . . . I have tasked myself to spend two days in the week, and have got through about one hundred pages. . . . The more I enter into this business, the better I am pleased at the undertaking, and frequently, I suppose, experience the same feelings that actuated me at the time of those transactions. I believe, that through myself, every thing past, relative to this country may be known."[24]

John Pope, an old acquaintance who was touring the South and West, visited Clark in December and noted the reunion in his daily journal. "I shall . . . proceed on to Louisville and its Neighbourhood, and rouse up Gen. George Rogers Clarke, who, the Kentuckians say, hath actually been in a profound Slumber for upwards of four Years." And,

> He immediately recognized me, and without Ceremony, entered into a familiar, though desultory Conversation, in which I was highly pleased with the Atticism of his Wit, the genuine Offspring of native Genius. . . . On serious and important Occasions he displays a Profundity of Judgment, aided by Reflection and matured by Experience. I cannot dismiss this Gentleman without observing, that some Years since he shown forth in all the Glory of military Prowess. He appeared from his Plans and Successes to have possessed an intuitive Knowledge of the Maneuvers and Designes of the Enemy, having in no Instance out of many concerted his Operations injudiciously.[25]

In the immediate aftermath of his retirement, influential friends and concerned family members carried Clark through the sudden reversal that reduced his standing from territorial leader and military hero to maligned marauder. It was Jefferson who collaborated with Brown initially to suggest Clark record his memories of the western Revolution, and when the narrative's progress stalled, it was Jefferson who enlisted Innes to push Clark along, and whose words brought the general to tears. "Will it not be possible for you to bring Gen'l Clark forward? I know the greatness of his mind, and am more mortified at the cause which obscured it. Had this not unhappily taken place there was nothing he might not have hoped. No man alive rated him higher than I did."[26]

It was about this time that Clark became related and closely connected to "Dr." James Fallon, an Irish fabulist who would entangle his family in the French Conspiracy and, in the process, marry John and Ann Clark's youngest daughter. Fallon was born in Roscommon County, Ireland, in March 1749, although he later claimed a Spanish heritage. He attended the University of Edinburgh, from which he did not graduate, before his arrival in North Carolina in 1774, where he immediately became an active revolutionary. A personal acquaintance of Thomas Paine, he aligned himself with the King of Spain, who later ordered his arrest, before he found his way to Kentucky.[27]

Disillusioned with the new American government in 1788, Fallon expressed his belief that the United States' control of territory south to Florida and west to the Mississippi inevitably would lead to conflict with Spain, and so he developed a plan to colonize the frontier with settlers who would organize politically under his control and buffer Spain from inevitable conflict. Spain turned down his offer, which differed from Clark's in that the Irishman envisioned a colony along the northern border of Florida rather than on the Mississippi. Also, unlike Clark, who specifically disdained religious tests in his proposal, Fallon planned a colony limited to Catholic settlers.[28]

Within the year, he altered the spelling of his name to O'Fallon and turned his attention to a new scheme on the eastern bank of the Mississippi River. He thought for some time that the Spanish governor at New Orleans supported his plan, and wrote Miró early in 1790 to boast that the incentive for the creation of a new colony was his. "Through my persuasion and influence the members . . . all dissatisfied with the present Federal Government, have immediately and spontaneously, fallen in with my plan . . . and, without their having suspected in the beginning what I was aiming at . . . led them to consent to become the slaves of Spain."[29]

He appeared in Lexington, Kentucky, later in the spring, ostensibly as a Revolutionary veteran who held the title "General Agent in the Western settlement for the company of South Carolina relatively to the Yazoo territory." His purpose was to recruit settlers in association with the larger Yazoo Company, a group of Carolinians, Georgians, and Tennesseans who sought to develop a southern colony free from the authority both of the United States and Spain, but who were unaware of his secret connection to Spain. Wilkinson, as Miró's agent, insinuated himself into the plan and reported to the Spanish governor on 20 June. "I have had several favorable occasions to converse with Dr. O'Fallon, and have the satisfaction to assure you that his plan, his principles and his designs agree perfectly with ours. . . . He appears to be a man of light character, although he is not lacking in education and intelligence, because, being forty-five years old and with many gray hairs, he allows his flightiness and puerile vanity to peep out." After he consulted with Madrid, Miró recommended it would be better for "Spain to populate that territory," but advised Wilkinson to feign support for the company as a means of staying abreast of its progress.[30]

Wilkinson worked behind the scenes to secure the company's ruin through the revelation that its directors attempted to bribe several state legislatures to provide twenty million acres on the Yazoo River for development, all the while appearing to work with O'Fallon. By summer, O'Fallon bragged that thousands of settlers were prepared to follow him to the Mississippi, but most of his claims were little more than pipe dreams.

Wilkinson abruptly resigned from his position with the Yazoo Company on 4 November, saying O'Fallon was a man "destitute of sincerity," but his reasoning probably was more influenced by his knowledge that O'Fallon had discovered his Spanish connections and forwarded the news to Washington: "an influential American has been engaged in trade to New Orleans and now acts the part of secret Agent for Spain in Kentucky." The letter, read by the US Senate in January 1791, made it obvious O'Fallon now knew Wilkinson's reasons for associating with the Yazoo Company.[31]

James O'Fallon married Frances Eleanor "Fanny" Clark in February 1791 at her parents' home, Mulberry Hill, after he signed a 21 February prenuptial agreement in which he promised to provide her with £500 sterling upon his death. The marriage was tempestuous, at best—the bride had turned eighteen only weeks before the wedding—and was further complicated both by O'Fallon's desire to move his wife to Lexington and her resistance to his Catholic faith. O'Fallon asked her brother, George Rogers Clark, to assume a role as military leader of his Yazoo settlement sometime between Wilkinson's resignation and his wedding, but the entire project fell apart when a proclamation published by George Washington appeared in the 14 May 1791 *Kentucky Gazette*. "It is my earnest desire that those who have incautiously associated themselves with the said James O'Fallon, may be warned of their danger . . . that all persons violating the treaties and act aforesaid, shall be prosecuted with the utmost rigor of the law."[32]

O'Fallon would not be the only figure targeted by Washington in his attempts to shut down Mississippi land schemes. Patrick Henry soon was condemned for organizing a Yazoo Company in Virginia, and a Supreme Court justice was cited in a Georgia examination. Washington's concerns were real; the land companies compromised the tenuous diplomatic relationship the United States had forged with Spain. Also, the president genuinely hoped to negotiate the fair acquisition of territory south of Kentucky to Florida, without military action.

The temporary stimulation brought to the Clark family by O'Fallon's presence was short-lived, but for George Rogers Clark, it initiated a period of nostalgia for old triumphs and enthusiasm for the future. Consequently, the 128-page manuscript known as Clark's *Memoir*, created at Jefferson's gentle insistence at the time of Clark's withdrawal from public life, was not completed and remained buried among other papers while its author engaged in *la guerre française*.

11

French Major General

> If it is lawful for any one citizen of the state to leave it, it is equally so for any number of them to do so.
>
> —Governor Isaac Shelby to Secretary Thomas Jefferson, 13 January 1794

A decade or so before their deaths, John Adams and Thomas Jefferson reconciled well enough to begin a correspondence, in which each man clarified his early grievances with the other, and remarkably, each man attempted to understand the other. In one letter, Jefferson asked Adams to explain the American government's hysteria over Citizen Genêt's 1793 tour, and Adams responded. "You certainly never felt the terrorism excited by Genêt . . . when ten thousand people in the streets of Philadelphia, day after day, threatened to drag Washington out of his house and effect a revolution in the government, or compel it to declare war in favor of the French Revolution and against England. The coolest and the firmest minds . . . have given their opinions to me that nothing but the yellow fever . . . could have saved the United States from a total revolution of government."[1]

When George Rogers Clark submitted his original application to Virginia for reimbursement, Jonathan Clark acted as his brother's liaison in Richmond, and it was he who delivered the bad news late in 1791. "I am sorry to inform you that the whole of your claims against the state are by the assembly rejected. The Assembly appears to me to be determined to let no money go out of the Treasury." Clark's response foretold his future. "I have given the U. States half the Territory they possess and for them to suffer me to remain in poverty in consequence of it, will not redound much to their honor hereafter. . . . I am more capable of Negotiations and the Military life now than ever, because I have untill the present day studied it.

Suppose my principles would permit me to change sides, don't you think the continent would have cause to trimble?" He added, "I shall follow your advice and present another Memorial this fall. [I] am now making preparations for it. If I meet with another rebuff I must rest contented with it, be industrious, and look out further for my future Bread."[2]

War between Spain and France appeared inevitable (it would come 7 March 1793, one month after France declared war on Great Britain and the Netherlands), and westerners saw an opportunity through an alliance with France to secure river access. France had followed the United States into revolution in 1789, and radicals seized control of the government less than two years later, which led to the executions of Louis XVI and his queen, Marie Antoinette. Although many Americans repudiated their French affiliations at that time, westerners continued to view France as their strongest ally. The French revolutionary government reciprocated with a plan to "liberate" Louisiana, Florida, and Canada from Spanish and British control and a promise to open Mississippi trade to settlers in the western territory of the United States.

With the Yazoo plan in limbo and westerners in near solidarity in their opinion of the Spanish government at New Orleans, Clark abandoned his hope for the colonization project and offered his services and those of a western army to assist France in an invasion of Spanish Louisiana. O'Fallon later explained, "This plan was digested between Gen. Clarke and me last Christmas [1792]. I framed the whole of the correspondence in the General's name, and corroborated it by a private letter of my own to Mr. Thomas Paine, of the National Assembly, with whom, during the late war I was very intimate."[3]

The proposal, written in tortured French by O'Fallon in February 1793 and displaying the Irishman's dramatic rhetoric, was deliberately made to appear to have been penned by Clark.

> I can raise an abundance of men in this western country, men . . . who have repeatedly fought, obtained Laurels, and never yet were met with a repulse under my command, men through whose courage, fidelity to their country and confidence in my arrangements, which . . . took the Illinois & Post St. Vincennes from the Britons, saved St. Louis and the rest of Louisiana from the Spaniards . . . humbled the whole Northern and Southern tribes of Indians . . . ,

> preserved Kentucky, Cumberland, and the whole territory north west of the ohio to the United States, and protected the western frontiers of Virginia and Pennsylvania from British & Indian depredations. These are not exaggerations. All America will concur with this my unexaggerated testimony in their favor, and these are the men, who, with me, will instantly expatriate ourselves, (as the Law directs), and are ready to become citizens of the French Republic, if my proposals shall have been approved of.[4]

Paine, who received a private letter from O'Fallon enclosed with the Clark proposal, responded from Paris on 17 February, advising that Clark's offer was under serious consideration by the French revolutionary government, in part because of Jefferson's warm support of the general. The letter also referred to the Yazoo Company, obviously the subject of O'Fallon's private correspondence, and introduced the name of a new French liaison: "Give me every intelligence, and write often. Please to direct under the cover of the Ambassador, Mr. Genet's address. He is my sincere friend, and yr. name is already made known to him by me. He is to set out for America speedily."[5]

Edmond Charles Genêt, who had begun his diplomatic career in 1787 as secretary to his embassy in Russia, arrived in Charleston weeks after Paine wrote to introduce him to O'Fallon. Genêt's enthusiasm for the French Revolution had resulted in his expulsion from Catherine the Great's court in 1792, but it had earned the approbation of his countrymen and an assignment to the United States. To the distress of Washington, who feared the French anarchist government, thirty-year-old Genêt began a southern tour in April 1793 that concluded twenty-eight days later with much celebration in Philadelphia, despite a cool reception from the president. Genêt's goal was to establish a favorable commercial relationship with the increasingly pro-British Washington administration, and to drum up support for France's influence in the center of North America. Jefferson, who served as the minister to France from 1785 until September 1789, was America's leading Francophile and was more involved in the French government's mission than he admitted to Washington. His well-known affection for French culture probably played a role in Clark's initial decision to offer his services to France.

By the time Paine's letter arrived in Louisville, O'Fallon had experi-

Francois Andre Michaux by Rembrandt Peale. Courtesy of the American Philosophical Society.

enced a very public separation from the Clark family, which threatened the general's French affiliation. Spain's commander in the Natchez District wrote Carondelet in December 1793, after it was over, to inform him that Fanny O'Fallon had returned to her parents' home after her husband had abandoned her and that Clark, according to Manuel Gayoso de Lemos, was so offended he broke "his stick over his [O'Fallon's] head."In his last known letter to his pregnant wife, written only months before his death, O'Fallon blamed her parents and George Rogers Clark for their marital problems.[6]

Samuel Fulton was quickly assigned the role of Clark's French liaison, and after he secured the Kentuckian's commitment to the expedition, he began plans for the campaign. Momentum grew through the autumn of 1793 with the appearance of French botanist André Michaux, who arrived in Louisville with letters of introduction from Jefferson and John Brown. Brown recommended Michaux to Clark as a man of science who was about to undertake a "Journey to the Westward from a desire to examine the plants and natural productions of that Country," but a Genêt letter written to Clark earlier in the summer clarified Michaux's true instructions.[7]

> General, it is time that the free Americans of the West are liberated from an enemy that is unjust as well as despicable. . . . It is in you, General, that the direction of this honorable mission has been vested and you will be able to cover yourself with glory and you will earn the gratitude of a great number of men whom you will have freed from Tyranny. . . . The citizen Michaux who will hand you this letter, acting as an agent of the French Republic, will be in charge of the administration side of this affair. . . . Citizen Michaux will also hand over to you your commission of Commander in chief of the independent and revolutionary army of the Mississippi. I will write to the Minister of foreign Affairs to ask him to submit, to the Council, your request for the rank of field Marshall of the armies of the French Republic, and I have no doubt that this honor and others even more important will be awarded to you.[8]

Thomas Jefferson wrote James Madison on 11 August to suggest that, although he wouldn't care one way or another about the business in Louisiana, "enticing officers and soldiers from Kentucky to go against Spain was really putting a halter about their necks, for they would assuredly be hung." Whether prompted by the disturbing turn the French Revolution had taken, or concerned about the implications a French invasion would have on his own reputation, Jefferson now understood the severe penalty Washington was prepared to enforce on participants and attempted to extricate himself and those he had encouraged from the risky undertaking.[9]

The president ordered Jefferson to alert the Kentucky governor that his administration would mobilize to combat the proposed French campaign. The secretary of state consequently sent a carefully worded warning to Governor Isaac Shelby, which specifically failed to rebuke the French intrigue. "Spain [has] complained to the President . . . that certain persons are taking measures to excite the inhabitants of Kentucky against Spanish

Dominions. . . . If you have reason to believe any such enterprise, put them on their guard against the consequences."[10]

In a direct challenge to the federal government, Genêt sent five agents, led by Michaux, to organize Kentucky's citizens behind Clark. The botanist visited Mulberry Hill on 17 September to present George Rogers Clark with his French military commission, and to offer support for the trials that lay ahead. The flattery of attention and promise of opportunity worked their magic. Clark informed Genêt on 3 October of his decision to leave the United States and wrote he had no doubt that "the greatest part of the Government of Louisiana will fall into our hands without a probability of the spaniards ever recovering of it and by proper conduct increas our force by making friends of the people. There is no knowing whare our carear will stop. This kind of Warefare is my Ellement. I have served a long aprintiship to it. . . . I find that I shall have to be very circumspect in my conduct while in this cuntry and guard against doing any thing that would injure the U States or giving offence to their Govt."[11]

Carondelet alerted Manuel Godoy, the Duke of Alcudia and Spanish prime minister, of the growing American threat. "A numerous body is being raised in Georgia [by General Elijah Clarke] to invade the Creek nation's territory. It is known that the nephew of General [George Rogers] Clark entered the Mississippi by the Ohio. . . . He returned by land with his soldiers to Cumberland, promising that within a few months he would bring a second convoy of the same nature. If the Americans attempt any hostilities against these [Spanish] dominions, they will have occasion to repent of their audacity."[12]

Carondelet erred here, possibly because the transient French governments were confused about their dealings with two former Revolutionary militia generals named Clark(e) who were willing to lead military campaigns into Spanish Louisiana and establish settlements for France. Genêt coordinated George Rogers Clark's planned activity in the West even as he organized a military invasion of Florida under the command of Georgia's General Elijah Clarke. Both men were promised salaries of $10,000 and the rank of major general in the French army, and each was disillusioned with the federal government they had fought to create. It was Elijah Clarke's nephew, however, who was related through his wife, Hannah Arrington (Harrington), whom Carondelet referenced.[13]

George Rogers Clark's former Revolutionary men rallied around him.

John Montgomery wrote from Clarksville, Tennessee, on 26 October, "I have received a letter from a friend of mine in Kentucky Announcing that you had received a Commission from the National Assembly of France and that you had accepted the same . . . and find that it will be in my power to raise several Hundreds for your service in a very short time." Within weeks, fifty-year-old Ben Logan volunteered to leave his Shelby County, Kentucky, farm to follow his former commander to Louisiana.

> If it appears to be the general opinion that the interest of this country requires that a spirited Enterprise be undertaken against the spanish posts on the Mississippi in order to carry this business into effect I have once more offered my feeble aid knowing you are honored with a commission from the Minister of france and is to be at the head of the business undertaken. . . . I have taken leave of appointments in this state of the united states and do presume I am at liberty to go to any foreign country I pleas and I intend to do so.[14]

Philadelphia's 1793 yellow fever epidemic scattered members of Congress across the countryside and, by John Adams's estimation, saved the Union, but France's objectives ultimately failed because its government expected the United States to finance its North American machinations as a means of repaying the United States' $5.6-million Revolutionary War debt. By the time Jefferson was directed to request Genêt's recall from the United States, the ambassador had lost favor with the new French government and faced execution in Paris. Genêt chose to marry the daughter of New York's governor and spend his remaining forty-four years on the Hudson River as a country gentleman, but the events his tour set in motion inadvertently led to the passage of the Proclamation of Neutrality, which ensured the young nation a long period of stability. Ancient European hostilities continued to be played out in the American West, however, and Clark maintained an inert connection to France, where the Paine-supported Girondist government was about to be swept from power by extremists who established the Reign of Terror. In the midst of Paris' domestic chaos, France's plan to invade New Spain was shelved, but neither Clark nor Spain knew this immediately.

In New Orleans, Spanish authorities grappled with problems that grew from the administration of a large and dissatisfied French population and a threatened slave revolt. Officially at war with France, Carondelet turned his attention at the beginning of 1794 to the possibility of simultaneous sea and river invasions aimed at his city. "All the western country is in favor of the French side and to not heed the orders . . . of the President and . . . in particular the inhabitants of the American part of Illinois and those of the Cumberland are ready to unite with the French who . . . applied to General Clark to command the expedition, which is said to consist of 5000 men." Anthony Wayne, wrote Gayoso de Lemos, had sent a detachment to "dislodge the rebels," and Wilkinson had been paid $12,000 to ensure Kentucky's peace with Spain.[15]

The Washington administration grew edgy and pressed Isaac Shelby to arrest Clark and his followers, but the governor responded on 13 January 1794, speaking for the West: "I have great doubts, even if they attempt to carry this plan into execution . . . whether there is any legal authority to restrain or to punish them, at least before they have actually accomplished it. For, if it is lawful for any one citizen of the state to leave it, it is equally so for any number of them to do so." Clark continued to recruit and provide certificates of authority and announced his intentions in Cincinnati's *Centinel of the North-Western Territory* on 25 January 1794, which were reprinted in the *Kentucky Gazette* on 8 February.[16]

In response, Wilkinson carried on with the farce of appearing to support Washington's Proclamation of Neutrality. His report to Anthony Wayne on 2 February was oddly similar to that Carondelet had forwarded to Alcudia the month before. "You have doubtless seen the audacious proposition of Gl Clark, added to which, I am informed that a Coll McGommerry from Cumberland, has taken Part with 200 Men on the Ohio below, & seizes every Boat bound to N. Orleans with Provision. I have also authentic Intellijence that this Seditious flame, has Spread itself as far as Kaskaskias, & that the People of that place & St. Vincennes, are preparing to join Clark."[17]

Anthony Wayne had initiated a vigorous military rebuilding program after St. Clair led a disastrous Wabash campaign on 4 November 1791. He had moved his army to Fort Massac, in part to monitor the expected French activity, but when a native coalition attacked Fort Recovery (Ohio) on 30 June 1794, the army moved quickly to counter. Fifteen hundred mounted reinforcements arrived from Kentucky in July under the command of generals Charles Scott and Thomas Barbee, and on 8 August, the United States "gained possession of the grand emporium of the hostile Indians [70 miles from Greenville, Ohio] in the West without loss of blood." On 20 August, Wayne's army of nine hundred men, screened by the Kentucky volunteers, rode into woods where an army of Ohio and Great Lakes natives lay hidden among scores of trees scattered across the ground by a recent tornado. Wayne's troops included young Lieutenant William Clark, who commanded a column of experienced riflemen. As the battle began, the militias absorbed the first assault and fell aside, but Wayne won the struggle decisively by pinning the native warriors between his army and the Maumee River. Despite pleas, the British troops at nearby Fort Miami did not come to the Indians' aid, choosing not to attack the army of a nation that remained neutral in its war with France. The outcome of August's Battle of Fallen Timbers ended the northwest war that had been conducted since 1783 by the Miami, Delaware, and Shawnee coalition. It alleviated lingering fears of Indian attacks in most of Kentucky and quieted the Indiana and Ohio territories until Tecumseh and his brother, Tenskwatawa (the Prophet), led the Shawnees' last resistance some fifteen years later. Furthermore, it deflated France's hopes for generating a legitimate cause for a French Louisiana Expedition.[18]

The Treaty of Greenville, drafted after the battle, recognized the surrender of the southern and eastern portions of Ohio to the United States. In agreeing to the pact, the participants ended the coalition's occupation of the Ohio River valley, which had existed as long as native memory could recall. Wayne's treaty was signed on 3 August 1795 by Blue Jacket and Little Turtle, who had led the Shawnees and Miamis against St. Clair and Josiah Harmar, and by representatives of the Wyandot, Delaware, Ottawa, Chippewa, Pottawatomie, Wea, Piankeshaw, Kickapoo, and Kaskaskia nations. It was witnessed by Quartermaster General James O'Hara, Wayne's aide-de-camp, William Henry Harrison, and interpreter Francis Vigo, George Rogers Clark's old Vincennes friend. The wife of Little Turtle, whose son-in-law was the brother of Richard Clough Anderson's next-door neighbor, died the next day, and American soldiers served as her pallbearers.[19]

News of Wayne's victory reached London, where John Jay had been sent as Washington's special envoy to conclude a commercial treaty with Britain. In addition to placing the United States on a most-favored-nation trading basis with London, Jay's Treaty stipulated Great Britain would abandon its forts in the territory ceded to the United States in 1783. The treaty, made public in March 1795, was greeted favorably by Kentuckians to the extent they believed the British army had continued to incite the various native nations against American settlements since 1783, but the treaty's failure to secure navigation rights on the Mississippi River ultimately carried the weight of western opinion against it.[20]

While his youngest brother remained in Ohio, George Rogers Clark tarried in Louisville during the Jacobin rule in France, in part, because Wayne's Ohio campaign had depleted his potential supply of volunteers. He became anxious and wrote Genêt that France's continued failure to reimburse him and others who were waiting with impatience would be "sufficient to rune me." Repeated requests for money made to Genêt's replacement, Jean Antoine Joseph Fauchet, resulted in promises, but little action. When he learned of Maximilian Robespierre's execution and the restoration of French civil order, Clark again harbored hope for the campaign against Spain and contacted his liaison, Sam Fulton. The letter arrived as Fulton prepared to leave France in the spring of 1795, but he found time to answer Clark familiarly. He grew "d-d tired of paris," he wrote, and asked to be remembered to Clark's "worthey Father & Mother & Sisters, Colo. Anderson, Major Croghan and my Worthey Friend Marstin," a clear indication the general's family was well-aware of the French proposal.[21]

Fulton soon sent word from Philadelphia that the expedition surely could be revived through Clark's application to the French national convention, and he left immediately for Louisville. Richard Clough Anderson, as a Jefferson County justice of the peace, certified an itemized bill of $4,805 from Clark to France on 25 October at Mulberry Hill, and Clark dictated a letter addressed to the French Committee of Public Safety that explained his actions against Spain.

> Citizens, Colo. Fulton hath arrived with the satisfactory inteligence of your having Ratified the proceedings of Mr. Genêt and my self relative to the plan of an attac on the Governments of Louisiana and the two Floridas. . . . The peculiar situation of Kentucky is such that their only natural Door to Foreign Commerce is the Missisippi. They despair of ever getting it opened through

> the mediation of the present American Ministrey. This is not the only reason for their desire to assist France but a more powerfull one that of gratitude towards you and the Idea they posess of the rights of Man. I am Citizen yours with esteem.[22]

Fulton left Mulberry Hill with Clark's bill and his letter in hand. He again wrote Clark after his return to Paris. "You may rest asuered that I Shall Do eavery thing in my power to obtain indemnefycation to you and all those that have sufferd by the Disappointment. If we are not able to obtain a renuel of the expeditiond I Shall Return early in the Spring and Settle my self Some whare near you. . . . Remember to give my Complyments to the Famely if you pleas. Adieu."[23]

The Jay and Greenville treaties calmed Kentucky, but unsettled Mississippi River valley politics continued to rouse Anti-Federalist sentiments. Wayne was well aware of Clark's movements and, in a countermove designed to unbalance both Spanish observers and the general, ordered William Clark to conduct a reconnaissance mission on the Mississippi. The lieutenant was directed to gather any information that was required for the defense of the United States, which presumably included his brother's French activities. Because he believed, as he reported to Jonathan, that their brother's "expedition that was going to Louisiana I believe is given out," William focused his attention on New Orleans. He met with Gayoso de Lemos aboard *La Vigilante* near New Madrid in October 1795 to deliver Wayne's demand that Spain withdraw from the newly established post among the Chickasaws (Memphis), which established the United States' claim to the southern Mississippi River. By the time Clark's full report was submitted in November, however, news of the Treaty of San Lorenzo had reached the West. The new treaty, frequently referenced for its American negotiator, Thomas Pinckney, documented Spain's agreement to allow American access to the Mississippi and the right of deposit in New Orleans. It satisfied Kentucky's decade-long demand and removed any legitimate necessity for a western war with Spain.[24]

With western concern about Spain temporarily put aside, new French minister Pierre Adet anticipated a possible war with the United States in response to the Americans' increasingly pro-British policy and sent General Henri Victor Collot to map the Ohio, Mississippi, and Missouri rivers and gauge the mood of the population. The general arrived in Louisville in the spring of 1796 eager to meet French general Clark, who was now without a mission and remained unpaid. Collot left deeply saddened by the encounter.

> A person of great military talents and who had acquired considerable reputation in the war which procured independence to America; who had also gained from the natives almost the whole of that immense country which forms now the Western States; the rival, in short, of General Washington; who is conversant only with military affairs and has no taste for the charms of nature, is soon wearied of still life. . . . We were the witnesses of a scene most humiliating. . . . We returned about 7 in the evening . . . when we perceived in the midst of the square a number of persons who were crowding around something that lay extended on the ground on which a blanket had been thrown and which a man was about to take up and carry off. I asked the man, who appeared to be a shoemaker, what was the matter. "Do you not see, Sir, it is that hero, that great man; *he has forgotten at this moment the important services which he has rendered us; but it is our duty to remember them.* I cover him thus, to preserve him from the contempt of the people." [He] carried him into his house, where we were witnesses of the affectionate care with which he treated him.[25]

Legal and financial difficulties continued to plague Clark despite efforts by his brothers to rectify the situation. Jonathan Clark worked with lawyers in Richmond to influence the Virginia legislature to clear up its outstanding military accounts, and after William Clark resigned from the army in July 1796, he acted as his brother's agent in the West. During William's enlistment, George Rogers Clark had fallen into the darkest period of his life and, in an effort to repay his family and local creditors for the Vincennes debts, was forced to sell his most valuable possession.

He had bought 73,962 acres on the southeast side of the Ohio River at the mouth of the Tennessee River in 1780. Although the land had been surveyed, it was proven to lie within territory still owned by the Chickasaw Nation, but after Kentucky achieved statehood, Clark was able to secure it in two grants, dated 15 September 1795. He and Humphrey Marshall, a distant cousin whose political leanings diverged strongly from those of the Clarks, came to an agreement about the transfer of the land even before the governor's grant came to Clark's hands, and Marshall agreed in writing on 24 October 1795 to pay Clark "half a dollar per acre" for the tract, or $36,981.00.[26]

As soon as William Clark returned from service, George Rogers appointed him to manage the transfer, but before the transaction could be concluded, Marshall sold the land to prominent Philadelphia merchant Robert Morris. Morris paid Marshall for the land, but never received the deed still held by Clark, who had not been paid by Marshall. Morris consequently ran an ad on 15 October 1796 in the *Kentucky Gazette* that announced he had purchased the tract on 3 June from Humphrey Marshall and warned off potential buyers. Marshall later testified he had suffered a stroke and turned the contract over to his son, who failed to pay Clark for the land. The contentious legal entanglement lasted beyond George Rogers Clark's life and left him without available funds for the remainder of his days.[27]

William Clark wrote their brother, Edmund, in August 1797. "Our Bro: Gs business in this Countrey is in a disagreeable Situation. I have been agreeable to his particular request Surveying his lands and to doing what parts of his business I could, which I found a verry unfinished Situation and Shall proceed to attend to his Suit at Vincennes (which I fear will go against him tho unjustly) after which I shall not [have] Money of my own to attend any longer." Four months later, William advised Edmund the Vincennes suit had been settled. "I have rode for Bro: George in the course of this year upwards of 3000 miles . . . and have been serviceable to him in several instances. I have but a few days returned from Vincennes attending a sute broug for Tresspas on a Fereign Attachment for 24,000 dollars against him, after . . . some expense & hard pleading had it Dismissd, and have secured his property on that side of the Ohio." George Rogers Clark now lived with his brother and aged parents, and with the exception of the lingering Marshall case, he could put the financial struggles of the last decade behind him. William, having served both country and family throughout his short adulthood, looked to his own future.[28]

The John Adams administration upset this peace. Well into the nineteenth century, historian Mann Butler would write, "In the year 1798, an agitation took place, which has scarcely ever been equalled in Kentucky, produced by the passage of two acts of Congress, familiarly known as the alien and sedition laws. The sentiments of Kentucky were never more unanimous than in the condemnation of these measures."[29]

John Adams. Library of Congress.

Adams, who became president in 1797, determined that Washington's Neutrality Act failed to protect the United States adequately from foreign intrusion, and he introduced a number of acts designed to limit European influence in America. The series of bills, known as the Alien and Sedition Acts, successfully passed through a Federalist Congress on 18 June 1798 and gave the president the power to imprison or deport aliens considered dangerous to the "peace and safety of the United States." As they were intended, the bills made it more difficult for immigrants to be granted citizenship, and in a happy outcome for the president, resulted in the shuttering of pro-Jefferson newspapers across the country.

Adams represented the pro-English interests of his fellow New Englanders and personally was averse to the establishment of economic or political ties with the French revolutionary government, now embodied in foreign minister Charles Maurice de Talleyrand-Perigord. When the hypersensitive administration restricted civil liberties to secure the nation's borders, southern and western men answered by joining popular democratic societies viewed by the administration as thinly disguised pro-French organizations. Because Europe had not been unprepared for a shift in American foreign policy when Adams became president, Talleyrand responded to Adams with the revival of the French plan to acquire Louisiana from Spain, which reignited western interest in the trans-Mississippi.[30]

In a letter to Fulton, Clark expressed doubts for the future of his role in this new campaign, but maintained his allegiance to the Revolutionary spirit.

> I received, attached to your letter of last December, the copy of the patents of the rank of brigade general that the Directory of the French Republic has graciously accorded me. . . . We have here English agents coming from Canada to enlist volunteers destined to march against Louisiana. Several days ago I received propositions from the governor of Canada to march at the head of two thousand men against the Spanish establishments in New Mexico. You may be sure that I refused, for you know that I detest despots in general, and the English in particular. . . . Their plan is to take possession of Saint Louis, then to divide their army. One part will go down the Mississippi and the other will march on Santa Fe.[31]

Clark appeared to have been unconcerned or maybe unaware of Congress's activity as he traveled to Philadelphia in late May 1798, to finalize his business with France. His reception in the capital changed his plans, as he explained to Fulton on 3 June.

> I am eager to tell you of the unfortunate situation in which our country is on the point of being plunged into by an English faction which seized the reigns of government. . . . On my arrival here I was immediately threatened of incarcination but after a more mature deliberation, I was invited to give my resignation to the counsul general of France or to retire from the United States.
>
> I refused to do the former, as you would well be able to imag-

> ine but I believe that I shall be obliged to subscribe to the second proposition. . . . I went to find the French consul . . . but I found him a timid man and little inclined to give advice. Being unable to obtain anything satisfactory from him, I went immediately to the house of the minister of Spain and, informed him of my situation.
>
> He offered me at once all the protection that a friend and allie of France could grant to one of his officers, and he even asked me to go to St. Louis on the Mississippi and to cooperate there with the commander of that country to thwart the many tentative hostilities that our common enemy could make against the Spanish establishments along the Mississippi, until such times as I could obtain the orders from the Directory. I shall accept this proposition until a new order arrives. . . . From Kentucky I shall go at once to St. Louis where I shall remain until I hear from you. If you intend to come yourself, I advise you to disembark at some southern port where you are not known and to travel as incognito as possible until you arrive at the edges of Mississippi.[32]

Clark understood the federal government's new policies might force him to move to New Spain for his personal safety and, with no apparent awareness of impropriety, was prepared to travel to Paris to collect payment and, should circumstances merit, join the revolutionary forces there. Just as Steuben, Pulaski, and Lafayette had fought alongside Washington twenty years earlier, Clark had no qualms about considering travel to find work as an officer. If acceptance of citizenship from his employer was required, the Adams administration had just made the separation more palatable than at any earlier moment in his life.

After he first sent word of his situation to his revolutionary companions, Clark found his way out of Philadelphia, crossed the mountains, and raced to Spanish territory just ahead of federal forces. "The president of the United States gave the order to have me arrested. But the detachment that he sent to take me was attacked and disarmed by a certain number of men, volunteers, that my old comrades had the time to assemble. I then withdrew to the west bank of the Mississippi. . . . If the executive Directory wishes to possess Louisiana, there is no time to lose. In nine months at the most, it will be too late. This country [too] will be conquered by America or England."[33]

For a majority of Kentuckians, their opposition to the Alien and Sedition Acts was captured neatly in the language of the Kentucky Resolutions, covertly drafted by Thomas Jefferson and endorsed by the Kentucky legislature in two resolutions dated 16 and 22 November 1798. Jefferson and the state legislators argued, and Clark joined those in agreement, that the states were united through a compact drafted for the purposes of mutual security and prosperity, but that each state constituted a sovereign government that autonomously determined the extent of its participation within the union. The Virginia legislature passed a similar act, drafted by Madison, on 24 December. Together, the Alien and Sedition Acts and the Kentucky and Virginia Resolutions articulated both sides of the federal versus states' rights debate that would erupt sixty-three years later as a fundamental cause of the American Civil War.

Part 4

Settlement

12

Country Houses

> Only a few scattered Cabbins, with one indifferent farm.
> —Dr. George Hunter, describing Clarksville, Indiana, 1796

As the long statehood debate dragged on, and while Spanish and French schemes consumed thought, and sometimes, action, Kentuckians did what people do everywhere: they fell in love, built homes, and created societies. With the threat of native warfare receding, settlers of both affluent and modest means were induced to come to Kentucky. A number of wealthy Virginia planters established prosperous farms in the extended Lexington area, and near Louisville, along the Beargrass Creek. These communities were built for the most part by men who had served as Revolutionary officers, and because they brought their enslaved labor with them to Kentucky, the Virginians provided the district with a second population of original settlers.[1]

A late 1783 diary notation made by Jonathan Clark indicated he had traveled from the Shenandoah Valley to look for land for his parents in the Louisville area, where he selected a 256-acre tract on the south branch of Beargrass Creek. The ground Clark selected was a high, flat expanse known as the Poplar Level, located about three miles south of the Falls. The tract was adjacent to the infamous Wilderness Trail, which, at that point, almost wended itself to completion at Fort Nelson. Several miles to the south lay the dreaded Wet Woods, but they had no impact on John Clark's farm, which benefited from the plentiful water provided by the creek and the soft, rolling hills to the east, which offered adequate timber for all his needs. A large log house and several outbuildings were completed on the site before the summer of 1785, and it was here that John and Ann Rogers Clark had come to live with their son, William, and daughters, Lucy, Elizabeth, and Frances Eleanor "Fanny." George Rogers was so pleased with the Beargrass seat that he informed his brother, Edmund, that his parents were "by far the best settled of any persons in this part of the country." Some of the neighbors took notice of the Clarks' arrival as well, but for entirely different reasons. "There are many agreeable young Ladies On Bear Grass now Settled Namely Old Mr. Clarke's Daughters, who is my Nearest Neighbour."[2]

Clark joined his family at their new home, soon called Mulberry Hill, but initially lived there only sporadically while the Indian commission and other public responsibilities kept him occupied in other regions. He was exiled in St. Louis when his mother died on Christmas Eve 1798, but had returned to Mulberry Hill before his father's death the following July. The loss of John and Ann Clark marked the conclusion of a bleak decade for their second son, but the family had undergone darker trials.

Elizabeth Clark Anderson had died in 1795 following childbirth, leaving four young children. More than a decade earlier, Richard Clark had been a lieutenant under the command of his older brother at Vincennes before he volunteered for Robert Todd's company in the relief of Cahokia, served through the dangerous year of Fort Jefferson's existence, and accompanied his brother on the 1782 Shawnee campaign. Dickie disappeared while traveling between the Falls and Vincennes in March 1784, his body never recovered.

Third son, John, had been a nineteen-year-old captain when he was taken prisoner at the Battle of Germantown. He spent six years in captivity, the last aboard a prison ship in New York harbor, before he returned to his father's Virginia home as a lieutenant in broken health. Alarmed by his son's condition, John Clark sent the young man to the West Indies in hope of recovery from the tuberculosis contracted as a prisoner, but Johnny did not improve. Jonathan Clark's diary records his brother's death, "29 October [1784]: Rain my brother John Died—at my fathers." The day after they buried their son on 2 November, John and Ann Clark, with their four youngest children in the wagon, left for Kentucky.[3]

Under the terms of his father's will, William Clark received Mulberry Hill, "my stock of horses, cattle, sheep, hogs. My still and all my plantation utensils . . . one Negroe man named York, Also old York, and his Wife Rose, and their two Children Nancy and Juba, also three old Negroes James, Cupid, and Harry." George Rogers's inheritance was limited to the receipt of "One Negroe man named Lue. Also one Negroe woman named Venice, With her present and future Increase except Peter." The general transferred his inheritance, "Lew a small black man about 38 years old, Venos and her two Children Frankey and Tenar," as well as "Kitt, a yallow negroe man about thirty years of age" to William to offset debts owed his younger brother, but the enslaved servants continued to live with him for years. Kitt remained with George Rogers Clark throughout the general's life.[4]

The transfers of Kitt, Lew, and Venos were token actions; they had lived with George Rogers for years, and would continue to do so after their legal ownership reverted to William Clark. John Clark's decision to leave his home to his youngest son rather than to George Rogers has been explained through the certainty that the elder son's creditors surely would have claimed the farm, but the will also recognized the state of George Rogers's life in 1799. The stark contrasts between the complicated existence of his most famous son and the prosperous lives of his surviving children could not have been ignored by John or George Rogers Clark.

Elizabeth had been the first of the younger Clark children to leave Mulberry Hill, when she married Colonel Richard Clough Anderson on 14 August 1787. Seventeen years his wife's senior, Anderson had worked as a teenager for a Richmond merchant who frequently sent him to New England, where he was a surprised witness to the Boston Tea Party. Soon afterward, he secured a captaincy in the Virginia Continental Line's Fifth Regiment and fought at the battles of Trenton, Brandywine, Germantown, and Monmouth. Like William Croghan, he emerged from Valley Forge as a major. Anderson suffered a severe wound at the Battle of Savannah and witnessed the death and burial of General Casimir Pulaski before his capture at Charleston, but, after he was exchanged for a British officer, he was active in the Battle of Yorktown as a runner who carried information between Lafayette and Anthony Wayne.[5]

Anderson ended the war as a lieutenant colonel and joined Croghan as an original member of the Society of the Cincinnati, as did Jonathan and Edmund Clark. He had been named primary surveyor for the society and, as an extension of that position, acquired the role of principal surveyor for the soldiers of the Virginia Continental Line. Soon after he opened his Louisville office, Anderson had regularly joined the Clarks at Mulberry Hill.[6]

Richard Clough Anderson, probably by John Wesley Jarvis. The Society of the Cincinnati, Washington, DC.

He purchased five hundred acres on Beargrass Creek near the road from Louisville to Frankfort in the spring of 1789, and began to build Soldier's Retreat, a two-and-a-half-story stone house that essentially mirrored the brick home William Croghan was about to build several miles away. Elizabeth had given birth to Richard Clough Anderson Jr. on 4 August 1788 in a stone house Anderson had built in the center of Louisville, but the couple was living on the grounds at Soldier's Retreat when their three daughters arrived. Elizabeth Clark Anderson died on 15 January 1795, days before her twenty-seventh birthday, following complications from youngest daughter Betsy's December birth. After her burial—the first in what would become the Anderson family cemetery—Elizabeth's children were taken to Mulberry Hill, where the aged Clarks cared for them while Anderson spent most of 1795 in Virginia. He returned to Louisville and married Clark cousin Sarah Marshall, who would bear him twelve more children, on 24 November 1797.[7]

William Croghan, too, was a frequent guest at Mulberry Hill, attracted to George Rogers Clark's tiny, flame-haired sister, Lucy. Before he reached an understanding with her, however, Croghan had to compete with a former Continental Congress representative from New Jersey. John Cleves Symmes, who was appointed Ohio Territory federal judge in 1788, had spent some time at John Clark's home a year earlier when he traveled through Kentucky in search of land investments. Six weeks before Richard Anderson's marriage to Lucy's sister, Symmes wrote to him to acknowledge the coming wedding and his own connection to the Clark family.

> God bless you my friend and give you many happy days in the arms of your Betsey, and while you riot in bliss if you can for a moment sustane a thought on any other subject honor me with a line. . . . I have taken the liberty to enclose a letter to the unfeeling mistress of my affections which I beg you will deliver. I will this once give her a little more trouble, God knows whether I shall ever have it in my power to do it again. . . . I beg dear friend that you will present my best references to Mr. and Mrs. Clarke, to the young Ladies and the two brothers. I assure you that I [hold] affection for them all. This I desire Miss Lucy to do, but tis possible that she may be ashamed of her correspondent, in that case she will not be very communicative on the subject. . . . Tell me whether there is like to be a second wedding soon at the house of Mr. C— the first I consider is certain. . . . Let me have your guess, for sure I am that you will have it in your power to make a good one. If you see William is like to be crowned, tell me, and I shall then know what part I am to take.[8]

Symmes appears to have been more aware of Lucy Clark's feelings than her father, who rode to the Jefferson County courthouse two years later to secure a bond for his daughter's marriage. Writing somewhat cryptically on 13 July 1789, "Whereas there is a Marriage suddenly intended to be

Lucy Clark Croghan. Unknown artist.

had & solemnized between . . . William Croghan & Lucy Clark, I am willing a Licence should issue out of your office for the Marriage of my Daughter Lucy Clark to Majr. William Croghan," Clark gave his permission, unnecessary in light of Lucy's age, and the couple was married that week at Mulberry Hill.[9]

John Clark surely considered his son's former surveying partner an excellent husband for his twenty-four-year-old daughter. At the time of his marriage, Croghan had lived in Louisville for five years and already purchased "a good many Lotts of Louisville & had a considerable Acquaintance with the Situation of Town Property & the Town Arrangements in general." His associations with Revolutionary officers stood him in good stead with the community, and he willingly participated in public service through repeated jury duty and election commission activity. Croghan had been given the responsibility by the Jefferson County Court to lay out a courthouse on the public square in 1788, and had worked tirelessly to survey and record military grants for Virginia militia veterans. Although a significant portion of his post-Revolutionary life would be committed to the measurement and distribution of land, he also worked before his marriage to become a successful businessman, frequently in partnership with his future brothers-in-law. Croghan had maintained old New York and Pennsylvania connections after his move to Kentucky, and while others in the West bemoaned their lack of access to the port of New Orleans, he took action and contacted the heir of a family connection.[10]

Daniel J. Clark, a Philadelphia merchant who was unrelated to George Rogers Clark but was George Croghan's cousin and a former Pennsylvania militia officer, had left Philadelphia and moved to the east bank of the Mississippi River in West Florida before the Revolution. After he established Clarksville (now Mississippi) two miles below Fort Adams, Clark carefully nourished his relationships with Spanish officials in New Orleans and soon was allowed to access the port, through which he moved slaves, liquor, and other goods from the Caribbean for sale to American merchants. His nephew, also Daniel Clark, but known in the United States as Daniel Clark Jr., was James Wilkinson's early contact in New Orleans. Clark Jr. arrived in Philadelphia from Sligo, Ireland, before 1786, after reputedly completing his education at Eton, and in a short time he assumed his uncle's business responsibilities in New Orleans. He would become an American citizen and the first territorial and, later, Congressional representative from New Orleans, and he amassed a fortune in US dollars and influence.[11]

Croghan wrote George Rogers Clark from New Orleans early in 1788, on the heels of Wilkinson's success there, about "opening a Commercial Intercourse with this place, if it should be practicable." He had asked Daniel Clark for help in acquiring permission to bring goods through the Spanish port of New Orleans but, in consequence of his increasing closeness to the Clark family, also may have asked for clarification regarding the establishment of American settlements in Louisiana or West Spain.

Daniel Clark Jr. responded in June, after Croghan had returned to Kentucky. "Governor Miró . . . granted me the Permission I now send you. It is very general, and possessing it no danger or risque will attend any Shipment you may make in Virtue of it, at any time within 10 Months from its date. . . . Families who come to this Country to settle are allowed to import their Negroes, Furniture, Stock of every kind, and a sufficient Quantity of Provisions and Clothing for Two years free of all Duty." Although Clark Jr. and James Wilkinson briefly were business partners, he would become Wilkinson's leading critic in connection with Aaron Burr's treason trials early in the nineteenth century.[12]

Croghan and Anderson had become business partners after they moved to Louisville, and while Croghan was one of the very few Americans who were successful in receiving a passport to trade in New Orleans, he remained guarded in his enthusiasm for a commercial association with the Spanish circle. He notified Anderson, "I am informed that the Governor of Orleans, Mr. Daniel Clark, & General Wilkinson Are Actually entered into partnership. This partnership was Entered into Shortly After My Passport was sent. . . . If you Should be any way Apprehensive that the partnership above Mentioned Might be detrimental to us in our Intended trade down the river, and think that by Selling the Tobacco &c we have purchased we might do as well as by sending it to Orleans, I am perfectly Satisfied that you Should Sell it."[13]

In this letter, written 20 November 1788, Croghan also informed Anderson that George Rogers Clark had resigned his post as surveyor. "Gen Clark has sent his resignation as Surveyor to the Superintendts of the State line. If Offered to me I shall Accept of the place, but Suppose they will appoint a State Officer." Those close to the situation, including Virginia's governor, realized Croghan, in fact, had been in charge of the surveying office since its inception, and Croghan took the oath of office as principal surveyor for the Virginia Line two months before his wedding, on 7 May 1789.[14]

Croghan initially brought his bride to one of his houses in the center of Louisville, where they immediately began a family. Days before the birth of his first child, he placed an ad in the *Kentucky Gazette*: "To Be Sold . . . A two story log house thirty by sixteen feet well roofed, and with an excellent ground cellar under the whole house, and another house one and an half story high, twenty-four by sixteen with a compleat store for goods at one end and a counting room or bed-chamber at the other . . . and an excellent stone chimney."[15]

The houses either remained unsold or the couple moved to another nearby, as one year later, Croghan again advertised in the *Gazette,* "Notice is hereby given, that agreeable to direction from the superintendants of the Virginia State Line, I will open the office at my house near the falls of the Ohio, on Monday the first day of August next, to receive entries, and proceed to surveying the military state lands on the south side of Green river &c."[16]

No Virginia militia land warrants had been filed in Kentucky since Clark's retirement, and now recognized as principal surveyor, Croghan was ready to establish a home that would be built and furnished to reflect his status as a gentleman. The house would be built upon ground acquired by Croghan on 10 April 1790, two days before the *Kentucky Gazette* advertised his town house for sale. The April date is a traditional one, accepted only because a county clerk noted twelve years later that Croghan had paid £340 for the 387 acres on that day; the seller, Hancock Lee, did not come from Fauquier County, Virginia, to Louisville to record the transfer until 19 July 1802.

Lee had been George Rogers Clark's pre-Revolution surveying supervisor, and had acquired part of Col. William Peachy's (Peachey) thousand-acre French and Indian War grant through a family connection. Peachy's land abutted another Colonial Wars grant awarded to Hancock Eustace; but neither Peachy nor Eustace ever came to the Falls of the Ohio because each man opted instead to sell his tract as a means of receiving payment for military service. The four men who acquired the Peachy grant (Lee among them) subsequently sold the northern part of the land to Croghan, and on 12 March 1792 in a transfer witnessed by William Croghan and Clark relatives Marston Clark and Edmund Rogers, the southern section was sold to Richard Taylor, father of the future president. The remaining 253 acres that ran along the eastern boundary went to Richard Terrell, son-in-law to Thomas Jefferson's sister, Martha, and a friend and neighbor to the Peachy family in Virginia. Both Terrell and Taylor built prominent homes on the former Peachy grant, which abutted Croghan's larger house, known as Locust Grove.[17]

Croghan's new house was patterned upon a center hall plan that was traditional—Jefferson would have said old fashioned—but its imposing size (including its segmented cellar, the house rose four stories) and its handsome Flemish bond brick made an immediate impression. He began construction no later than 1791, and his small family was settled in the house before 1795. Locust Grove was built on a bluff overlooking and extending to the Ohio River, about six miles northeast of Louisville, which provided Croghan with a grand vista and easy commercial access. To secure his river operations, he had bought thirty acres of Six Mile Island at the foot of his farm from Jacob and Mary Kuykendall on 1 February 1791, and although he sold this acreage to Terrell in 1798, he continued to operate a ferry that ran from his landing to Indiana into the next century.[18]

Croghan went on to consolidate his estate; in 1792, he purchased

104.5 acres that adjoined Locust Grove's western boundary from Ambrose Madison, who had acquired the Eustace grant. Madison died of yellow fever before he could file the deed transfer in Virginia and left his Kentucky land to his brother, James, and sister, Nelly. A prolonged correspondence between James Madison and Croghan resulted, as Croghan had paid £94 for the property at the time the deed was signed. Croghan enlisted Richard Taylor, who was related to the Madisons, to help plead his case; but ultimately he was forced to sue, as he explained in an 1802 letter to Madison. "In consequence of the Death of your Brother Ambrose, Colonel Richard Taylor & myself were under the necessity of bringing Suits in Chancery against you & Nelly Madison for Lands we bought from your Brother belonging to you & he." The suit resulted in the recognition of Croghan's ownership in September 1802 and ended a decade of contention between William Croghan and the future president.[19]

A deed that recorded the purchase of an additional 202 acres from Taylor to Croghan was filed in Jefferson County on 18 July 1811, which expanded Croghan's farm to 693.5 acres. This portion of Taylor's land, called Springfields, had been purchased from the Eustace grant and probably reflected the long-standing presence of a mill operated by Croghan since 1797. By 1812, Croghan's Locust Grove property consisted of approximately four hundred acres cleared for domestic activity, pastures, and cultivation above the flood plain, and nearly three hundred acres left in timber along the Ohio River, where his landing was located.[20]

The estate was not built or managed without enslaved labor. Extant Jefferson County tax assessment records, which began in 1789, did not list anyone associated with the Locust Grove parcel until 1791. At that time, the assessment counted six enslaved men above the age of sixteen living at the site, who were surely carrying out the foundation work for Croghan's new home. By 1792, Major Croghan was taxed for 516 acres and for one white and seventeen black men and women. The tax notation of thirty-four horses and cattle indicated the land was functioning as a farm even as the house and other buildings remained under construction. And in this way, Dublin-born Major William Croghan and his wife, Lucy Clark, settled into Kentucky's gentry and emulated the Virginia lifestyle neither had known before the Revolution. The union resulted in the births of nine children, eight of whom survived to adulthood. In addition to John (born 23 April 1790), were George (15 November 1791), William (2 January 1794), Charles (13 February 1796—died in infancy), Ann Heron (20 October 1797), Eliza (9 April 1800), Nicholas and Charles (19 June 1802), and Edmund (12 September 1805).[21]

Clark siblings Ann and Jonathan each had married in Virginia even before their parents left for Kentucky. Ann had become the wife of Owen Gwathmey, son of a Virginia planter, and when the couple joined her family in the Louisville area in 1797, they built a comfortable house on nearby Harrod's Creek. Jonathan married Sarah (Sally) Hite, granddaughter of Jost Hite, in 1782 and settled in Spotsylvania County, Virginia, to rear a large family. The lieutenant colonel had continued public service as a magistrate and militia major general after his parole from Charleston, and achieved financial and social success before he reunited with his six remaining siblings near Louisville.[22]

Youngest brother, William, spent some time with Jonathan and Sally Clark at their Virginia farm late in 1801 to draw up plans for the couple's new Kentucky house. William had bought a wooded tract for his brother near Beargrass Creek and, after leaving Spotsylvania with most of Jonathan's enslaved laborers for a wintry journey to Louisville, was able to report progress in March. "George has fixed on a Spot in the Clearing, which is thought greatly preferable to the One at the spring I mentioned to you near Capt. Sullivans." Brother George had selected the location for the farm that would be called Trough Spring on the Poplar Level, just east of Mulberry Hill. William wrote Jonathan in April to let his brother know the work on the house was coming along, probably with the help of George Rogers and both brothers' enslaved men. "We . . . expect you out in June I flateer my Self I Shall have a house for you a garden &c. by that time. . . . I shall indeavor to have every comfort in as great forwardness for you as possible at your arrival." As always, William proved to be as good as his word. Jonathan's brief 26 May 1802 diary entry memorialized the move in typical style. "Clear. Moved from Spotsylvania for Kentucky," and when the new home welcomed its family on 14 July 1802, all was in readiness.[23]

George Rogers and William Clark were joined at Mulberry Hill by their widowed sister, Fanny O'Fallon Thruston, a year after their father's death. After the death of O'Fallon, Fanny had remarried in 1796, this time to Charles Minn (Mynn) Thruston, who had participated in the Revolution at the age of eleven as an aide to his father. Thruston was killed by Luke, an enslaved man, at his Westport, Kentucky, farm in December 1800, and now a twice-widowed mother of four, twenty-seven-year-old Fanny returned to her brothers with her children. Fifth Clark son, Edmund, reenlisted as a captain in the Seventh US Infantry in the late 1790s to participate in the movements planned to counteract the French threat, which assuredly created tense conversation at Mulberry Hill. After an unsuccessful stint in western Kentucky, Edmund returned to Louisville, where he lived as a merchant.[24]

John and Ann Clark's adult children prospered in Kentucky with the exception of the difficulties created by George Rogers's legal and financial entanglements. Hindered by the monetary outlay needed to appease the Vincennes plaintiffs, William Clark was forced to make difficult decisions. Although George Rogers had sold many of his possessions (William Croghan bought a large Indiana tract belonging to Clark on 26 May 1801), most of the transactions resulted only in paper profits. With no other option available to help his brother, William gave up Mulberry Hill. He sold 111 acres, including the gristmill, to Edmund, and 232 acres, including the house and its dependencies, to Jonathan on 2 May 1803. Without obvious bitterness, William packed his belongings and moved the few miles to the Indiana Territory, where George Rogers had acquired twelve half-acre lots from the trustees of Clarksville in 1796. There, the brothers established a little settlement overlooking the Falls of the Ohio River at Point of Rocks, on the land Tobacco's Son had awarded George Rogers. Fanny and her children joined her brothers regularly, and the men willingly assumed the roles of the boys' deceased fathers. Fanny's great-niece would remember that young Charles Thruston was taken to school for the first time riding "behind his uncle George."[25]

The Clarks found themselves somewhat isolated from society as they began the initial construction of their home. Clarksville, the nearby commercial center, had been characterized in 1797 as "a poor place hardly deserving Notice consisting of Six Cabbins and One Logg Hous with a Stone chimney," and little had changed. Clearly, there was much opportunity and more work to do to make Virginia's revolutionary payment a worthwhile investment, but hopes of economic gain temporarily were forgotten soon after the Clarks moved to Indiana. Global events were moving quickly, and Thomas Jefferson was looking up old friends.[26]

13

The Expedition

> Ocian in view! O! the joy.
> —William Clark, 7 November 1805

The 1795 treaty that succeeded in allowing Americans access to the Mississippi River had tempered the initiative that drove Kentucky's Mississippi land schemes, but shortly after his inauguration in 1801, Jefferson was made aware of Spain's secret agreement to transfer ownership of Louisiana to France. The world would soon know France reacquired Louisiana on 21 March 1801, but the normal delay in official transfer again would give Spain the opportunity to close New Orleans to the United States.[1]

Jefferson appointed Robert R. Livingston as minister plenipotentiary to Paris with orders to discover France's plans for Louisiana. Livingston left for France aboard the USS *Boston* in October in the company of his family and a retinue of secretaries and servants, with his coach lashed to the deck of the ship to serve as the women's parlor. Lafayette greeted the ambassador in Paris early in December. Talleyrand accepted his credentials without enthusiasm, and on 6 December, Livingston was presented at the Tuileries to Napoleon Bonaparte, who was rude.[2]

Jefferson's public response to France's reacquisition of Louisiana was limited to private negotiation, which led frustrated Hamiltonians, who were openly hostile to the president's French attachment, to demand invasions of New Orleans and the Floridas. Camped in his unfinished executive residence in Washington City, Jefferson considered and rejected strategies with Secretary of State James Madison and protégé, former French ambassador, James Monroe. Only after expatriate Pierre Samuel du Pont de Nemours successfully argued that the purchase of Louisiana would cost less than a war with France did Jefferson dispatch Monroe to Paris to bro-

Thomas Jefferson by Cornelius Tiebout after Rembrandt Peale. Courtesy of Yale University Art Gallery.

ker a deal. Unaware that France had failed to obtain the Floridas, Jefferson authorized Monroe to pay as much as $9,375,000 for New Orleans and East and West Florida.[3]

Livingston wrote Madison the day after Monroe arrived in Paris to announce Napoleon's unexpected willingness to sell the entire Louisiana Territory, save New Orleans, to the United States. Livingston anticipated competition with Monroe for the privilege of recognition as Jefferson's primary French liaison, so he backdated the letter. "They ask for only one town of Louisiana [New Orleans]; but I consider the whole colony as completely lost, and it seems to me that in the hands of that growing power, it will be more useful to the policy and even the commerce of France than if I should try to keep it."[4]

Within the week, Napoleon directed his ministers to negotiate the sale of 828,000 square miles of Louisiana to the United States, which induced Talleyrand to summon Livingston to begin the negotiation that would result in the acquisition of the massive Louisiana Purchase. The asking price was $25 million; the United States countered with $4 million. Louisiana finally was purchased for $15 million with a deduction of $3,750,000 as compensation to Americans who had lost goods to the French navy. Livingston and Monroe signed the purchase agreement on 2 May 1803 unbeknownst to Jefferson, who did not receive the news until 3 July. The president announced the triumph at an Independence Day celebration in Washington City, and his secretary, Meriwether Lewis, left the next day to rendezvous at the Falls of the Ohio with William Clark, who had prepared for his arrival.[5]

In an attempt to counteract objections to the purchase, Jefferson had begun to put it about that he meant to discover a water route to the Pacific and open trade with Asia even before Monroe reached Paris. He assigned Meriwether Lewis the task of leading the exploration and gave him the option of selecting the remainder of his company. Lewis nominated his former army companion as the expedition's coleader rather than second-in-command, and Jefferson, who knew the Clark family well, drafted instructions to be forwarded immediately to Clark in Clarksville, Indiana. Essentially, the company was to "explore the Missouri river, & such principal stream of it, as, by it's course & communication with the waters of the Pacific Ocean, may offer the most direct & practicable water communication across the continent, for the purposes of commerce." All this was completed two weeks before Jefferson knew the United States had acquired Louisiana, but not before he had requested $2,500 from Congress to finance the expedition and had informed British, French, and Spanish envoys of an anticipated scientific journey up the Mississippi.[6]

Notwithstanding strong opposition from New Englanders, who feared competition from western ports, and others, once including Jefferson, who considered the purchase to be unconstitutional, the United States Senate voted to approve the House bill to buy Louisiana on 3 November 1803. The authorization preceded the official transfer of power on 30 November, and doubled the size of the United States of America. Jefferson appointed

William Clark by C. W. Peale. Independence National Historical Park.

Meriwether Lewis by C. W. Peale. Independence National Historical Park.

William C. C. Claiborne to be the territorial governor of "Orleans," and he, along with James Wilkinson, now the US Army's senior officer, accepted Louisiana from France in a ceremony conducted in New Orleans on 20 December. Lewis and Clark were in their Illinois camp by then, assembling the last provisions for their expedition to the Pacific Ocean.[7]

Why was William Clark chosen to cocaptain Jefferson's expedition to the Pacific? As the cabinet wrestled with the Louisiana issue in May 1801, William, ever restless, had begun a trip to Philadelphia, Baltimore, and Washington City to examine opportunities in general and take care of a little business, specifically. He found Meriwether Lewis installed in the partially completed East Room of the executive mansion, where he lived as Thomas Jefferson's private secretary. Clark had stopped in Washington to ask for Lewis's help in retrieving papers to support his brother's financial claim against Virginia, and during the course of the visit, he met with Jefferson. In anticipation of western activity, the president sought to refortify the confluence of the Ohio and Mississippi rivers, and Clark's knowledge of the area, supported by a recent inspection at the site of old Fort Jefferson, undoubtedly was a topic of conversation.[8]

About the time the Jonathan Clark family was settling into Trough Spring, Jefferson directed his secretary of war to request further information about the Mississippi from Clark; and when the letter finally arrived in December, George Rogers Clark took the opportunity to write Jefferson himself on the subject of his former fort. He concluded,

> I have long since laid aside all Idea of Public affairs, by bad for tune, and ill health. I have become incapable of persuing those enterpriseing & active persuits which I have been fond of from my youth—but I will with the greatest pleasure give my bro. William every information in my power on this, or any other point which may be of Service to your administration. He is well quallified almost for any business. If it should be in your power to confur on him any post of Honor and profit, in this Countrey in which we live, it will exceedingly gratify me.[9]

William Clark probably had learned all he needed to know about Indian customs and cultures from his elder brother before he joined the army. He had participated in native negotiations and Spanish conferences and had become as familiar with the Mississippi and Ohio valleys as his more experienced brother; and as a certified deputy surveyor and burgeoning river merchant, he had made at least two trips to New Orleans, transporting goods for Croghan and others. Along the way, he created excellent maps and drawings of Spanish outposts and artillery.[10]

Lewis was selected as captain specifically for his knowledge of the army and the western country, but as he knew well, Clark's backwoods skills, surveying expertise, and physical and emotional strengths would be critical to the success of Jefferson's expedition. Lewis wrote Clark on 19 June 1803 to provide the requested material for George Rogers Clark's suit, and included with the letter a brief outline of Jefferson's instructions, along with an offer to colead the expedition. The claim against Virginia would not be resolved in George Rogers Clark's lifetime, but William's correspondence with Lewis was of more lasting consequence.

> From the long and uninterupted friendship and confidence which has subsisted between us I feel no hesitation in making to you the following communication. . . . I make this communication to you with the privity of the President, who expresses an anxious wish that you would consent to join me in this enterprise. . . . Thus my friend, you have a summary view of the plan, the means and objects of this expedition. If therefore there is anything under those circumstances, in this enterprise, which would induce you to participate with me in it's fatiegues, it's dangers and it's honors, believe me ther is no man on earth with whom I should feel equal pleasure in sharing them as with yourself.[11]

Lewis left Washington City on 5 July, not yet knowing whether Clark had accepted his offer, but there was no confusion between the two friends as to the authentic purpose of the exploration. Jefferson, rattled by the publication of a British book that called for a trans-Canadian expedition to secure settlement and commerce in the American Northwest, determined to have the United States in the Northwest before British explorers arrived. He initially characterized the proposed expedition as a form of "literary pursuit" to explore and survey portions of the vast Louisiana Territory, but as early as April, he wrote Lewis, "The idea that you are going to explore the Missisipi has been generally given out: it satisfied public curiosity, and masks sufficiently the real destination." As for Clark, clearly in the know, he referred to Jefferson as "that great Chaructor the Main Spring of its action."[12]

William received the invitation at Clarksville on 17 July "with much pleasure," and accepted the following day. "This is an undertaking fraited with many dificulties, but My friend I do assure you that no man lives whith whome I would perfur to undertake Such a Trip &c. as yourself, and I shall arrange my matters as well as I can against your arrival here." In his next communication with Lewis, written on 24 July, Clark explained he had rejected a number of local "Gentlemens sons" who had offered themselves for the expedition because they were not accustomed to labor, and assured Lewis he was eager to get started. "My friend, I join you with hand and Heart."[13]

Lewis received Clark's acceptance letter in Pittsburgh on 29 July and responded, "I could neither hope, wish, or expect from a union with any man on earth, more perfect support or further aid in the discharge of the several duties of my mission, than that, which I am confident I shall derive from being associated with yourself." The two men met in Louisville on 14 July to begin the work of organization of the Lewis and Clark Expedition. In the hectic days before Lewis's arrival, William had recruited seven Kentuckians, "good hunters, stout, healthy, unmarried men accustomed to the woods," just as Lewis, who brought George Shannon and George Gibson with him, had suggested. Charles Floyd, Nathaniel Pryor, Joseph and Reubin Field, John Colter, John Shields, and William Bratton joined Shannon and Gibson to become the first men selected for the company soon to be known as the Corps of Discovery, but the expedition would benefit equally by the addition of its single unrecruited member. Clark's enslaved man, York, would have no choice but to join the greatest American adventure of his generation.[14]

Jonathan Clark noted the beginning of the expedition in a journal entry dated 26 October 1803. "Rain at Louisville at Clarksville Capt Lewis and Capt Wm Clark sot [set] of[f] on a Western tour." In addition to mapping and surveying the course of the expedition, William Clark kept a regular journal and maintained sporadic correspondences with family members, especially Jonathan, and it is through these documents that the frustrations and achievements of the Corps of Discovery primarily are known. He wrote William Croghan from winter quarters early in 1804. "I have postponed writing to you until this time with a view of having something worth informing you relative to this Country. . . . My situation is as comfortable as could be expected in the woods, & on the frontiers; the Country back of me is butifull beyond description." Clark again wrote his brother-in-law on 21 May from St. Charles, Missouri, to announce that the real work of the Corps was about to begin.

> My friend Capt. Lewis expressed some sorrow that you happened not to be at home at the time he passed down [the Ohio River], but hopes to see you on his return to the U. States. . . . And I hope that in less than two years to see you & [your] family whome I have every affection for, at your own house. . . . The law authorizing the president to explore the Countrey has just come to my knowledge. . . . I have been at this place five days waiting for Capt. Lewis who has been detained at St. Louis to fix off the Osage chiefs. He has just arrived and we shall leave this Village immediately & proceed on our journey.[15]

In mid-June 1805, Croghan would receive a somewhat ominous notice of the expedition's progress in a letter written on 2 April. "We shall leave this place in two days on our journey. Country and River above this is but little known. Our information is altogether from Indians collected at different times and entitled to some credit. My return will not be so soon as I expected, I fear not sooner than about June or July 1806. . . . (P.S.) I send my sister Croghan some seed of several Kinds of Grapes."[16]

Three months later, nearly eighteen months into the trek and more than two years after they left the Falls, the Corps cleared a rocky bluff to make camp in what would become the state of Oregon. Not unlike so many other nights, a hard rain was falling on 6 November and the men were cold and wet. They awoke before dawn in a heavy fog and stiffly broke camp before they again moved west into unknown territory. Incredibly, as the sky cleared, the men of the Lewis and Clark Expedition realized they had reached the estuary known as the Columbia River. Now able to hear the crash of the ocean, Clark wrote, "Great joy in camp we are in *view* of the *Ocian*, this great Pacific Octean which we been so anxious to See."[17]

Clark's journal entry of 7 November reflected the euphoria with which the cocaptains greeted the end of their trail, but the men spent three more weeks rowing against tidal forces and fighting a windstorm in a futile attempt to reach the Pacific. Clark's journal described the events of 22 November: "The wind increased to a Storm . . . blew with violence throwing the water of the river with emence waves out of its banks almost over whelming us in water, O! how horriable is the day." Sometime after the twenty-seventh, the starving explorers made their ways across the estuary and bought fish from local Clatsop people. From there, the Corps of Discovery climbed around what today is called Point Ellice, where they ended their journey west. The men made a rainy winter camp at Fort Clatsop (near present-day Astoria) in December, where Clark set about charting the first specific map of the Pacific Northwest to be seen in the United States and Lewis created impressive drawings of the area's flora and fauna.

Initially thrilled, Lewis and Clark could not sustain their jubilation in the weeks and months ahead following the realization that a major river course to tie the Mississippi River to the Pacific Ocean did not exist. The expedition started home on 23 March 1806 and arrived to a warm greeting in a steady rain at St. Charles on 21 September. The Lewis and Clark Expedition ended officially two days later in St. Louis, having completed an eight-thousand-mile journey through territory unknown to anyone east of the Mississippi.

Dispatches to various government officials and family letters were forwarded between public dinners and toasts, and Clark invited Jonathan to make his summary of the expedition known to the public. The story consequently appeared in the Frankfort *Palladium* on 9 October, well ahead of the Corps's arrival in Kentucky. The explorers reached Louisville on 5 November 1806, as recorded by Jonathan Clark. "A little rain. Captains Lewis & Clark arrived at the Falls on Their return from the Pacific Ocean after an absence of a little more than three years."[18]

Three days later, on 8 November, Jonathan Clark wrote, "Rain at Majr Croghan with Capt Lewis & Clark lay Ditto." Lewis, Clark, and, at least, Jonathan, were at Locust Grove, the guests of William and Lucy Croghan. With the Mandan party in tow, led by Chief Sheheke, Lewis soon left Louisville for the capital by way of his mother's Charlottesville home. Pierre Chocteau guided the Osage delegates directly to Washington, where they arrived by 24 December. With his base established at Trough Spring, William Clark remained at the Falls until 15 December, moving between the homes of his siblings before he set out with York, who again left his wife for an extended period. Unlike Lewis, Clark rode by way of Fincastle, Virginia, and Col. George Hancock's home, Santillane, where he arrived on 8 January 1807 in search of a bride.[19]

The safe return of Lewis and Clark was celebrated across the nation, but few Americans knew that before it began, the expedition almost ended at the hands of George Rogers Clark's old nemesis. James Wilkinson had taken aim at the captains when news of the pending exploration was announced in 1803, just weeks after he and Claiborne officially took possession of Louisiana for the United States. After a meeting between Wilkinson and Vizente Folch, Miró's nephew and the governor of Spanish West Florida, Folch noted Wilkinson's eagerness to offer Spain "various reflections" concerning the United States' purchase of Louisiana and the planned expedition. He also recorded Wilkinson's embarrassment at having to mention that his annual $2,000 salary as a Spanish spy had not been paid in ten years. Because he was about to leave for Washington City, where he said he would meet personally with Jefferson and learn all there was to know of the expedition's *secret* mission, Wilkinson offered to put his thoughts in writing, and suggested a single $20,000 payment would be equal to his value to Spain. In the end, he provided Folch with a document, but settled for a $12,000 payment.[20]

Wilkinson's submission, entitled "Reflections," was a well-constructed summary of North America's political status, punctuated with specific strategies aimed to benefit his covert employer. Spain should offer to trade Florida for Louisiana, he advised, and repay the United States for the cost of the purchase. Otherwise, Mexico stood in danger of invasion by "an army of adventurers similar to the ancient Goths and Vandals." Moreover, because Lewis and Clark had not yet left St. Charles, Wilkinson argued Spain should "detach a sufficient body of chasseurs to intercept Captain Lewis and his party . . . and force them to retire or take them prisoners." In response to Wilkinson's report, the acting governor of Spanish Texas was ordered to stop this "daring undertaking" and to "divert and even destroy such expeditions." Consequently, two militias were sent out at least three times under Captain Pedro Vial with orders to kill or capture Meriwether Lewis and William Clark. Spanish forces would interrupt Jefferson's subsequent western expeditions; Zebulon Pike, clearly moving beyond Louisiana, was arrested by Spain the year after Lewis and Clark returned, but the president's first and most significant exploration arrived home with the loss of but one man, to appendicitis.[21]

When William Clark reported to Thomas Jefferson at the conclusion of the expedition, he agreed to stop at Big Bone Lick, near the Ohio River, on his way back to the Falls to collect mastodon and other megafauna specimens for the president. A few months later, having received some items and cognizant of William Clark's impending marriage to Julia Hancock, Jefferson sent George Rogers Clark a friendly reminder to forward the remainder of the bones collected by William.

> As I think it possible your brother will have left you before the inclosed comes to hand, I have left it open, and request you to read it, and . . . have the bones packed and forwarded for me to William Brown, Collector at N. Orleans, who will send them on to me. I avail myself of this occasion of recalling myself to your memory & of assuring you that time has not lessened my friendship for you. We are both now grown old. You have been enjoying in retirement the recollection of the services you have rendered your country, and I am about to retire without an equal consciousness that I have not occupied places in which others would have done more good. But in all places & times I shall wish you every happiness, and salute you with great friendship & esteem.[22]

This would be the last communication between the two men. Jefferson returned to Monticello the following year after he completed his second term as president, while Clark continued to reside in his little house near Clarksville, in decline. At first read, a letter written at this time by William Croghan's son appears simply to be laudatory, but with closer examination, a truth concerning the general's state becomes evident. "Give my respects to Mama and Family, and likewise to Uncle George whenever you happen to see him; he is an Uncle for whom on account of his noble, independent, and patriotic spirit, on account of the services he has rendered his Country . . . I am very partial to. He possessed truly a magnanamous Mind!" He *possessed* truly a magnanimous mind.[23]

14

Burr

> I never saw a man of so much natural capacity and general knowledge as George Rogers Clark.
>
> —Aaron Burr to Samuel Gwathmey, May 1805

The solitude that surrounded George Rogers Clark while his brother was away encouraged memories of lost opportunity that occupied his thoughts and sapped his energy. Now Clark was beyond fifty, the celebrated red hair had faded, and the intense eyes that once saw clearly through the moonlight had begun to cloud. One last chance for material success appeared literally at his doorstep in 1804, and without the intervention of an improbable and notorious western quest, it would have answered his unmet financial needs for the rest of his life.[1]

Neither interested in nor able to build a home that would compete in grandeur with those of his siblings, Clark had built a small, gabled house, situated near the Falls and facing the river. The only chimney on the place stood in the kitchen, situated behind the house. Fanny's daughter, Ann, recalled the little homestead with fondness. "My earliest recollection was going with my dear mother to see him at Point of Rock, a lovely bluff opposite Shippingport, and old Uncle Kitt, his devoted body servant in attendance. He had a nice little cottage, and I think farmed it on a small scale (for the watermelons were glorious)." Lucy Green, the wife of Clark's cousin, Marston, recalled, "General Clark had a large specimen of the vertebrae of the mammoth, as he called it, petrified—found at low water on the falls—had it before his door and would sometimes use it as a seat."[2]

Josiah Espy visited Clark here in 1805.

> I had the pleasure of seeing this celebrated warrior at his lonely cottage seated at Clark's Point, . . . situated at the upper end of the

> village . . . commanding a full and delightful view of the falls, particularly the *zigzag* channel which is only navigated at low water. The General has not taken much pains to improve this commanding and beautiful spot, having only raised a small cabin, but it is capable of being made one of the handsomest seats in the world. General Clark has now become frail and rather helpless, but there are the remains of great dignity and manliness in his countenance, person and deportment, and I was struck on seeing him with (perhaps) a fancied likeness to the great and immortal Washington.[3]

Clark had known the value of a canal around the falls since the June 1778 day he held his breath and led the Illinois Regiment through the rocks and on to Kaskaskia. Twenty-five years later, just before he left for the expedition, William Clark received a grant to construct a small canal near their Clarksville house in anticipation of increased river traffic, and he was not alone in foreseeing development. During William's absence, George Rogers Clark worked to create a commercial canal enterprise at the Falls of the Ohio; the project, in fact, would become his last passion. He and William Croghan were instrumental in the organization of the Indiana Canal Company after they envisioned a canal that would arc from the Indiana Territory's Jeffersonville to the east side of Clarksville, and they succeeded in gaining an official charter from the Indiana Territory on 24 August 1804, along with $120,000 in start-up funds. The company, which eventually raised more than one million dollars to attest to its legitimacy, initially was not threatened when supporters of a southern route developed a competing plan that devised a cut from the western side of Louisville through John Campbell's Shippingport to the river. Caught up in the canal business, the elder brother remained active while the younger crossed the continent. That is, until his Indiana Canal Company found itself embroiled in the quixotic adventures of a kindred spirit.[4]

Seven hundred fifty miles away and with no forewarning, shortly after six thirty on the morning of 11 July 1804, the vice president of the United States shot and mortally wounded the former secretary of the treasury in a duel at Weehawken, New Jersey. Neither William Croghan nor George Rogers Clark knew Aaron Burr in 1804, but Croghan had lived with and fought beside Hamilton and Burr throughout the New York and New Jersey campaigns, and had shared the brutal Valley Forge winter and tor-

Aaron Burr by John Vanderlyn, c. 1802. Courtesy of Yale University Art Gallery.

rid Monmouth battle with both men. Additionally, since 1782 Burr had been linked to Croghan through an almost chimerical family connection. Whether the coming 1805 Croghan–Burr reunion was the result of influence exercised by Wilkinson and/or Daniel Clark Jr., or was spontaneous opportunity, is not understood, but the men soon were in one another's company again, and George Rogers Clark found himself in the thick of the conversation.

The circumstances of Alexander Hamilton's death frequently define Aaron Burr's legacy today, but Burr's was a well-educated and improbable life, formed by the unforeseen Revolution and hardened in the country's initial political discord. The son of the president of the College of New

Alexander Hamilton by Benjamin Tanner. Courtesy of Yale University Art Gallery.

Jersey (Princeton University) and grandson of famed theologian Jonathan Edwards, he unsuccessfully applied to college at the age of eleven, but graduated at sixteen. In 1782, Burr married his brilliant Theodosia and established a law practice on Wall Street under the patronage of the powerful Livingston family.[5]

It was through his union with Theodosia that Burr was drawn into a complicated family connection to his Revolutionary companion, William Croghan. Croghan's cousin, Susanna, had married the nephew of Theodosia's first husband in 1765, which made Susanna a member of Theodosia's extended family, and when Susanna's half sister, Catherine Croghan, married Mohawk chief Joseph Brant, the three families were intertwined, or, as Burr later said, "amalgamated." Burr accepted the Irish and Mohawk factions of Theodosia's family as his own and adopted Prevost's five children when he married their mother. When his only surviving child with Theodosia, also called Theodosia, was married in 1801, the bride and her new husband honeymooned at the Canadian home of Joseph and Catherine Croghan Brant. The children of William Croghan's two cousins, along with Burr's stepchildren, remained lifelong British loyalists, which further amplified Burr's odd reputation among Federalists and Democratic-Republicans alike, but it was his selection as New York's senator over Alexander Hamilton's father-in-law, followed by Hamilton's consequential support of Jefferson over Burr in the tied 1800 presidential election, that set the scene for Weehawken.[6]

Burr went into hiding immediately after Hamilton's death, but returned to Washington City to resume his role as president of the United States Senate shortly before his term was to expire. His exit from the national stage came midway through the Lewis and Clark Expedition, just as the population, particularly westerners, began to imagine what lay beyond the Mississippi. The United States initially declared that the Texas territory lay within the Louisiana Purchase, and, therefore, land companies formed quickly to establish large trans-Mississippi grants. The boundary between Louisiana and Texas was not determined at the Sabine River until 1819, so, in the interim, many Americans saw Texas as an opportunity for financial boon. As early as 1804, Aaron Burr, by then a forty-eight-year-old widower and Revolutionary War hero who had lost little standing among westerners with the death of Hamilton, concluded he was one of those Atlantic Coast men who considered Texas to be his future.

When he offered his farewell address on the Senate floor on 2 March 1805, Burr assumed his political life in the nation he had fought to establish had come to an end, and with the words, "This house is a sanctuary, a citadel of law, of order, and of liberty . . . and if the Constitution be destined ever to perish by the sacreligious hands of the demagogue, its expiring agonies will be witnessed on this floor," he accepted a standing ovation and put public service behind him. Burr directed his daughter to forward his mail to Sen. John Brown's Liberty Hall in Frankfort, Kentucky, and advised James Wilkinson to meet him in Louisville, as he began a "grand" seven-month tour in April.[7]

He traveled down the Ohio in high style; his "floating house," provided by Wilkinson, consisted of two barges strapped together to create a sixty-by-fourteen-foot vessel that housed a dining room, kitchen, and two bedrooms. Before he arrived in Louisville, he visited the island paradise of Irish expatriate Harman Blennerhassett and his wife/niece, Margaret, and introduced Blennerhassett to his plans for a western "adventure." He then stopped in Cincinnati to meet with Ohio senator John Smith and childhood friend and recently retired US senator, Jonathan Dayton, who had just become a director in the Indiana Canal Company.[8]

In Louisville, the next-door neighbors later reported Burr dined at Locust Grove, and he soon expressed interest in the Indiana Canal Company. John Brown, whose term as Kentucky's US senator ended the day Burr's run as vice president concluded, joined Clark, Croghan, Marston G. Clark, Davis Floyd, John Gwathmey, John Harrison, Benjamin Hovey, Josiah Stephens, Samuel C. Vance, and Dayton in inviting Burr to join them as a company director, and the men announced their intention to begin work shortly. James Wilkinson also surfaced as a supporter of the Indiana group, but was not invited to join the company. Burr left the Louisville area appearing to be enthusiastic about the project, but the degree to which his interest in the canal extended beyond his desire to move men and supplies more easily from the upper Ohio to New Orleans remains unknown.[9]

His travels took him to Nashville, where he accepted the public hurrahs of a hero and enjoyed the hospitality of Andrew Jackson, and on to New Orleans, where Daniel Clark Jr. became his principal contact. The city's Roman Catholic Church emerged as another Burr supporter, and long conversations with Edward Livingston, the former mayor of New York City and future senator from Louisiana, drew him into an investment in the Bastrop Tract, a Louisiana colony set aside by Spain for private development. Burr returned to Washington in November 1805, apparently still unsure of his western commitment. In a letter to an unknown recipient, he guardedly summarized the prospects of his fellow canal company directors. "Whether I shall . . . return westward or go to the Atlantic is not yet resolved. The Indiana Canal people would really do something if they had the aid of more talents and information." He spent the winter considering various options, dining with Thomas Jefferson, and lobbying for a position on Pennsylvania's Supreme Court, while old friends worked to reestablish him in New York's political activity. Through it all, he toyed with the idea of creating a settlement at the Bastrop Tract.[10]

The words of Thomas Jefferson, who announced that his former vice president was guilty of treason ahead of trial, have characterized Aaron Burr's intentions in the West for more than two centuries. In reality, Burr attempted to lead a filibuster in 1806—a term for what in the nineteenth century meant a privately organized military action that occurred without government sanction. Setting aside original European intrusions into Native American lands, Burr had participated in one of America's earliest filibusters when he followed fellow New Yorker Richard Montgomery into Canada in 1775 before a declaration of war against Britain was made, and his efforts to carry the mortally wounded Montgomery from the field first brought him to the nation's attention. George Rogers Clark had attempted throughout the 1790s to stage a filibuster against Spain with French support, and he consequently was a primary subject of Congress's 1794 Neutrality Act, which classified a filibuster as a misdemeanor except in time of war, and permitted personal diplomacy by private citizens.[11]

As long as war with Spain appeared inevitable, Burr's plan for a filibuster fell within the law. His ostensible plan was to sever the Mexican people from Spain, and he meant to use the land he purchased in the Bastrop Tract as a staging area for the campaign. The lingering question concerning his actions revolves around his still unknown motivation: was Mexico to become part of the United States, or was it to become Burr's independent empire?

Speaking for Burr, Jonathan Dayton began to act as a double agent early in 1806. He informed Spanish minister Carlos Martínez de Yrujo that Burr planned to seize the federal government and take all its funds and ships to New Orleans, where he would establish an empire separate from the United States, and then attempted to extort $40,000 in exchange for the information. Historians disagree on the subject of Dayton's and Burr's intentions with Yrujo, but most assume the exaggerated information was an attempt to confuse and, with luck, earn enough money from Spain to finance the expedition to Mexico. When known, it rattled the Jefferson administration and inspired many men in the West who had, at best, tenuous allegiances to Washington City.[12]

Meanwhile, Burr's reintegration into eastern society was under way when Jefferson received a letter from Kentucky's US district attorney, Joseph Hamilton Daveiss, that identified a number of dangerous western insurrectionists, all Democratic-Republicans. Jefferson did not react immediately, perhaps because Daveiss was a well-known Federalist, but primarily because he had no interest in waging a Spanish war and knew secret truce negotiations then under way soon would cool western animus for Spain and deflate talk of a Mexican invasion.[13]

Aware of the administration's determination to avoid war, yet unable to secure a suitable position, Burr began a second western tour later in the year. He recruited New York followers and sons of fellow Revolutionary War officers for an expedition that appears to have been something more than settlement, but perhaps less than treason. He arrived in Pittsburgh in early August and stayed for some time with George Croghan's former protégé, George Morgan, identified more than a decade earlier by Wilkinson as a pro-Spain conspirator. Morgan, alarmed by Burr's belief the West might secede from the United States, immediately wrote Jefferson to inform him of Burr's conversational rummaging. Apparently unaware of the offense he had given Morgan, Burr moved on to Blennerhassett's, where he made arrangement for the construction of fifteen boats, each capable of transporting fifty men. In Cincinnati, he again met with Smith, whose sons joined the procession, and traveled on to John Brown in Frankfort before going to Jackson in Nashville. There, he encouraged Jackson to call up the state militia and go with him, but settled for the recruitment of seventy-five men.[14]

The Mississippi River valley was now alive with rumors of Burr's intentions, and a thousand Spanish troops moved to within ten miles of the US post at Natchitoches. Secretary of War Henry Dearborn ordered Wilkinson to the post; Wilkinson tarried, but responded that he would gladly move ahead if Spanish negotiations failed "to soon plant our standards on the left bank of the [Rio] Grande." To Burr supporters John Adair and John Smith, Wilkinson's distortion went further when they were assured that the time had come for a fair chance of subduing the Spanish government in Mexico, and that their conquests might "extend as far west as California."[15]

In the early fall, Burr's daughter and her husband, Joseph Alston, joined him in Lexington, where he formalized his intention to acquire forty thousand acres in the Bastrop Tract. In the months ahead, Alston publicly would disavow any knowledge of a planned invasion of Mexico, and the appearance of his family in Kentucky, coupled with what seems to be a genuine commitment to his Bastrop settlement, lends doubt to the belief Burr was mounting a military campaign for Mexico at that time.[16]

Western World, a Federalist newspaper in Frankfort, Kentucky, whose editor opposed Burr when both men lived in New York, began a series of alarming articles that depicted Burr as a "little emperor," and called for a defense against an inevitable invasion. Daveiss again contacted Jefferson and forwarded articles from the *Western World* to the president. The president called a cabinet meeting for 22 October to consider news of Burr's plan "to separate the western from the Atlantic States, and erecting the former into an independent confederacy," adding that his intelligence indicated Wilkinson was considered to be Burr's "second-in-command." Jefferson closed his initial investigation three days later when he informed his cabinet that letters from the West indicated Burr was up to nothing and that he "is committing no overt act against the law."[17]

Jefferson's information probably came from Wilkinson, who was attempting to remove Burr and himself from the brewing calamity. Prior to Jefferson's cabinet meeting, Wilkinson had realized the administration had turned against Burr, and that he, too, was about to be discovered. He wrote Jefferson that day and acknowledged that a conspiracy to take New Orleans was in the making, but he feigned ignorance of its source. Soon after, he received a cipher letter from a Burr associate, written in the code he and Burr had devised earlier, and seized upon the opportunity: he changed the words "*our* project" to "*the* project" and forwarded the letter to Jefferson with a cover document that suggested Burr was prepared to capture New Orleans and all Louisiana. To separate himself further from the invasion, Wilkinson then arrested all known Burr accomplices (including his own "project" connections) and their attorneys.[18]

By the time the Corps of Discovery reached the Falls in November 1806, the Louisville area was so enthralled by Burr that local newspapers placed reports of his activity above headlines that announced the safe return of the explorers. Daveiss charged Burr on 5 November with planning an invasion of Mexico and asked for the arrest of the New Yorker, who hired Lexington lawyer Henry Clay to represent him. The case died for lack of evidence, but after he received word that Wilkinson had implicated Burr to Jefferson, Daveiss subsequently organized a Frankfort grand jury to hear the evidence. This jury was dismissed on 12 November for lack of evidence. A second grand jury convened, but ended with jury members ridiculing Daveiss after his witness, *Western World* editor John Wood, admitted the paper's Burr articles were fabricated from rumors alone.

Long before Burr had become his vice president by virtue of placing second in the 1800 election, Jefferson had distrusted and disliked him, and although his disdain for Hamilton was equal to that he held for Burr,

Jefferson's animosity for Burr soon would test the limits of presidential authority. Jefferson, who had known what Wilkinson was when he warned George Rogers Clark of the man's deception in 1782, had not cared in 1793 "what insurrections should be excited in Louisiana" by Clark or, apparently, Wilkinson. The antagonism he directed at Burr after 1806, however, was personal.[19]

When William Clark finally reached Washington City the week of 18 January 1807, he brought a letter from Jonathan that informed his brother of Burr-related news from the Falls, but both Clarks apparently were oblivious to Wilkinson's role in the activity. William responded to his brother later in the week. "I have received [your letters] one of which I have Shewn to the president it contains Some information respecting Mr. Burrs Expedition which he wished to See or know." After he reviewed the letter, Jefferson supplied Clark with a summary of the situation as told by Wilkinson, which the younger man condensed in a famously irregular spelling pattern. "The Expedition of Mr. B. has excited the greatest alarm and his views as are maid known to the Exctve. (and which will be laid before Congree tomorrow or the next day) are of the most desperate and violent aspect (and little Short of a Second Boneparte to the Nateal Convention). Genl. Wilkinson has been giving information to the Government for Some time."[20]

Jefferson publicly accused Burr of attempting to separate the western states from the United States on 22 January 1807 with an assurance to Congress that his information came from a trustworthy source whose name was withheld. Furthermore, he reported, Burr had twenty thousand men at Blennerhassett's Island. Fully aware of Wilkinson's connection to the plot, but unwilling to implicate his source, the president was about to use his wayward general to trap Burr, and received authorization to spend nearly $100,000 to capture him.[21]

Burr was with Jackson at the Hermitage when he received word federal agents had raided Blennerhassett's home and had confiscated arms and boats meant for the foray. He rode quickly to Louisville, unaware Wilkinson had betrayed him to the president, and on to the mouth of the Cumberland River, where he met Blennerhassett, who had escaped his island with his wife and a few men. When he learned of Wilkinson's role in the federal action, Burr wrote the Mississippi Territory's governor on 10 January to claim the charges were the result of "vile fabrications of a man notoriously the pensioner of a foreign country," and placed himself under the authority of Mississippi officials at Bayou Pierre, near Natchez, on 17 January, before Wilkinson's soldiers could capture him.

Informed of the details of the arrest, acting governor Cowles Mead wrote Secretary of War Henry Dearborn with the news. "Thus, sir, this mighty alarm, with all its exaggerations, has eventuated in nine boats and one hundred men, and the major of these are boys, or young men just from school. . . . I believe that they are the dupes of a stratagem, if the asseverations of generals Eaton and Wilkinson, are to be credited." A local grand jury refused to indict Burr, but as Jefferson's declaration now was circulating throughout the country, he was held pending the arrival of federal forces. Burr, who fully understood the charges Jefferson meant to press, disappeared; this time he moved east, toward West Florida.[22]

Federal troops led by Edmund Gaines arrested him on 19 February 1807 in Wakefield, Mississippi Territory (Alabama), and he was taken to Richmond to stand trial. He and Blennerhassett were indicted for treason on 24 June, and Jonathan Dayton and John Smith were indicted the following day.[23]

The trial began on 3 August in the searing Virginia summer heat, with Theodosia and Alston at Burr's side and Chief Justice John Marshall, a Jefferson relation, presiding. US attorney George Hay was the prosecutor and Edmund Randolph, related to both Jefferson and Marshall, represented the vice president. Jefferson had provided Hay with signed, blank pardons, that allowed him to summon "all but the grossest offenders" to testify against Burr before the proceedings began. The highlights of the trial—aside from the spectacle of Burr himself—were the appearance of Wilkinson and the testimony of Daniel Clark, who implicated both Wilkinson and Burr in a scheme to seize Louisiana. Andrew Jackson, who appeared on Hays's list of witnesses, was not called. Early in the course of the trial, Randolph argued that he required the letters written by Wilkinson and held by Jefferson to defend his client; Jefferson refused, citing executive privilege. Judge John Marshall ultimately determined Jefferson was not above the law and thereby established the president's role within the American judicial process.[24]

At one point, Burr took the floor in his own defense.

> Our president . . . is a lawyer, and a great one[,] too. He certainly ought to know what it is, that constitutes a war. Six months ago, he

> proclaimed there was a civil war. And yet, for six months they have been hunting for it, and still cannot find one spot where it existed. There was, to be sure, a most terrible war in the newspapers; but no where else. . . . At length, however, the Spaniards invaded our territory, and yet, there was no war. But sir, if there was a war, certainly no man can pretend to say, that the government is able to find it.

Burr was acquitted on 31 August 1807 for lack of proof that he overtly conspired to create a war. Emerging from this debacle more disgraced than in the months following the Hamilton duel, he left the country for several years before he returned to open a law practice in New York, never again to entertain hopes of a western empire.[25]

The nation was left to guess what he had intended, and opinion eventually divided along political and geographical lines. He had written his daughter that the 1805 trip was contemplated "with gayety and cheerfulness" as a means of recovering from the previous year, but, "As the objects of this journey, not mere curiosity, or *pour passer le temps,* [it] may lead me to Orleans, and perhaps further." Aaron Burr had considered a campaign in Mexico to be plausible in 1805 and probably saw Wilkinson and himself as military and civilian commander, respectively, of what he hoped would be a newly claimed western acquisition.[26]

Jefferson's treaty with Spain had concluded before the 1806 trip began. Burr therefore understood war would not materialize to give his filibuster cover, and despite a two-year flirtation with British minister Anthony Merry that was designed to develop a union against Spain, no nation expressed official interest in joining his venture. Yet, Burr continued to recruit young men to come to his Bastrop settlement in preparation for the campaign he hoped would end with financial reward and, perhaps, personal restoration. Had he succeeded in driving Spanish claims south of the Rio Grande, even as far as Mexico City, Burr must have believed he would have become a recognized western figure, recovering his pre-1804 status as a gentleman despite the dangers he had risked to achieve it. Never a political ideologue, it is possible he had not anticipated the formation of a Federalist and Democratic-Republican alliance against him.[27]

For his part, Wilkinson may never have meant to join Burr, but instead used the opportunity to participate in the scheme at the request of his Spanish employers. Alternately, his initial commitment could have been genuine. As he began to fear that his usefulness to Spanish authorities had run its course, and knew that Jefferson was aware of his role in the conspiracy, Wilkinson could have chosen to escape the United States before the administration finally pulled the plug. Chronically strapped for cash, he required a backup career plan.[28]

Burr's association with the Indiana Canal Company, and the timing of his first Louisiana tour, led his enemies and many subsequent historians to connect the two enterprises. The overt involvement of company directors Dayton and Smith, and the public's memory of George Rogers Clark's long association with France, further fed the rumors. The Indiana directors denied any involvement with Burr's conspiracy, and public statements that blamed claims of collusion on the competing Ohio Canal Company accused the Ohio directors of deceit and misrepresentation of the Indiana Canal Company. Conclusive proof does not exist, but while the Indiana company was not accused of illegal activity, it failed to regain its former prominence after Burr's trial.[29]

With the disappearance of Burr from the scene, the West settled into a period of growth that would continue until the Panic of 1819. Clark did not know he had only a year more to live at Point of Rocks, so when he accompanied Owen Gwathmey to Jeffersonville's mineral springs spa in the summer of 1808, he told his brother-in-law he at last was busy completing his house. Fanny's new husband, Dennis Fitzhugh, provided him with a thousand bricks to construct a chimney, and Clark sent Kitt to Fitzhugh's Louisville store to bring additional supplies, a new handkerchief, and two pairs of stockings home to Clarksville.[30]

The cost of paying hired workers became more than Clark anticipated. In October, he sent Kitt to Trough Spring to borrow fifty dollars, with a promise to repay Jonathan at the new year. Remarkably, he added, "P.S. If you can honour this note send it by Kitt," who surely would have considered the money to be a small fortune in 1808. Kitt, indeed, returned to Indiana and the home he shared with Clark. The completed house was about twenty by thirty feet, with two rooms downstairs and two upstairs, divided by a stair. The chimney, built at the eastern gable in the smaller room, and a kitchen standing to the north of the house were painted white. The spring ran to the southeast, above an orchard that contained "perhaps a hundred" cherry, apple, and peach trees. Cabins in which "Cupid, Ceasar,

Ben McGee and his wife, Venus, lived stood near the house" long after Ben and Venus left for St. Louis with William in 1808.[31]

Clark continued to push for the Indiana canal project from his little house overlooking the Falls, and late in 1808 applied to the Clarksville trustees to grant his brother, William, land between the town lots and the Ohio River for "use of opening a canal . . . on which to erect Mills, Wharfs, Store Houses." By this time, however, William Clark lived in Missouri with his bride, Julia, and fate was about to make the canal subject meaningless for George Rogers Clark.[32]

15

Clark's Death

> The broken soldier, kindly bade to stay, sate by his fire and talked the night away; Wept o'er his wounds, or tales of sorrow done, shouldered his crutch, and shewed how fields were won.
>
> —Oliver Goldsmith, *The Deserted Village*, 1770

Jonathan Clark's characteristically terse diary entry recorded the date of the amputation. "25 March 1809 Clear at Louisville—brother George had his leg taken off by Doct Ferguson." Thirty-seven years after the event, George Rogers Clark's nephew described it for Lyman Draper. "In March 1809, Gen. Clark had his leg amputated above the knee. Had when alone, in fit, or somehow, fallen into the fire the prior winter. Never was known exactly how it was caused, & so burned it as to require amputation." A generation later, another nephew, George Washington Clark, told Draper that he had heard his uncle "had a fit of some kind, and thus got burned" but had been informed by others that his uncle was under the influence of liquor; thus, he could not tell Draper "really how it was." "He was paralyzed in the little home, fell in the fire, was burned badly," Elizabeth Clark Anderson's granddaughter, Sarah Jane Gamble, recalled. "Mrs. Samuel Gwathmey [Mary Ann Booth] of this place often rode on horseback behind her husband to dress the burn. But this loving niece, I knew her well, could not cure his leg."[1]

An 1846 interview substantiated the Clark family's account.

> South West Cor. of Main & 5th streets you remember is . . . now a fine, brick house . . . [but] about 1807 or 1808 a common log house was standing there in which was amputated the leg of Gen. Clark by Dr. R. Ferguson of this city. . . . Dr. Ferguson says that arrangements had been made at the time of the amputation of

> Clark's leg for a drummer to stand down in the street before the door and play some favorite tunes of Clark. The signal was given, the drum commenced and the Dr went to work. During the whole time engaged in taking off his leg the Genl was keeping time with the music with his fingers (both hands) on the bed. The Dr says he noticed his countenance and he says it was effected more by the music than the pain.[2]

Fanny's daughter, Ann, remembered, "He was afterwards brought to my mothers and step father's, Judge Fitzhugh, in Louisville, where the amputation of his right leg was performed, I think by Drs. Galt, Ferguson, and suppose others, for the house seemed full. . . . A band of music [was] playing all the time. The array of instruments attracted my curiosity, with my mother walking up and down listening at the door in the deepest grief, and often heard her and Pa speak of his fortitude and patience under the operation, never having murmured or groaned but once." Fanny's brother-in-law, William Croghan, who had purchased it in 1806 and would leave it to his widow to use as her town house, owned the building that housed Ferguson's office and Dennis and Fanny Fitzhugh's home in 1809.[3]

Clark had become lame in his thirties as the result of severe arthritis in his left leg, which necessitated the use of a cane and left his gait unsteady. Richard Ferguson summarized Clark's medical problem as "a violent Rheumatic affection of the left Hip & Knee joints . . . attended with such general weakness of the Extremity," and added "that in walking the body was rendered tottering and unsteady. . . . In addition to the above an unfortunate accident, which happened to him, in the month of March Last, made Amputation of the opposite [right] Limb necessary. It is the belief of the Genl. (nor do I hesitate to Subscribe to the opinion) that the Fatique and exposure to weather, which he underwent, whilst engaged in the Service of his Country, was the cause." Although younger generations repeated public doubts concerning Clark's sobriety at the time of his fall, no one who attended the general at the time suggested this was the cause.[4]

On or about 11 June, when he was able to be moved comfortably, Clark was taken to "Maj. William Croghan's capacious house about six miles up the river where he remained the rest of his life with his sister Lucy," but the arrangement may not have been meant initially to be permanent.

Ann Clark's husband, Owen Gwathmey, wrote an affectionate letter to his brother-in-law on 13 November, offering his own home to Clark.

> I have been anxious for several years past that you should come and spend the remainder of your days with me, I feel more desirous since you have met with so great a misfortune.... I will do every thing in my power to make your time pass off agreably. I have lately purchased me a set of the Dictionary of Arts & Sciences, with Three hundred plates, consisting of Machenery of every kind, Fish, Tools, &c. I think if you was with me you could make me understand many things I am now at a loss for.

In the end, the move to Locust Grove would be George Rogers Clark's last. General Clark "is now Seated in a Chair, depending upon the assistance of others to move him, even across his room," Ferguson wrote in December. He is "doomed, I am fearfull, never to walk again."[5]

Locust Grove was not a new experience for Clark, as he had been a regular guest over the years. The large house had taken years to finish, but Croghan apparently ordered a posh interior completion shortly before the arrival of William Clark and Meriwether Lewis. When George Rogers Clark became a permanent member of the household, the center hall wainscoting shone with a newly applied verdigris finish and wallpaper hung in the principal, or public rooms. The great parlor on the second floor boasted a striking American-made copy of a French Reveillon pattern, and carpets, an English one in the small parlor connected to his room, covered the floors. A punkah fan, no doubt discovered by Croghan in his many trips to New Orleans, swung over the dining room table. Locust Grove presented Clark with luxuries unknown in the rustic home he had occupied at Point of Rocks and was a significant departure even from the stark interior of the massive log house his parents knew at Mulberry Hill. Jonathan's son later wrote of his uncle's life at Locust Grove, saying, "Gen. Clark... had a servant Kitt, who used to wheel him around. [Clark] would take his place at table, beside Maj. Croghan, & fed himself. It had been arranged... as Maj. Croghan had the best accommodations, that he should go there, & arranged that he should have his toddy at dinner each day, & only then, & Mrs. Croghan or the Major would prepare it & leave it out to him."[6]

A loving family and faithful friends who sustained him before he moved to Locust Grove saved Clark from ignominy, but none was more important to his well-being than William Clark and Kitt. William was a child when George Rogers's star burned so brightly, but he was closer to his brother between 1796 and 1803 than at any period in his life. He devoted years and, indeed, his inheritance to his elder brother. It was William, with Jonathan's aid, who cleared his brother's Vincennes debts, helped establish his Clarksville residence, and prolonged George Rogers's life until the Croghans assumed the responsibility.

William had returned to Clarksville for a short time in 1807, but he became a resident of St. Louis in June 1808, never again to live permanently in the Louisville area. He was named first territorial governor of Missouri, a position he held from 1813 until 1820, and later, superintendent of Indian affairs. In bleak contrast to George Rogers's life, William lived happily with Julia (Judith) Hancock, and when she died in 1820, Julia's cousin Harriet Kennerly Radford became his wife. Four children survived him, as did several of Fanny's children, whom he essentially reared. The only Clark son not to serve in the Revolutionary War, William surpassed his brothers in fame and fortune and died on 1 September 1838 in St. Louis as an enduring hero. The last of John and Ann Rogers Clark's children to survive was buried at the St. Louis plantation home of Fanny's son, John O'Fallon.

Kitt, whose days were interwoven with those of William and George Rogers Clark, almost certainly began life as the son of a Virginia farmer. He was born within a year of William Clark, and although Kitt's first known mention is in John Clark's will, he lived with George Rogers for nearly two decades, until the older man's death. William Clark emancipated Kitt six weeks later. "Be it known that Kitt, having served faithfully and as the body servant of Genl. George R. Clark deceased, conducted himself for many years with entire approbation, is hereby liberated from any involuntary servitude to me or my heirs forever."[7]

Lew, probably the same man who had served Clark through the general's Revolutionary War trials, was emancipated with Kitt. Lew's expenses do not appear in Croghan's ledger book, however, which suggests he had lived with William in St. Louis and traveled to Louisville in 1818. It is also possible that Lew arrived at Locust Grove with George Rogers Clark in 1809, but that he occupied a lower social standing than Kitt, as the expenses Clark absorbed and the allowance of relatively free movement indicate Kitt possessed a singular position within the Clark family's master–slave hierarchy. James Harrison later thought Kitt had continued to live at Locust Grove and "died there some ten or fifteen years afterwards. My impression is that he was never treated as a slave after the death of Gen. Clark." Harrison continued, "Kitt . . . was about five feet eight inches high, robust built, weighing about 160 pounds, dark yellow complexion, good and cheerful temper, and greatly attached to Gen. Clark, & took pleasure in waiting upon him."[8]

Kitt, of course, would have had much to say about his service had he lived to be interviewed by midcentury historians. If Harrison's understandings were correct, Kitt died as a quasi-member of William Croghan's household in the small house Croghan had built for Clark, but some sources suggested otherwise. Meriwether Lewis Clark, William Clark's son, recalled Kitt died about 1840 at the Louisville home of Fanny's son, Charles W. Thruston, but his cousin, Dr. William Clark, remembered Kitt had struggled on his own before moving to St. Louis to live with William Clark. It is possible, of course, Kitt returned to Louisville after William Clark's death and, with William and Lucy Croghan also gone from the scene, found a home with Thruston. The result of each narrative is that Kitt lived and died at the home of a descendant of John Clark.[9]

Clark was strong enough to spend the summer of 1811 at the springs near Jeffersonville, Indiana, with old soldiers Jonathan and Edmund Clark, Richard Clough Anderson Sr., Alexander S. Bullitt, and others. James Harrison, son of the spa's owner, remembered that the general could speak with difficulty, and was able to get around in a large chair with rollers with the aid of his cane. Clark and his friends came regularly to the springs. "Some [stayed] in cabins near the Spring, & [they] would have their servants with them to cook & keep house; and these men would hunt some, play whist, &c. They paid every attention & respect to Gen. G. R. Clark," said Harrison. The first portrait of Clark painted from life was completed at Locust Grove about this time by an artist named Cook. The result of a month's work is a somewhat primitive image that portrays a stern Clark—the face perhaps already distorted by the first stroke—sitting in an armchair near a globe, surely a prop of his own choosing. Forgoing all military regalia, Clark posed in a good wool coat, his hair carefully combed, his posture upright.[10]

The family had tried for some time to secure a pension for Clark from the Virginia state assembly, but none had been successful. After Virginia legislator Charles Fenton Mercer learned of Clark's plight, he made the trip to Louisville to assess the general's condition for himself. "When I paid my first visit to Majr. Croghan," he recalled, "[Clark] was a member of his family, nursed with the tenderest regard by Mrs. C. his sister, and so helpless from a paralysis, which deprived him of speech, as to be moved about on a chair, by assistance of others. Touched by his condition, my object was to secure to him, the half pay of a Colonel for the residue of his life."[11]

Mercer returned to Richmond where, as he wrote James Monroe, "I succeeded in getting through both branches of the Assembly in one day a bill for the relief of General George Rogers Clark. I had the house in tears with me for many minutes . . . in bringing in a bill giving the largest pension that has ever been granted by the Commonwealth." The act entitled Clark to an annual pension and ordered a new sword to be forged by the State Manufactory of Arms in Richmond, inscribed, "A tribute to Courage & Patriotism," and, "Presented by the State of Virginia, to her beloved son General George Rogers Clarke who by the conquest of Illinois & St. Vincennes extended her empire and aided in the defence of her liberties." The decorative work was completed in October 1812, but the sword was dated 12 June 1779, the date an earlier, secondhand sword, had been refitted as poor recognition for Clark.[12]

Mercer was "deputed to convey the second sword Virginia voted to Gen. G. R. Clark & passing over the mountains," he worked up "a fine speech" to make to Clark early in 1813. At Major Croghan's, Draper wrote, the general sat in his chair in the parlor, where he received the sword and laid it across his lap while Mercer delivered the speech he had taken pains to compose. After the speech, Mercer told Draper, Clark responded, "Young man, go back to your State; and tell her when she needed a sword, I found one for her. I want bread."[13]

Draper's account of the presentation offers a striking similarity to the memoir attached to the 1860 publication of Ebenezer Denny's *Journal,* a book well known to the historian. In this, Clark is reported to have told Denny he destroyed the first sword on the banks of the Wabash in frustration, disappointed the Virginia messenger had not brought news of the legislature's approval of his submitted bills. "I asked for bread, and she

[Virginia] sent me a sword," Clark told Denny in 1786. Compounding doubt concerning Draper's report of the presentation is the contradiction between Mercer's characterization of Clark as a man "deprived of speech" in 1812, and the succinct response Clark was said to have managed in the winter of 1813.

From the time Virginia approved Clark's $400 annual pension, the general passed the income to Croghan who, as he had done since their surveying partnership had begun more than thirty years earlier, kept meticulous records of Clark's expenses. Croghan immediately deducted $200 per annum for expenses connected to Clark's "boarding, lodging, washing, etc." and backdated the payments to 11 June 1809. From 1 January 1812 forward, these expenses were valued nominally at $400 annually. With the pension income, Croghan paid Clark's household bills dating to 26 July 1809 with an outstanding 1s4p tavern account at Harrison's springs. Most of Clark's expenses beyond those owed Croghan were limited to clothing: he spent between eight and eleven dollars each year for a new hat, and Mr. and Mrs. Jonathan Mason and a Mr. Hardin were employed by the Croghans to create Clark's and Kitt's shirts, leather overalls, and other clothing. A greatcoat was made for Kitt in February 1815, followed by new summer clothes in May, and a new blanket the following fall. In March 1816, Clark again outfitted them both: Mason was paid for providing a new coat, jacket, and breeches for Clark and new shoes for Kitt. Cloth valued at $11.37 was purchased and tailored into clothes for Kitt in April 1817.[14]

Jonathan and Sally's son, Dr. William Clark, remembered the best of his uncle's days at Locust Grove. General William Clark, he reported, then the governor of the Missouri Territory, made a trip in the company of

> a delegation of some forty or fifty chiefs & warriors . . . from Missouri to Washington, soon after the close of the war of 1812, & visited Maj. Croghan [who] entertained them with a dinner in his yard. Prior to dinner they had been introduced to Gen. Clark in his room (subsequently a separate small building was erected for his occupancy) & he seemed much interested by the visit. Among the delegation was an aged chief (probably a Shawnee) now a short, bow[ed], shrivelled man, evidently well built when young. . . . This old chief seemed to eat his dinner hastily, & then went to Gen. Clark's room (as if he sought a fuller interview than he could

George Rogers Clark by Joseph Bush, c. 1815.

> have had with the crowd before). . . . Gen. C. seemed fully to comprehend his Indian mixture of words & pantomime. [The chief] said "You have saved the life of many a man." [Clark responded], "How so?" "I and my warriors waylaid the trails around the Falls & along the Beargrass many a time for the special object of killing you, and suffered many [to] pass untouched, hoping & expecting you might soon pass by, & we should destroy our mortal enemy, & receive a large reward for your scalp; & thus many escaped." "Ah," Clark sighed, "then I have saved the life of many a man." The idea seemed a pleasant reminiscence to him.[15]

Educator and historian Mann Butler recalled his only meeting with George

Rogers Clark years later. "He was staying at Major Croghan's, in his own private apartment, where every visitor to that hospitable mansion called to pay his respects. . . . His chamber was a public shrine, where every patriotic breast desired to offer worship." Soon after David Rozel Poignaud moved to Louisville in 1814, he "supped, slept, & breakfasted" with a "party of upwards of a dozen gentlemen and two ladies" at Locust Grove. Several in the group entered General Clark's room, and "the hum of conversation & the laugh of the parties was heard outside." In the summer of 1817, when Poignaud again visited, he discovered the general sitting on "a piazza" in a large armchair.[16]

Joseph H. Bush, a young Kentucky artist who would train under Thomas Sully, visited Locust Grove sometime between 1814 and 1817 to make a portrait of Clark. "Mr. Bush at my dinner table calling attention to the portrait told me that it was the first portrait he had ever painted," James Ann Pearce Pindell later wrote, "and that whilst he had painted many finer he had never painted one which was a truer likeness than this one of Genl Clark. He said that Genl Clark was the most striking looking man he had ever seen and it would have been difficult for an artist to fail to catch his likeness in a portrait." The portrait exists today as a reminder of the physical ruin conferred upon the once robust soldier. The work indicates that Clark's always dominant forehead had extended into a sweeping arc across the bald skull, and what remained of the once easily recognizable red hair largely had given way to gray. He was clean shaven, no doubt thanks to Kitt's steady hand, because the obvious signs of stroke appeared most severely around the turned-down mouth, particularly on the left side of his face. His dark eyes remained focused and heavily hooded by the notably untamed brows; his face was ruddy, depicting his life-long complexion.[17]

Clark's life wound down amid the comfort and protection of an indulgent family and increasingly appreciative community. The eight Croghan children grew to maturity in their uncle's presence, and the sons and daughters of Jonathan and William Clark, Ann Gwathmey, and Fanny Fitzhugh were his regular companions. Brothers Jonathan and Edmund Clark died while George Rogers lived at Locust Grove, and the failing general must have wondered how it was that he continued.[18]

Ann Gwathmey's son, William, was a student at Robert Tompkins's school, which adjoined Richard Clough Anderson's Soldier's Retreat, when Clark's life neared its end. After a messenger arrived at Anderson's home in the evening of 12 February 1818 to apprise the old colonel of the general's expected death, Anderson and Tompkins immediately rode the several miles for Major Croghan's, where they remained until after the funeral. George Rogers Clark died Friday, 13 February 1818. His last words, as communicated by Anderson and Robert Tompkins to their respective families were, "waving his hand, 'Come on my brave boys! St. Vin.'"[19]

Poignaud, who attended Clark's funeral, remembered Judge John Rowan's eulogy was delivered "at the coffin head . . . in a conversational tone. . . . There were only some 6 or 8 in the room. The relations & household were on the other side of the passage from the room where the services were conducted," which suggests that the family gathered in the small parlor across the hall from the Croghans' dining room. Jonathan's son, George, recalled a stormy and snowy day, which necessitated an indoor service. The Vincennes *Western Sun* reported, "The Rev. Mr. Banks officiated in his professional capacity by offering up an appropriate prayer . . . and was succeeded by the Hon. J. Rowan, in a pathetic and impressive eulogy on the character of the ever memorable hero." Future Clark biographer and relative, Temple Bodley, was told the judge closed the service with "The mighty oak of the forest has fallen, and now the scrub oaks may sprout all around." Another biographer would conclude Rowan's "sentence did not need to be written. No one ever forgot it."[20]

George Rogers Clark, until his dying day an inactive general in the French army, was buried in William Croghan's graveyard. Later that day, Croghan entered one of the few personal notations recorded in his ledger: "February 13th, the above Genl Clark died at my House & was buryed on the 15th. To cash paid for his coffin $50." As he closed the account he had maintained for Clark since 1783, Croghan reckoned his brother-in-law died owing him £311.15.2, or roughly $1,000.

Many years later, Dr. William Clark would recall, "Gen. Clark regarded himself as a pauper, & Maj. Croghan assured him he was not. He left a large body of wild lands on the Ohio & Tennessee, below the latter, which were devised among his brothers & sisters & their families." This information was correct by the time the doctor related it, but Clark's will had not mentioned his western Kentucky land because the general considered it to be the property of his brother, William. In a bit of pre–Lewis and Clark Expedition business between the brothers, George Rogers had given the two Ohio River grants that were the subject of contention between Humphrey Marshall and him to William on 28 July 1803.[21]

An 1821 lawsuit determined that the 1803 transfer of the two land grants from George Rogers to William Clark represented a mortgage rather than a deed, and ordered the land sold to satisfy the judgment. The property was sold at the courthouse door on 10 July 1826, when William Clark successfully bid $2,500, $400 more than the debt his brother owed him when he originally received the deed. With free title, Clark had Paducah, Kentucky, surveyed and platted in 1827. The town officially was created by the Kentucky legislature in 1830, thus ending William Clark's long struggle connected to his brother's complicated finances.[22]

Inexplicably, William did not produce his brother's will for more than twelve years after George Rogers's death. John Croghan, who wrote Clark's will on 5 November 1815 at Locust Grove, was not asked to prove it until 4 October 1830. George Woolfolk, an attorney married to Catharine Tompkins Gwathmey, was appointed administrator of George Rogers Clark's estate after the will was produced, and he was contracted by the Clark heirs to clear the general's outstanding accounts with Virginia. Woolfolk spent nearly a year in Richmond before he recovered more than $25,000 owed by the commonwealth and $6,500 from Henrico Circuit Court (Virginia), the balance of the debt owed Clark by Virginia.[23]

This money, even without the value of the Tennessee River tract, would have allowed Clark to live as well as any man in Kentucky, yet he benefited from none of it. The ultimate sorrow of his life was the utter lack of hope he harbored after 1786 for reestablishing his financial footing or his once brilliant reputation. George Rogers Clark remains an enigma. His motives and personal attributes, maligned by political enemies in his lifetime, rehabilitated at his death, and glorified in the hagiographic style that accompanied the nation's centennial, remain unclear today, when formula patriotism is revered and perceived failure denigrated. Clark was neither a formula man, nor a failure to any but himself, as the act that directed the initiation of his Revolutionary pension acknowledged. "The State of Virginia was indebted [to him] for the extension of her boundaries from the Atlantic to the Mississippi," or on today's map, the portion of the United States enclosed by the Mississippi and Ohio rivers and the Great Lakes.[24]

He began his career as a patriot in the only way he knew to express the fidelity: as a Virginian. The Native Americans Clark met in the Illinois understood him to be a Virginian; Mohawk chief Joseph Brant knew him to be the leader of the "savage Virginians"; and certainly, Pennsylvania settlers and militias near Fort Pitt had no doubt he worked for Virginia. It was clear he considered his work in Kentucky to be an extension of his allegiance to his home and to governors Henry and Jefferson, as this was the nature not only of the man, but of colonial and early Federal-era customs. Clark's later anger with the *government* of Virginia was profound, but his inspiration from the Old Dominion, permanent.

He decided it was possible to leave his beloved home when he took a break from public service in 1786 to nurse physical and psychological ills. His primary motivation was the war debt the commonwealth refused to reimburse, but the unsettled politics of the Kentucky district also influenced the decision. He was not in favor of separation from Virginia, but an increasingly large number of Kentucky pioneers were, which left him somewhat politically and socially isolated. Unlike Boone, who simply packed up and left the country to begin a new life and new tales in Missouri, or John Sevier, who abandoned independent nation building in favor of joining Tennessee's established government, Clark was at a loss. The avocational scientist and certified surveyor had discovered along the way that he was good at leading men through harrowing situations and negotiating potential enemies into submission, and he wanted to get back to work. When he offered to establish a colony for Spain, he joined not only such luminaries as Steuben and Boone, but also George Morgan, at the time a sitting trustee at the University of New Jersey, in working to weaken Spain's western hold through the introduction of "American" colonists on the Mississippi. Had Spain accepted the offer, Clark would be thought of today, with Austin, Houston, and others, as a successful western pioneer.

Jefferson's role in shaping Clark's geopolitical vision cannot be overlooked, and while the general's flirtation with France reflected a continuing financial need and an ongoing desire to rehabilitate his damaged reputation, it also served as an attempt to nurture the admiration he knew Jefferson once held for him. To the extent that Clark genuinely associated with any ideology, he was a Democratic-Republican in the Jeffersonian sense of the term. The president's expression of "natural aristocracy" suggested that people of the "first rank" owed it to their social inferiors to serve as exemplars in the new society and, through this service, they would teach others to create a sound republic. It could be argued that Clark's darkest hours appeared when he sensed he had failed to satisfy Jefferson's ideals (Jefferson's own profound failures notwithstanding), and his brightest coincided with the obvious pleasure the president, Patrick Henry, or George Mason took in his achievements.[25]

Jefferson's positions regarding nullification, states' rights, slavery, revolution, and France are reflected in Clark's words and actions, and it was not until Jefferson became president of the United States, particularly after William Clark accepted the expedition role, that Clark began to develop a federalist tone. The man who boasted to Genêt in 1793 that he had "no doubt . . . the greatest part of . . . Louisiana" would fall into his hands reconsidered his appreciation of the United States by 1805, when he no longer thought of the Illinois Expedition as "a local thing" but as one that would contribute to the defeat of the British army across the continent.

George Rogers Clark's postwar disillusionment does not diminish his earlier triumphs, and his contributions to the United States rightfully continue to be celebrated. He may have been surprised by a Vincennes newspaper's eulogy that correctly summarized his end with, "Although he may not have felt his country's gratitude cheering his declining age, yet his country did not, nor ever shall forget, that he well deserved it." Nevertheless, Clark had been witness to too much brutality and bore too much responsibility before time and experience prepared him, and the remoteness of place and position, coupled with the public humiliation of de facto poverty, had left him broken. He saw no role for himself in the federalist United States' army, and, unable to succeed in the place he claimed, and bewildered by a government that appeared to him before 1801 to be the mirror image of British colonial policy, he could not find his purpose in Washington's or Adams's United States of America.[26]

16

William and Lucy Clark Croghan

> The President of the United States and Gen. Jackson . . . were escorted . . . to Locust Grove, the seat of Maj. Croghan, where they remained until Monday morning.
>
> —*Kentucky Herald and Mercantile Advertiser,* 25 June 1819

After William Croghan buried his brother-in-law, he must have made his way slowly across the two hundred yards or so that separated the family cemetery from his house and, in deference to the weather and his own considerable age, settled near the fire to reflect upon the decades that had passed since he and Clark had been young men. In the autumn, next-door neighbor Zachary Taylor would write John O'Fallon, "Major Croghan . . . is rapidly declining, and I am fearful, unless a change for the better takes place shortly, he cannot stand it long." So many patriots had preceded Clark to the grave: Greene, Steuben, Scott, Hamilton, and of course, in 1799, the most important of them all, Washington. Croghan surely saw his future. Burr survived, and Lafayette; but Burr never again would travel to Kentucky and Croghan would not live to reunite with Lafayette.[1]

The Irish immigrant, reared to become a successful Englishman, had prospered in North America, able to grasp political and social structures at once and to make himself useful to those whose opinions mattered most. A shrewd judge of character, Croghan lived his life strategically and avoided embarrassment, if not conflict, with a focus on his own success and that of his family. He had remained at Clark's side through the dark days that led to searches for mercenary opportunity because Croghan's loyalty, which emanated in part from familial connection, extended beyond his normally careful boundaries. Genuine friendship, respect, or a commonly shared acknowledgment of nightmarish war trauma might have bound them, but

Lucy Clark Croghan by John Wesley Jarvis, 1820.

the letters or journals that could better identify the tie, if they were written, no longer exist.

Like Clark, Croghan was fifty-seven when the general joined his household. He had spent years in the saddle scouting for Washington, and afterward, riding regularly to conduct survey duties, oblivious to the tolls the work demanded. He rallied in June 1819, when fellow officer, now president, James Monroe set out to inspect the American frontier in the company of Andrew Jackson, whose popularity in the South and West was enormous. The *Kentucky Herald and Mercantile Advertiser* reported Friday, the twenty-fifth, that when the entourage arrived at the Falls, they "partook of a public dinner given on the occasion, at the Union Hall; Major Croghan was the president." After a dinner in Jeffersonville on Saturday "the President of the United States and Gen. Jackson, accompanied by

William Croghan by John Wesley Jarvis, 1820.

their respective suites, crossed the Ohio from this place to Jeffersonville, under an escort of citizens; after which they were escorted . . . to Locust Grove, the seat of Maj. Croghan, where they remained until Monday morning."[2]

William and Lucy had experienced other brilliant society, but none so splendid as their second son's Manhattan marriage to Serena Eliza Livingston, daughter of Revolutionary privateer and New York realtor J. R. Livingston and his wife, Eliza McEvers. A niece to Robert R. Livingston, who had administered the 1789 oath of office to Washington and served as Jefferson's emissary to France, Serena's hand was sought by eager New Yorkers despite her formidable father, who was said to have pronounced, "Poverty is a curse I can't bear; with it a man had better not exist." Hen-

George Croghan by John Wesley Jarvis.

ry Lee IV, son of Light Horse Harry and half brother to Robert E. Lee, admired Serena, but was warned by a friend in 1816, "If you possessed ten-thousand a year, she would long ere this been Mrs. Lee." Washington Irving also marveled, but withdrew. "[Serena] is the heroine of all my poetical thoughts when they would picture anything very feminine and lovely," he wrote. "But where is the hero . . . worthy to bear away so peerless a face? Not among the worthy young traders of New York, most certainly."

Serena found a bona fide hero in the form of Lt. Colonel George Croghan, who somehow, erroneously, convinced her father he could provide for her. The only one of William Croghan's sons to pursue a military career, George had graduated from the College of William and Mary and

Serena Livingston Croghan by John Wesley Jarvis.

briefly studied law before he joined the Kentucky militia to serve under William Henry Harrison at the Battle of Tippecanoe. He abandoned his formal education after the militia experience "to read history, biography and Shakespeare at Locust Grove," where he also could "give chase to the fox or battle the wild cat and raccoon," before he again changed plans to join the army in June 1812, when war was announced against Britain.[3]

Croghan received early promotions with the help of his father's influence and the association of his famous uncles, and soon he was placed in charge of Fort Stephenson (Fremont, Ohio) by General William Henry Harrison. After Harrison ordered Croghan to evacuate and burn the fort in July 1813, when a native force approached, Croghan replied tersely, "We have determined to maintain this place, and by heavens we can." He later swore Harrison's orders had arrived too late to execute. Three days later, on 2 August, the defense of Fort Stephenson was assured and Croghan became a national hero. He left "Maj. Jessup in command of L. Sandusky" and returned to Locust Grove to recover from an "ague" before he was made lieutenant colonel of the newly organized Second US Rifle Regiment on 21 February 1814. The regiment arrived in New Orleans after Andrew Jackson famously concluded the war, and Croghan was transferred to the Seventeenth Infantry in May 1815. He assumed command of the southern army's Eighth department under Jackson, again with Jesup, to whom he passed command on 1 June.[4]

Croghan had lobbied successfully for a seat at the New York court-martial trial of General Edmund Gaines, hinting in his correspondence with Robert Butler that his reasons were personal and "*known*" to Butler. After a disagreeable four-week voyage, he arrived in Virginia on 9 July and traveled overland to the Hudson River, where he stayed in the Albany area until 3 September. When it was time for Croghan to leave for Manhattan with General Jacob Brown, he first said goodbye to Serena Livingston. His 1816 correspondence with Butler suggests he had met Serena prior to his summer visit, and an 18 October furlough request that sought permission to return to "his father in Kentucky" probably was prompted by his desire to announce his plans to his family. The colonel arrived in Louisville at Christmas and resigned from the army before the end of February 1817. "I have left the army [and] am shortly to be married and I have resolved on establishing myself as a farmer in the neighborhood of Louisville and there to enjoy 'time cumdignity' (as the landowners have it)."[5]

The Wednesday evening wedding was celebrated on 7 May 1817 in Manhattan's St. John's Episcopal Church, with the Livingston and Croghan families and New York society in attendance. George Croghan's father, of course, was an experienced New Yorker, but the wedding is the first recorded appearance of his mother in the city.[6]

After the wedding, William Croghan brought his wife and children back to his Kentucky farm and continued his slowing pace on the Ohio. The now-married Zachary Taylor, who was a cousin to Julia Hancock Clark, took notice of Eliza and Ann Croghan in 1818 when he wrote John O'Fallon, "The young [Croghan] ladies look quite enchanting. They are both single . . . at which I am much astonished." Whether or not Julia's brother, a Yale graduate, considered Taylor's opinion, he married Eliza Croghan at Locust Grove on 29 September 1819, with the Rev. Banks again officiating.[7]

A year later, George Croghan interrupted a river voyage from Pittsburgh to New Orleans to visit his parents and brought with him artists Henry Inman and John Wesley Jarvis, who made portraits of the Croghans during the stay. Lucy's strong Clark features leap from the canvas, the physical comparison to brothers George Rogers and William inescapable. A prominent nose dominates her face, but the well-formed chin and soft, steady gaze capture the viewer's attention and announce to anyone in doubt that he or she is in the presence of a still formidable woman. Jarvis's brush depicted a more inscrutable William Croghan. At sixty-eight, what obviously once had been a strikingly handsome face had grown gaunt and his hairline had receded, but Washington's former spy maintained a glance that was at once direct and guarded. His sitting posture remained erect, and his clothes, like Lucy's, were a bit out of style but finely made and freshly starched. Croghan surely knew this would be the last image of his life, and took care to display prominently the Society of the Cincinnati medal, establishing forever his role as an American officer in the Continental Army.[8]

Within three months of the Jarvis visit, William Jr. returned to Louisville from New Orleans on his way east, but, shocked by his father's condition, ended the journey at Locust Grove. Major Croghan's health was not the only family concern. Youngest child, Edmund, was a student in the summer of 1821 at Lexington's Transylvania Seminary, with brothers Nicholas and Charles, when he wrote a last letter to his mother. "Should I find that my health will permit, I will commence the study of law next October. . . . Had I enjoyed any thing like health I would have taken my degree with the last graduates. I will go on to the springs, though I am confident that I shall never recover." He was correct. The sixteen-year-old boy left the springs to return to his parents and died at Locust Grove on Thursday, 20 September, probably as a result of tuberculosis; he was buried near his uncle.[9]

The last great occasion of William Croghan's life was the marriage of his elder daughter, Ann Heron, to the celebrated quartermaster general of the United States Army, Thomas Sidney Jesup. The wedding took place at his home on 17 May 1822 and was attended by Jesup's fellow officers

Ann Heron Croghan Jesup by Charles Bird King.

and members of the extended Clark family. The match was as celebrated as Ann's brother's had been, not because Jesup brought social and financial connections to the family—he did not—but because he was a true military leader whose character was obvious to all who met him.[10]

Ann's closest brother, William, had not arrived in time for the wedding, but wrote his father the following day from Pittsburgh to explain his absence. "All that is wanting is her mother's consent. . . . On learning the result, I will loose no time in returning home." He had fallen in love with Mary Carson O'Hara, the daughter of General James O'Hara, who had become fabulously wealthy through the establishment of Pittsburgh's first glassworks factory and several mining operations that fueled most of Pittsburgh. His wealth, further secured through the early acquisition of land, including the remains of Fort Pitt, and a lively involvement in various area industries, made his children among the wealthiest heirs in the United States.[11]

A yellow fever epidemic began to sweep through Louisville shortly after Ann's wedding, and while the extent to which it affected the health of those at Locust Grove is unknown, the summer proved to be a deadly one for the family. The end came for Major William Croghan at his home on 21 September 1822, in his seventieth year, at the conclusion of a long and useful life. The *Louisville Public Advertiser* enigmatically reported the death of "the independent country gentleman," but Washington's *National Intelligencer* published a fulsome obituary. "During the whole of that memorable conflict which resulted in the dismemberment of one, and the creation of another empire, he discharged the duties of an ardent and gallant officer in the dangers, as well as the glories of that eventful period." Dennis Fitzhugh, Fanny's last husband, already had died that summer, and the death of Lucy's sister, Ann Gwathmey, came at Locust Grove just days after William's funeral.[12]

Croghan left an estate that included 53,860 acres in Kentucky, Indiana, and Ohio, in addition to Locust Grove, which would be left to son William at Lucy's death. Various Louisville buildings and lots were distributed to his wife, children, and nephew, as were the tens of thousands of acres he had acquired through Revolutionary War service and later purchase. All debts were forgiven, but following the pattern known to most of Virginia's Revolutionary officers, William Croghan failed to emancipate any of his enslaved laborers.[13]

Croghan had lived in North America as a colleague or friend to most of the important men in the country, and his accomplishments largely erased much of the ill-repute associated with his extraordinary uncle. He died having seen three children successfully married, one of whom was an esteemed national figure, with his sons well-educated and his daughters admired by all who knew them. Everything that had been lost through William Croghan's first Pennsylvania investment at the outbreak of the Revolution had been recovered tenfold and had left behind, in its time and place, a legacy of dignity and public service.

If time stood still, the story would close here. George Rogers Clark died at the moment of his rehabilitation, and William Croghan followed

William Croghan Jr. by James Reid Lambdin. Copy.

four years later, in no need of any such remedy. William Clark, explorer, soldier, governor, and Indian superintendent, was newly remarried in St. Louis, and Lucy Clark Croghan was left surrounded by neighbors and family members who revered her. Time did move forward, however, and Lucy lived to see the glory fade, and the famous names and deeds replaced by others.

William Croghan Jr. was married to Mary Carson O'Hara Tuesday evening, 28 January 1823, in Pittsburgh. Four months or so after her husband's death, Lucy allowed her son to claim the role, if not the title, of his inheritance, and she began a temporarily peripatetic way of life to allow William and Mary room to establish their lives at Locust Grove. Sixteen years of widowhood lay ahead for her, but Lucy embraced each of them with characteristic gusto, as life had better prepared her for exertion than quiet retirement—a condition she found necessary in the coming years.

By the time of his marriage, William had spent nearly a year in the company of the O'Haras and was in a position to compare the relatively carefree life of a Pittsburgh gentleman to that of a Kentucky farmer; and not unlike each of his brothers, he found the management of the farm to be inexplicably difficult and dull. The sudden poor health of his family

Andrew Jackson by Anna Claypoole Peale, 1819. Courtesy of Yale University Art Gallery.

further complicated the feelings he held for the only home he knew and ultimately led him to abandon Locust Grove, a decision that could not have come as a complete surprise to his family.[14]

William had read law with Thomas Cooper at Pennsylvania's Dickinson College and with Tapping Reeve in Litchfield, Connecticut, before Henry Clay was enlisted to help him find employment. Clay dutifully wrote a perfunctory 1817 letter of introduction to the state department ("Mr. William Croghan . . . is desirous of being appointed Secretary of Legation to the first foreign embassy. . . . All the accounts I have received of him concur in the most favorable representations of him"), but the application was unsuccessful. William returned to Locust Grove to assume his declining father's farm responsibilities and entered into a law partnership with a Mr. Dunbar, a "gentleman from New York [who] has performed in the theatre in that place with some applause." A year later, with his association with Dunbar ended in favor of a new partnership with William Tompkins, he remained indifferent to the law, but found what he knew would be a solution to financial and career uncertainty when he traveled to Pittsburgh in 1822.[15]

Life at the farm was not without some excitement. Andrew Jackson returned to Louisville early in April 1825, this time with his family, who were the dinner guests of Lucy and the young Croghans. "General Jackson and Family . . . dined at Locust Grove and made frequent mention of Ann and Eliza," wrote elder brother, Dr. John Croghan, who went on to share his opinions of the Jacksons with the Jesups. A month later, ten thousand Louisvillians greeted Lafayette on 12 May when the French general made a grand tour through the United States. A community ball given in his honor that evening was attended by Lucy Croghan and Sarah Anderson, and the marquis stopped at Soldier's Retreat the next morning. Now seventy-five, Richard Clough Anderson welcomed Lafayette on the steps in his "homespun knee-breeches and buckles," where "they were clasped with kisses and tears." "Our recognition of Lafayette was creditable to the town and gratifying to our esteemed guest," John informed the Jesups days later. "The ladies of the town and country generally waited on him & among them were Aunt Anderson and my Mother."[16]

Mary O'Hara Croghan was in Pittsburgh with infant son, William III, at the time of Lafayette's visit, and young Nicholas Croghan was completing a tour of Mammoth Cave and the Green River property he had inherited from his father. He returned to Louisville within weeks, but soon fell ill. Nicholas died on 11 July 1825, a few days after Locust Grove received word from St. Louis of Fanny Clark Fitzhugh's death, and his mother was left inconsolable. Lucy and Nicholas's twin, Charles, left for the Jesups' Washington home in August for, as George wrote, "a change of scene is necessary to both of them." Never strong, Charles Croghan probably was dying of tuberculosis even then, and although John would take him to Europe in a futile attempt to regain his health, he would die in Paris on 21 October 1832.[17]

Mary Croghan returned from Pittsburgh amid the grief and gave birth to Mary O'Hara in October 1825. Her husband's bitterness was evident in a letter written to Thomas and Ann Jesup two weeks after the little girl died on 18 July 1826. "I am sick & tired of farming, incessant toil and anxiety & no profit, if this place were mine I would convert it into a grazeing farm for sheep. . . . I am now firmly resolved so soon as my difficulties will allow to make arrangements for moving to Pittsburgh, unless the ponds between this and the river are drained this place can not be healthy."[18]

The couple's third child, Mary Elizabeth, was born in Pittsburgh and

John Croghan by Gennarino Persico, c. 1817.

baptized at the city's Trinity Church on 1 May 1827. Mary Elizabeth and her parents had returned to Locust Grove before her mother died on 15 October, at the age of twenty-three. William's young wife was buried in the family cemetery next to baby Mary before Croghan took his surviving children to Pittsburgh and delivered them into the care of his sister-in-law, Elizabeth O'Hara Denny. He was called back to Pittsburgh early in April, when his four-year-old son died of whooping cough. After he returned to Kentucky and found, as he wrote his sister, that he was "sickened at the thought of farming at Locust Grove," William decided with his mother's permission to sell the farm to George Hancock, Eliza's husband.[19]

Before he left Louisville, William rode to the courthouse with Charles, his forty-eight-year-old enslaved manservant, to emancipate him. Charles Goldman then agreed to a seven-year indenture with Croghan before the men left for Pittsburgh, where they arrived at the end of April. There, on 12 May, Croghan manumitted his last enslaved servant, thirteen-year-old Matilda Richardson, who would live with him as an indentured household member until 1843. Resettled and financially comfortable as a result of his wife's estate, Croghan dabbled in law and doted on his surviving daughter, and within a few years, he began construction of a twenty-two-room Greek Revival home, called Pic Nic. Although he would make many trips to Kentucky, he never again considered Locust Grove to be his home.[20]

Dr. John Croghan never had been interested in running the farm, and with Nicholas dead, William in Pittsburgh, and Charles unable to help, he and his mother reluctantly resigned themselves to the sale of the family home. The eldest son of William and Lucy Croghan had graduated from the University of Pennsylvania's medical school in 1813, and on his return to Louisville the next year, he advertised his intention to practice medicine and surgery. John Croghan became one of the Louisville Marine Hospital Company's incorporators and served as its director until 1832; yet, although some considered him to be Louisville's most prominent physician, he had no passion for medicine.[21]

John sporadically practiced in "his residence . . . three doors below the U.S. Bank and adjoining Forrester's Apothecary Shop," and he traveled to Louisiana in connection with his brother's plantation before he chose to spend some time in 1825 exploring the lands he had inherited from his father. The doctor also used his inheritance to buy various salt production businesses as a source of income, one of which accidently struck oil in 1829. He explained that should the salt business fall through, he would revert to buying ten or twenty acres near Louisville and grow market vegetables, botanical plants, and grapes, and "derive a revenue amply sufficient to supply my grounds, my books & my practice. I will be fully occupied and this is what the most of us require to make us happy."[22]

Just shy of thirty-six, John wrote, "If I can meet with a woman of good sense I would have no objection to marry, provided it suited my convenience." His fitful attempts designed to maintain a "courting" appearance amused his siblings, as William confided to Ann in a gossipy letter. "The Doctor . . . has met with quite a calamity. . . . He obeyed the prescription of some quack, as to the method of restoring the hair. He writes me, he is in consequence to loose all his hair & begs me forthwith to send him on a wig. . . . The truth is, he could not be much worsted by the prescription." Not surprisingly, John Croghan never married. He never bought a twenty-acre gentleman's farm, either. Between regular stints in town to accommodate his practice, John Croghan always had returned to his father's farm, but now decided to let it go.[23]

George Hancock announced his arrival in Louisville to William Croghan on 15 December 1828, in a letter richly infused with condescension. "I found the place not so much out of sorts as I had expected—though it will take one years hard labour to get it in order. Since bringing out my Negroes I find that there are too many on the farm, and most of them here entirely worthless—so much so that I intend on getting them off the place. The food they eat is to be sure a trifle, but the example set my own of idleness is intolerable."[24]

Established as the mistress of her parents' home, Eliza remained busy until she became feverish and seriously ill in the summer of 1832. Her husband was not concerned about her ultimate recovery and characteristically informed Jesup that the cholera outbreak affected others, as the "deaths [are] almost entirely among the dissolute; the Better clases almost without exception are cured of it." Indeed, Eliza appeared to recover before she relapsed in June 1833, a victim of the epidemic that claimed thousands in Kentucky. Hancock first alerted the Jesups of Eliza's final illness the week of 24 June, begging them to send Dr. Croghan home immediately if he had reached Washington. John Croghan arrived from Europe too late to help his sister, and Eliza died at Locust Grove on 12 July, her brothers absent and her mother with Ann in Washington.[25]

Eliza was buried with the growing number of family members in the farm's cemetery, even as the epidemic continued to ravage the region. "The cholera is with us," Hancock wrote Thomas Jesup three months later. "You can conceive nothing to equal the gloom spread over the country here. No one leaves home. Crops of wheat standing uncut, cornfields abandoned to the winds." Eliza had made a dying wish that indicated she understood the man who was her husband. Her enslaved woman, Anna, along with Anna's children, were to be taken to Washington to live with her sister rather than be condemned to inevitable sale and separation by Hancock.[26]

Lucy's return from Washington would have been difficult even for a young woman to bear. The grave of her youngest daughter, freshly filled, was about to be sold by Hancock, along with the rest of the farm and its enslaved residents. After consultations with his brothers and cousins, and in consideration of Lucy's bereft state of mind, John Croghan bought Locust Grove and its laborers on 1 February 1834 for $3,500, and although the transaction became a point of acrimony between Croghan and Hancock for years, Locust Grove remained the doctor's home for the rest of his life.[27]

Thomas Sidney Jesup by Charles Bird King. The Washington National Cathedral.

Lucy returned permanently to her home and settled into a first-floor room in recognition of rheumatism and failing sight, happily going to work. "My Mother has been very busy in having cotton, wool &c spun for a carpet. It is for her room and judging from the variety of colours it will be a flashy affair. She is in fine health, and there is not a day we do not speak of you all & regret your not being here," John wrote Jesup later in 1834. In part to answer the repeated invitation, and in part of necessity, Ann Croghan Jesup and her five children came to Locust Grove in November 1835, when her husband began construction of a new F Street house in Washington City. Her stay was extended in May 1836, when Andrew

Jackson assigned Jesup the task of transferring the Creek Nation to the Arkansas Territory.[28]

Jesup had joined the army in 1808 and served under General William Hull early in the War of 1812. Following Hull's surrender, Jesup spent a year in Montreal as a prisoner of war, and after his exchange, he served as commander of the Twenty-Fifth Regiment under General Winfield Scott. He participated in the Niagara campaign at the battles of Chippewa and Lundy's Lane, where he sustained four wounds, one of which shattered his right hand and permanently disfigured it. Two years later, he was given command at New Orleans and, in 1818, was appointed quartermaster general at age twenty-nine.

The dismal work with the Creek Nation was interrupted when Jesup was made commander of the army during the United States' Second Seminole War, which lengthened the separation from his family to three years. Ann remained at Locust Grove to manage the household for her bachelor brother and aging mother, both of whom helped with the children, who suddenly rejuvenated the otherwise quiet home. "Billy Boy [William Croghan Jesup, four] and the Big Man [Charles Jesup, two] walk a good deal with me over the farm and occasionally we pay old [enslaved] Uncle Jim as he is called a visit at the mill," the doctor wrote Jesup in January 1837. "Although it is some time before our breakfast, Big Man is seated to my left, talking away and ready to take with me our accustomed cup of coffee. . . . Wishing that you soon terminate the war." The war did not end quickly, and Americans who had been opposed to Jackson's aggressive Indian reassignment program were outraged when Jesup ordered the arrest of Seminole chief Osceola.[29]

It was against this backdrop that the son and daughter of Lucy Clark Croghan watched over their mother's decline. John expanded her bedroom with the addition of a bathroom and dressing room early in 1837, and the construction of a small porch adjoining the suite allowed her to enjoy the activity of the farm and tend to grandchildren while the days wore on peacefully. Indeed, her last years were spent in the company of friends and relatives and were made vastly easier by the work of her well-established household staff and the presence of Ann and her children. She died on 4 April 1838 at the home she and Major Croghan had built more than four decades earlier, and her body was placed in the cemetery between those of her husband and daughter-in-law. Nearly seventy-three, and with her younger brother William's death only months away, she lived to be older than any of her siblings, and had survived nearly a generation longer than any of her children would do.[30]

Jesup was replaced in Florida by Zachary Taylor days after Lucy died, allowing him to be reunited in July with his family at Locust Grove, where they remained until they moved to their new Washington home in November 1839. With George Rogers Clark and William and Lucy Clark Croghan gone, along with so many of the enslaved who had given their lives to work and die beside them, Locust Grove and the new nation were passed to a second generation.

17

Emancipation

> For no consideration would I ever rent this, my home; . . . for more than half a century it has been recognized as a homestead for my relatives, and as long as I live . . . [I] wish it viewed in this light.
> —Dr. John Croghan, January 1848

The phenomenon of fame confounds and fascinates, indiscriminately raising some to glory while consigning apparent equals to exile. In its most satirical form, fame dooms an occasional soul to both states. George Rogers Clark knew the experience in all its facets, as did some of his nephews, but with one exception, the sons and daughters of William and Lucy Croghan lived unremarkable existences in extraordinary places, among the shadows of uncommon beings. The same held true for the sons and daughters of many Revolutionary figures across the country. The next generation found glory in the War of 1812 (in some ways an extension of the Revolution, it ended in a draw), discovered a religious fervor unknown to their parents, and, below the Ohio River, spent their lives in the reflected luster of national expansion, attempting to ignore the looming threats associated with slavery and nullification. Adversity eventually arrived, of course, but before it called at Locust Grove, it knocked at the door of Soldier's Retreat.[1]

The last of the old Revolutionary soldiers, Richard Clough Anderson died deeply in debt, having educated his brood of fine boys beyond his means and overspeculated in business. Elizabeth Clark Anderson's first child, a graduate of the College of William and Mary, became the Speaker of Kentucky's House of Representatives, a United States congressman, and, in 1823, the first US minister to Colombia. Anderson Jr. feared the South American climate, but he had placed himself in debt to repay his father's many debtors and, consequently, required the income the ambassadorship would provide. "My father has been too affectionate, too indulgent, too devoted to all his children for me to hesitate. . . . My responsibility continues for him and I see no way of clearing myself soon."[2] After they had lost five of their eight children, Anderson's wife (and first cousin), Betsy Gwathmey, died in childbirth in Bogota in 1825; he followed her to the grave a year later. His ashes were buried beside his mother at Soldier's Retreat, two weeks before his worthy father died.

Widow Sarah Marshall Anderson, who would tell her grandson that of all the luminaries who visited her home, Miami war chief Little Turtle was the most memorable, left with most of her children for Ohio after Colonel Anderson's death. Youngest son, Charles, an active abolitionist, would become a lawyer and serve as a colonel in the Union army and governor of Ohio. He was a memorable chronicler of people and events connected to his Kentucky childhood and described his parents as the wisest in every other respect, but wondered aloud how they could have reared their children in an environment of involuntary servitude. Aware of his mother's change of mind, he concluded she, too, had become an abolitionist as a result of the influence of his own Soldier's Retreat "mammy," Patsy, "who weaned and long nursed me and kept me in her own cabin and bed and who ever loved me."[3]

Charles's brother Robert, who had served as Richard's secretary in Bogota after his graduation from West Point, achieved dubious fame in 1861 as the US commander of Charleston's Fort Sumter, where he endured ridicule in some quarters as the slaveholding major who defended and lost the fort for Lincoln. When Major Anderson later carried the flag that was lowered over Sumter to a New York Unionist rally, the thirty-three-star banner became the symbol of American patriotism, a status the flag continues to enjoy today. Robert Anderson was replaced as commander of the Cumberland district by William T. Sherman in 1863 after he disagreed with Lincoln's decision to issue rifles to border state Unionists, and died in France after the war.

At nearby Locust Grove, Lucy's death had marked the essential end of formality for the once proud home. John Croghan discovered a new infatuation in the form of Mammoth Cave, a sprawling grotto found under the rocky central Kentucky terrain one hundred miles south of Louisville. He had been aware of the cave for most of his life, as it lay at the Green River, where his father had spent decades surveying for Revolutionary veterans.

Hyman Gratz, son of his father's Philadelphia benefactor, had purchased the property in 1812, and Croghan bought the cave in 1839 from attorney Franklin Gorin to create a hospital for victims of pulmonary consumption. Should that fail, he wrote, the cave might be converted to a tourist attraction. "I have no hesitation in affirming that for enjoyment, for the gratification of ones curiosity, for the restoration & preservation of health it stands unrivaled and in fine is worth all the Niagaras and watering places in the Union put together."[4]

The sanatorium proved disappointing; the cave's atmosphere did not aggravate the disease, but neither could it prevent the inevitable, so the doctor turned to tourism. He named the wide pathway at the entrance of the cave "Audubon Avenue" as a tribute to his father's Revolutionary friend and the ongoing esteem he and the family held for the Frenchman's son, artist John James Audubon, and Audubon's son, Victor. Audubon recorded his memory of the Clark brothers and William Croghan in his 1843 journal, recalling raccoon hunting with young George Croghan on his father's "plantation in Kentucky . . . , and whose father and my own were well acquainted and fought together in conjunction with George Washington and Lafayette during the Revolutionary War, against Merrie England." When Audubon published his double-elephant folio edition of *Birds of America,* the doctor was counted among his first subscribers.[5]

Croghan published an updated illustrated guidebook, *Rambles in the Mammoth Cave during the Year 1844,* to bring the cave to the public's attention. The book featured an 1842 cave map drawn by enslaved cave guide Stephen Bishop. Croghan had purchased Bishop's services along with other guides, Mat Bransford and Nick Bransford, enslaved men once belonging to prominent Tennessean Thomas Bransford, when he acquired the cave from Gorin. Mat was the son of Bransford and an enslaved woman; Nick, a son of an enslaved couple owned by Bransford. It was Stephen Bishop, however, who was the undisputed star of Mammoth Cave.[6]

Gorin spoke of him in a letter written years after the guide's death. "I placed a guide in the cave—the celebrated and great Stephen—and he aided in making the discoveries. He was the first person who ever crossed the Bottomless Pit. . . . Stephen was a self-educated man; he had a fine genius, a great fund of wit and humor, and some little knowledge of Latin and Greek, and much knowledge of geology; but his great talent was a perfect knowledge of man. . . . Stephen was certainly a very extraordinary boy and man." Mat Bransford discovered the beautiful cave grotto that would be called Serena's Arbor, but Bishop remained Croghan's closest advisor regarding the cave that would be owned by Croghan's nieces and nephews and their heirs until 1926. The cave later became a United States National Park and a designated World Heritage Site.[7]

The marriage of George and Serena Livingston Croghan had begun joyously, and the couple moved to his newly acquired Louisiana plantation, near Baton Rouge, after some months at Locust Grove. Through a combination of incompetence and lethargy, however, George vastly mismanaged the place and fell into debt. Serena and her baby joined him in fleeing the sheriff, and they left an enslaved workforce and farm animals without an immediate means of survival.[8]

With the support of James Monroe and Andrew Jackson, with whom he remained close throughout the Tennessean's life, Croghan was able to secure a lucrative position as New Orleans' postmaster, but was discovered a year later to have withdrawn thousands of dollars from the office illegally against anticipated insurance payments that never appeared. William Croghan Jr. and Serena's brother made restitution, which eliminated the need for penalty, but George's mounting humiliations led to a suicide attempt within the year and an eventual temporary break in the formerly close relationship he had enjoyed with his mother.[9]

He managed to retain some standing in Washington and New York through the influence of their families and was appointed inspector general of the US Army in 1826, one of only two such positions in the country. The Croghans established a succession of homes in New York, Georgetown, and Philadelphia, and an 1829 letter to Lucy in which he described a White House dinner, indicated his relationship with Jackson remained strong. "I dined with the President the other day, he enquired very particularly after your health, spoke of the Doctr and I enjoyed the dinner the more because it was a family one." The army, too, particularly generals Jesup and Scott, stood with him. Scott wrote Jesup in the autumn of 1830, concerned he had not seen Croghan for several months. "There is no man, out of the Colonel's immediate family more devoted to him than I am. Nay, I feel for him much the affection as brothers usually bear to each other. He is honorable & affectionate, gallant & high-minded. There are

E. W. H. Schenley by Swellie Watson, 1824. Copy.

but few individuals in the late war [War of 1812] who shed equal glory on his country."[10]

Croghan's Ft. Stephenson heroics led Congress to present him with a ceremonial sword and the prestigious Gold Medal on 13 February 1835, the seventeenth anniversary of his famous uncle's death, but his life continued to unravel. When he removed himself to Locust Grove in 1840 in an attempt to restore his health and reputation, the colonel joined the temperance society, farmed, and devoted months of work to improving his brother's investment at Mammoth Cave.[11]

William Croghan Jr. also arrived at Locust Grove that May, in a state of shock as a result of his fourteen-year-old daughter's 22 January elopement. Mary Elizabeth Croghan had been reared in near opulence in Pittsburgh; her indulgent and frequently absent father provided her with a carriage and horses when she was six so she could maintain her "social obligations" in proper style. She entered the fashionable Brighton School, operated by Mrs. Richmond McLeod on Staten Island, early in 1840, but her elopement two years later with McLeod's brother-in-law, Captain Edward W. H. Schenley, twice married and thirty years her senior, made headlines across the country.

Edward Wyndham Harrington Schenley, born in 1797 or 1798 as the son of an Irish Royal Artillery lieutenant who died in the Peninsular War, had been christened William Henry Shanley, a common Irish surname. His granddaughters later would vow they had been told Schenley was an illegitimate grandson of George III, but there is no proof of this. Schenley and his brother graduated from the Royal Military College shortly before he was wounded at the Battle of Quatre Bras, two days and twelve miles from his brigade's defeat of Napoleon at Waterloo. Shortly thereafter, he began to conflate his own war experiences with those of his father and became known as a veteran of the Peninsular War *and* Waterloo. He had become "Edward William Henry Shenley, Gentleman," by 1823, when he married Catherine Anne Inglis. Catherine's sister, Richmond McLeod, later moved to the United States, where she and her mother opened a school for young ladies, first in Boston and then at Staten Island.[12]

After Catherine's November 1828 death, Shenley won a position as judge in His Majesty's Mixed British and Spanish Court of Justice at Havana, where he oversaw efforts to adjudicate West Indian slave trafficking. In 1833, and by then spelling his name as Schenley, he married Jane Maria de la Pole, daughter of Sir William Templer Pole of Shute House, Devon, and heir to a nearly three-hundred-year association with English monarchs. Jane died in Cuba in 1837, after which Schenley became arbitrator to the British and Netherlands Mixed Court at Surinam. When he visited his former in-laws in New York in 1841, Mary Croghan, thirteen, apparently committed herself to the man by then known as Edward Wyndham Harrington Schenley, Esq.[13]

Mary Elizabeth Croghan Schenley by Thomas Lewis, 1842. Thomas Lewis, British, active 1835–1852, *Mrs. Schenley,* 1842, oil on canvas, 90×58 in. Carnegie Museum of Art, Pittsburgh.

In the days and months immediately following the elopement, William Croghan Jr. ruined Richmond McLeod, caused the Pennsylvania legislature to prohibit the couple access to Mary's inheritance, and refused to acknowledge his daughter's correspondence. Meanwhile, Edward and Mary Schenley returned to Surinam, where she gave birth to two daughters. After an early 1845 citywide fire destroyed nearly a quarter of Croghan's Pittsburgh rental property, he lamented his reduced circumstances to the Jesups and grew increasingly bitter toward the Schenleys. "For the sake of peace & in order to keep the property left my wife in my *own* hands, I have entered into a compact to pay her, my child, so much a year. . . . If I were to yield it up to her as she my daughter thinks (*in confidence*) I *ought,* the Lord knows what would become of it, for I am greatly apprehensive he is in debt."[14]

Probably because of the "compact" his father-in-law accepted, Schenley resigned from diplomatic service that year and took his family to London, where Mary finally was reconciled with her father, who was present for the 1846 birth and death of William Croghan Schenley. William made the purchase of the Schenleys' first London home possible and furnished the couple with a lifestyle that permitted Schenley's membership in London clubs and paved the way for an audience with Queen Victoria. Croghan returned to Pittsburgh to expand Pic Nic in anticipation of a visit from his daughter and her family, but he placed Mary's O'Hara inheritance in a trust, limiting her access to the spoils of General O'Hara's wealth.

The Schenley family eventually spent extensive time in Pittsburgh, but they were with William at Pic Nic only once, in 1848. After Croghan's death, the couple would live as few people on any continent could do; they purchased a home across the road from Hyde Park and next door to John Pierpont Morgan, joined the Royal Yacht Club, and vacationed at Cannes. When Schenley died in 1878, Mary began to make liberal donations to the City of Pittsburgh, through the direction of her close friend, Andrew Carnegie, most memorably three hundred acres that became Pittsburgh's famed Schenley Park.[15]

After Mary Croghan Schenley died at her London home on 4 November 1903 at the age of seventy-six, Morgan bought her home and, combining his house with hers, created a larger one that retained Mary's address, No. 14 Princes Gate. The large residence was bought by the United States in 1921 and, from 1929 to 1955, served as the home of the US ambassador to the Court of St. James, housing such notables as Robert Worth Bingham and the Joseph P. Kennedy family. Mary, the infant who lost her mother in 1827 at her grandparents' Kentucky farm, left an estate roughly valued in today's economy as ninety-three million dollars, and it remains under the authority of the trusteeship established by her father.[16]

William Croghan regularly forwarded money to his brother George after he moved to Pittsburgh, but the entanglement in his daughter's 1842 elopement had left him with taxing legal fees and little patience. On his return to Pittsburgh, he angrily wrote Jesup in November of that year, "I wish here to remark, only three days before the presentation of [this] draft, I took up a[nother] note of his, money lent some three years since of a fellow Steam Boat passenger who came here and made his appeal to me after being refused by the Doctor." Less than a year later, John Croghan, "in order to protect what he dreaded, *public* exposure," applied to a Louisville bank for a loan large enough to cover the debts that threatened to drive his brother George into prison: Croghan's long service in the significant post of inspector general again had been marred by an incident of salary overdraft as a result of recurring bouts of gambling and drinking.[17]

With his family's money and Jesup's influence, President James Polk was convinced to revoke the call for Croghan's court-martial, but the career Croghan had begun in 1826 was effectively ended. The colonel officially remained connected to the army, but resigned his office after making a last, reduced tour of western forts in 1845. In New York, at the insistence of her father and brother, who wished to protect her from bankruptcy, Serena finally severed the relationship and filed for a separation, and the colonel permanently returned to Kentucky.

John Croghan penned a forlorn letter to his sister's family in Washington on Christmas Day 1844, with his brother's behavior in mind. "This is Christmass, merry Christmass. To me it has been a day of gloom and melancholy forebodings." The entire Jesup family gathered at Locust Grove in May, and again in November 1845, which no doubt improved John's humor. The second stay was a happy one despite John's ill-health, and included a trip to Mammoth Cave, made more lighthearted by Navy Lieutenant James Blair's proposal of marriage to Mary Jesup. After the autumn visit, Willie Jesup's indulgent uncle John continued to keep the boy abreast of events at Locust Grove, and wrote in January to tell him of the antics of old Bill, the horse, and reminded him that his uncle George and "Zach Taylor" wished to be remembered.[18]

Ann Heron Croghan Jesup died suddenly in her Washington home on 24 April 1846, three months after daughter Mary's wedding. "I am distressed beyond measure at this unexpected and melancholy event," John wrote Jesup. "My only sister is gone, gone to a happier & better world. My grief is that of a sincerely attached brother. Most deeply do I sympathize with you, dear Genl. and my distressed nieces & nephews." The United States and Mexico declared war the day after Ann's death, but before Jesup left for active duty, he ordered two posthumous portraits of Ann to be painted by Washington artist Charles Bird King.[19]

George Croghan had responded favorably, even eagerly, when Zachary Taylor appealed for his help in the Mexican War. His marriage essentially ended and awash in debt, the fifty-three-year-old colonel, who once wished only to read and hunt at his parents' home, left Louisville in June 1846, hoping to reconstruct his earlier military glory. He was with Taylor in September during the three-day battle at Monterrey, where, a year later, he reported the loss of twenty pounds due to ague, fever, and stomach disorders. He returned to Louisville in December 1847 on his way to Washington and apparently fell into "old habits," which led John to sit in the weak winter light a month later and lament his once-lauded brother's state. "His past life and *family considerations* render him the most miserable & reckless man I have ever seen, and painful as it is to me, I now look upon him as entirely lost." The colonel returned to Locust Grove early in the spring of 1848 to put his affairs in order and settle financial differences. After failing to be reinstated as the army's inspector, he halfheartedly returned to New Orleans, where he died of cholera on Monday, 8 January 1849, having fallen short of achieving significant notice on the Mexican battlefield.[20]

John Croghan never knew his brother was dead. He had spent much of the last years of his life at Mammoth Cave, building a large hotel able to accommodate ninety guests. His own hotel quarters were supplied simply, but richly. The two-bedroom apartment featured a fully stocked kitchen and finely furnished drawing room; an English teapot, a French coffee pot, and German silverware decorated his table. He initially moved regularly between Louisville and the cave; but, unable to continue the travel by 1848, he leased the cave's management and returned permanently to Locust Grove.

His nephew, George Gwathmey, later reported to Jesup that he had been called to the doctor's side at 4 p.m. (on the day of George Croghan's death), and although Gwathmey thought the end was imminent, the doctor did not die until "35 minutes after six on Thursday [11 January] morning," in the bedroom suite he had built for his mother. "Judge Brown came up into my room to announce his death. . . . Just as his boy [Isaac] got to the bedside, the Doctr was seen to throw up his hands and before the judge got to him he was no more. . . . On Friday the 12th he was buried in the family burying ground."[21]

Isaac was emancipated immediately by the terms of Croghan's will. The remaining enslaved workers at Locust Grove and Mammoth Cave were to be liberated after a period of seven years, during which time the men and women were to live and work elsewhere in preparation for freedom. Stephen Bishop had married Croghan's enslaved cook, Charlotte Brown, probably during the 1842 winter break when the cave map was drawn. He and Charlotte and their son, Thomas, and Hannah Brown, probably Charlotte's niece, along with Alfred and his wife, Hannah, and their children, Ellen, Wesley, and Charles; Sara and her sons, Jake and James; Sarah and her daughters, Malinda and Maria; Gabriel, Jeke, Peter, Gibson, Cynthia, Humphrey, Sylvia, Rachel, Mary, and David were emancipated legally on 4 February 1856 in Jefferson County (Louisville), Kentucky. Ben, who had been seventy-one in 1849, Louisa, forty, and Susan, eighteen months, unfortunately did not survive to know freedom. Most of the emancipated men, women, and children were born on the farm established by William Croghan, and had known from their own perspectives the celebrities who visited the home. Some of the newly freed workers chose to remain at Locust Grove, and all the people connected to the cave initially remained there. Many of the former Croghan/Clark slaves, however, moved to the city and into the oblivion of history after 1856. Bishop, whose fame had spread across the globe, died at the cave in 1859, and Charlotte, who continued to work in the dining room at the cave hotel, subsequently married Nick Bransford. Finally, Dr. John Croghan's will, written the day before his death, left Locust Grove to his brother, Col. George Croghan, and forgave a $2,000 loan he recently had made to his brother.[22]

William and Lucy Croghan's last surviving child, William Jr., died in his Pittsburgh home Sunday morning, 22 September 1850. A collector of internationally recognized art and owner of what many considered the finest home in the Pittsburgh area, William left everything he possessed in trust for his daughter, Mary Elizabeth Croghan Schenley.

General Thomas Sidney Jesup was reunited permanently with his family at the conclusion of the Mexican War, but by then his eldest son, now called William, lived with relatives in southern Kentucky and appeared to be lost to his father. Alcoholism, and its attendant affliction, debt, coupled with the loss of parental oversight, had taken their toll. Aware of his standing within the family, William Jesup wrote his eldest sister, Lucy Ann, " I will . . . see my Father if I can, but know that meeting will be very painful to me, as Father will meet me as he would any stranger, and that would be almost too much to bear. . . . I shall continue to write to my married sisters until they prohibit me from doing so [and youngest sister,] Julia will have one brother that she can love and respect, but me her unworthy brother it will be better to forget." This letter survives with the addition of a note made by Lucy Ann Jesup Sitgreaves: "To burn—Do not let *anyone see these letters.* L.A.J.S."[23]

With his father's hesitant support, William Jesup's acceptance to West Point was assured, and so he agreed to enter the academy where his younger brother already was enrolled. The experience did not make the man of him his father had hoped, and William abandoned the commitment to return to southern Kentucky, where he accrued large bills for liquor, clothing, and jewelry. Charles Jesup, correctly deemed the worthier of the two brothers, graduated from West Point in 1858, which occasioned his proud father to write, "There is a singular coincidence between the commencement of your military career and mine. I was . . . appointed in the Infantry; and my first station was in Newport, Kentucky. General George Rogers Clark was an officer of Infantry as was Colonel Croghan, as were both your grandfathers."[24]

When Quartermaster General Thomas Sidney Jesup died in his F Street Washington home on 10 June 1860, President James Buchanan spoke at his funeral. Older than any of the second-generation Croghans, Jesup would be the last of them, having been a source of intelligent advice and generous support from the day of his marriage. William Jesup inherited the general's Todd County, Kentucky, land, but died in his small Elkton house five months after his father's funeral, having already mortgaged his inheritance. Brother Charles, ill, retired to his uncle's nearby farm, where he died in 1862, a month after he turned twenty-seven.[25]

Epilogue

William Croghan's extensive land acquisitions are long forgotten, and Locust Grove itself was nearly so in the years following the deaths of his children. It began when George Croghan sold most of his inheritance soon after he acquired it; John Croghan, too, had sold 172 acres of the western portion of the farm in 1847, and as his health failed, leased many of his fields to area farmers. It was St. George Croghan's inheritance of Locust Grove, though, that triggered a series of events that nearly led to the loss of his grandparents' home.

After Serena reluctantly gave her approval, General Jesup had recommended St. George for placement at West Point on 15 April 1840. The sixteen-year-old eagerly entered the academy as an at-large cadet on 15 August, but left within the year because of his "deficiencies in arithmetic." He settled on Louisville as his home as early as 1845, when he sold three hundred acres inherited along the banks of the Ohio to finance the construction of three tenement houses "now being erected on the corner of Main and Fifth streets," the site of his grandmother's Louisville town house. He married Livingston cousin Cornelia Adelaide Ridgely on 1 July 1846 in Baltimore, and immediately brought her to Locust Grove, where he attempted to manage the farm under his uncle's disapproving eye. A year after the 9 May 1847 birth of his first child, St. George mortgaged his newly built tenements to cousin Charles Thruston for $6,500 and purchased an eighty-six-acre farm at Flatbush, near Saugerties, New York, directly across the Hudson River from his Livingston grandfather's estate at Barrytown. With the understanding that his father would inherit Locust Grove upon his uncle's death, the young family settled in on the Flatbush farm to wait.[1]

George Croghan's unexpected death made St. George the owner of

Locust Grove and brought him to Louisville in the early summer of 1849. He left Cornelia with his mother in New York, while he supervised the July appraisal of his property and conducted an estate sale of his family's belongings. Excellent oil portraits and his father's sword, along with the magnificent ceremonial sword presented to George Rogers Clark, already had been sent to Serena for safekeeping, but most of the furniture and household goods purchased by William and Lucy Croghan were sold at public auction on 2 August 1849. A silver service for twelve, glass decanters, champagne and wine glasses, five beds and a French day bed, each fitted with feather mattresses, mahogany and gilded chairs, a cherry dining table, case clock, mirrors, and carpets were among the items, which were appraised at $1,315 in value, but brought only $915 through the sale. The values of the enslaved farm and cave workers were not counted in the appraisal, as John Croghan's will ensured their emancipations.[2]

St. George and Cornelia remained in New York through the birth of their second daughter in May 1850, but upon their arrival in Louisville, they spent their available resources to modernize Locust Grove in the Italianate style of the day. The couple searched fruitlessly for additional income through a series of suits filed against Cornelia's Livingston uncles, who refused to permit the sale of land she had inherited in trust from her mother; but most significantly, they soon found their affluent upbringings had failed to prepare them for the management of a Kentucky farm. St. George, his sisters, and Jesup cousins had inherited equal parts of the income derived from the management of Mammoth Cave, but when he asked his cousins for permission to manage the cave as a means of alleviating his financial situation, the Jesups refused.[3]

He borrowed $6,000 from his mother in November 1851, for which Serena charged him 6 percent interest; and now with a third child on the way and desperate for cash, St. George secured a loan for $1,390.50 from Thruston, offering his interest in the cave and title to Locust Grove. The Croghans permanently abandoned Louisville for Saugerties at the close of 1852. When Cornelia died in October 1857, she left her husband only the land that remained from her mother's Sullivan County, New York, property, most of which had been forfeited.[4]

Locust Grove was leased as early as 1853, and inaccurate reports of the farm's function through the Civil War abound, nearly all of them apocryphal. In reality, a succession of documented tenants lived there between

1858 and 1878. Early in 1860, St. George again mortgaged the property, listed as "about six hundred acres more or less," although he knew full well that Locust Grove, which had once amounted to nearly seven hundred acres, had been reduced to less than four hundred. He sold the Flatbush farm and moved his small family to nearby Kingston, where, in the late winter of 1861, he made another ruinous decision.[5]

He determined to follow his prominent relatives into war and, hoping to capture both fame and subsequent fortune, St. George Croghan chose the Confederate Army as his vehicle for success. He sold his interest in Mammoth Cave to his uncle, John R. Livingston Jr., who promised Croghan two equal payments of $237, with the second payment forgiven if Croghan did not survive, and he pleaded for Serena to care for his children before he reported for duty. St. George was thirty-nine years old when he died in the Tenth Virginia Cavalry's retreat from Cotton Hill near McCoy's Mills, [West] Virginia, on 14 November 1861. His mother took his daughters to Oakland, California, where they all lived until the girls' marriages. With the exception of an extended New York City visit in 1870, Serena Livingston Croghan, too, lived the remainder of her life in Oakland, where she died at the age of eighty-nine.[6]

At St. George's death, his son George (1852–1911) became the ward of Christopher Wyatt. He secured title to Locust Grove from the sole remaining trustee, J. R. Underwood, in 1868, but the Westchester, New York, heir had no intention of living on his great-grandparents' farm. Heavily mortgaged, the property was for sale in 1876, and although it was advertised as "The Finest farm in Kentucky—The Celebrated Croghan Farm," no buyers materialized. At last, in late December 1878, he sold the remaining 369 acres for $28,000 to steamboat captain James Paul, who died in the house two months later.[7]

Christopher C. Graham, who had spent two weeks at George Rogers Clark's cabin in 1805, wrote Draper in the fall of 1882. Now an old man, he recently had been to Locust Grove, but no one there "has any knowledge of the former occupants. The locusts that gave name to the place have felt force of storms and the decay of years. The lawns have put on the garb of fields of culture, and the old family graveyard where sleep our pioneers is a tangled thicket through which none may creep to read the inscriptions which tell of the honored dead."[8]

After they owned Locust Grove for not quite five years, the Paul family sold the farm on 1 October 1883 to Richard Waters of Oldham County, Kentucky, for $25,000. John Scott Waters acquired the farm upon his mother's 1899 death and soon created the Fort Stanwyx Realty Company. He claimed most of the company's shares by virtue of his provision of the land—Locust Grove. The acreage on the bluff overlooking the Ohio River was sold first and supplied fortunate Louisvillians with smart addresses and splendid views, but Dr. John Croghan's will, which specifically protected his family's cemetery "forever," was ignored through the succession of deed transactions.[9]

Years before Waters sold the cemetery, the Kentucky legislature had moved to have George Rogers Clark's body reinterred in Frankfort, in the cemetery "to which those [remains] of Boone and his wife had been removed." The effort revived in 1869 when a bill passed by the General Assembly directed the governor to carry out the provisions of the earlier legislation, but the Clark family acted first and moved Clark's body from Locust Grove on 29 October 1869 to the new Jonathan Clark plot in Louisville's Cave Hill Cemetery. The *Evening Post* reminisced about the reburial 104 years after Clark's death. "The same negro sexton who had made the [original] interments and two old friends of the Clarks and Croghans met [at Locust Grove] and opened one of the two graves, in one of which Gen. Clark had been buried. The second grave gave up the remains of a man which showing a part of the left thigh bone missing." The article was incorrect in identifying an amputated left leg; Clark's right leg was removed in 1809.[10]

The ornate casket of Col. George Croghan was exhumed in June 1906, after the Daughters of the American Revolution erected a handsome monument in Fremont, Ohio, as a memorial to his victory at Fort Stephenson. The bodies of the remaining family members, Mary Carson O'Hara Croghan and her infant daughter, along with Eliza Croghan Hancock, Major William Croghan, Lucy Clark Croghan, and John, Nicholas, and Edmund Croghan, and that of Mrs. McSorley, a family connection, and child were removed to Cave Hill on 3 May 1916.[11]

Jefferson County and the Commonwealth of Kentucky jointly purchased Locust Grove's remaining 55.15 acres, including the historic residence, for $250,000 on 24 July 1961, with the intention of restoring the farm to its original appearance as "a shrine" in memory of General George Rogers Clark. The remnant of Croghan's farm now is owned by Louisville

Aerial view of Locust Grove by Jason Heiner. Courtesy of Jason Heiner.

Metro and is a National Historic Landmark, a federal designation awarded not in recognition of the restored eighteenth-century buildings, but in consequence of the people connected to the site. One of Kentucky's oldest structures and the only extant one to shelter Lewis and Clark together west of the Appalachians, Locust Grove joins the White House, Monticello, Montpelier, Mount Vernon, and three sites well-known to Major Croghan, Valley Forge and the Brandywine and Monmouth battlefields, in signifying the highest standard among the nation's monuments.

William Croghan's home today is managed as a historic house museum by Historic Locust Grove, Inc., a not-for-profit organization created solely for the purpose of preserving and managing the site. Croghan's former home reflects the appearance known to the family at the time of George Rogers Clark's residency, and boasts reproductions of the original ca. 1790 wallpaper and period paints proven to have once covered its walls. Interestingly, with the exception of Mount Vernon's red, Locust Grove's original palette was exactly that which George Washington chose for his post–Revolutionary War refurbishment. Jarvis's portraits of the major and his wife join those of George and Serena Croghan, and Ann Jesup, and most importantly, the Bush painting of Clark, in their timeless watch over rooms once known to Burr, Jackson, and Monroe.

The locations of many farm buildings, including the house Kitt and General Clark once occupied, have been lost since the mid-nineteenth century. And, although archaeology remains a significant component of the museum's planning process, the sites of Charlotte's house, and those of Peter, Maria, Isaac, and all the other enslaved men, women, and children who knew Locust Grove as their home, remain elusive. Tens of thousands of visitors nevertheless find their ways to Locust Grove each year to participate in interactive programs or to sit quietly, listening for the sounds of Kitt, the legendary Clarks, or Washington's Irish scout.

Acknowledgments

I extend my sincere appreciation to Dr. Carol Ely and Julia Parke, who are as familiar with these stories as I by virtue of their experiences at Locust Grove, for their critical reviews and encouraging words as writing progressed, and to Mary Beth Williams, who maintained serenity as she met multiple requests for museum images. This project was invaluably enriched by the informed input of Clark scholar James J. Holmberg, Curator of Special Collections at The Filson Historical Society, and the manuscript could not have been submitted without Ursula Beam's adept assistance. Anne Dean Dotson and the University Press of Kentucky staff have provided cheerful and much-needed assistance through the writing and editing processes, and Western Kentucky University's history department deserves my enduring appreciation, as does Historic Locust Grove, which brings the story of western settlement to the world every day. Finally, *many* thanks to Grover, Scott, and Jack for their cheerful perseverance.

Notes

Abbreviations

Denny Journal	William H. Denny, *The Record of the Court at Upland . . . and A Military Journal Kept by Major Ebenezer Denny* (Philadelphia: Lippincott & Co., 1860)
Draper MSS	Draper Manuscripts, Wisconsin Historical Society, Madison, WI
Etting MSS	Etting Manuscripts, Historical Society of Pennsylvania, Philadelphia
JCDB	Jefferson County Deed Book, Metro Archives, Louisville, KY
LOC	Library of Congress, Washington, DC
Mason Letter	George Rogers Clark to George Mason, 19 November 1779, TFHS
Memoir	George Rogers Clark's memoir; text of memoir available on IN.gov, https://www.in.gov/history/2425.htm.
TFHS	The Filson Historical Society, Louisville, KY

1. George Croghan

1. Brian O'Neill, *The Paris of Appalachia: Pittsburgh in the Twenty-First Century* (Pittsburgh: Carnegie-Mellon University Press, 2009).

2. Nicholas B. Wainwright, *George Croghan, Wilderness Diplomat* (Chapel Hill: University of North Carolina Press, 1958), 6; John Bannister Gibson to Lyman C. Draper, 24 April 1849, Draper Manuscripts [hereafter cited as Draper MSS] 10E100, Wisconsin Historical Society, Madison; Sewell Elias Slick, *William Trent and the West* (Harrisburg, PA: Archives, 1947), 1–3, 10; Thomas Perkins Abernethy, *Western Lands and the American Revolution* (New York: Russell and Russell, 1959), 6; Robert Grant Crist, "George Croghan of Pennsboro" (unpublished paper presented at Cumberland County Historical Society, 7 May 1964), 9–16.

3. The council was the governing body of the Mohawk, Oneida, Cayuga, Seneca, Onondaga, and Tuscarora nations. The collective cultural and linguistic society of these nations was known to the French as Iroquois. The "Buck" referred to the enormous number of skins Croghan exchanged with the Indians.

4. Wainwright, *Croghan,* 22–23, and 49; Crist, *Croghan of Pennsboro,* 22.

5. Samuel Hazard, ed., *Pennsylvania Archives from Original Documents* (Philadelphia, 1853), 2:144.

6. *The Colonial Records of Pennsylvania* (Harrisburg: T. Fenn & Co., 1831–1853), 6:148.

7. Seymour I. Schwartz, *The French and Indian War, 1754–1763: The Imperial Struggle for North America* (New York: Simon and Schuster, 1994), 27–28.

8. Andrew Wahll, ed., *Braddock Road Chronicles, 1755* (Bowie, MD: Heritage, 1999), 338. French commander Pierre Contrecoeur sent out small scouting parties who "picked off stragglers" and left "pornographic insults on trees"; they regularly brought news of Braddock's progress to the fort.

9. John Bakeless, *Daniel Boone: Master of the Wilderness* (New York: William Morrow, 1939), 20–25; Wahll, *Braddock Road,* 364–365. These numbers reported by Frenchman M. Roucher, as recorded in Paul Kopperman, *Braddock at the Monongahela* (Pittsburgh, PA: University of Pittsburgh Press, 1977); Schwartz, *The French and Indian War,* 46.

10. Born in Ireland, Johnson arrived in the Mohawk Valley in June 1738.

11. Schwartz, *French and Indian War,* 65–68; Max W. Reid, *The Story of Old Fort Johnson* (New York: G. P. Putnam's Sons, 1906), 8–10. 14 December 1756, in *Colonial Records of Pennsylvania,* 7:354–356.

12. Reid, *Fort Johnson,* 10, 152–155; Isabel Thompson Kelsay, *Joseph Brant, 1743–1807, Man of Two Worlds* (Syracuse, NY: Syracuse University Press, 1984), 47–62, 137–138.

13. Kelsay, *Brant,* 62, 109–110, 134; Schwartz, *French and Indian War,* 97–99.

14. Ralph Birdsall, *The Story of Cooperstown* (New York: Charles Scribner's Sons, 1917), 36. "At the close of the [Easton] conference [1758], one Nichos, a Mohawk, made a speech. . . . This Nichos is G. Croghan's father-in-law"; George Croghan to Richard Peters, 18 December 1757. William Henry Egle, ed., *Pennsylvania Archives, Third Series* (Harrisburg, PA: William Stanley Ray, printer, 1894) 3:319–320; Kelsay, *Brant,* 279–281; Draper MSS 1F98 and 1F105; William C. Bryant, "Joseph Brant, Thayendanegea, and His Posterity," *American Historical Record* 2, no. 19 (July 1893): 295. Brant, who helped translate the Gospels into the Mohawk language and assisted in the 1769 publication of a Mohawk Anglican prayer book, gave Catherine a ring engraved, "Thayendanegea to Catherine."

15. Schwartz, *French and Indian War,* 100–104 and 135–138. Growing numbers of historians now consider the Great Lakes–area Native American fight

against trans-Appalachian settlement to have begun in 1754 and lasted until the conclusion of the War of 1812, which would include Clark's Revolutionary activity.

16. Entertainment Folder, Cadwalader Collection, Historical Society of Pennsylvania, Philadelphia.

17. Walter Isaacson, *Benjamin Franklin: An American Life* (New York: Simon & Schuster, 2003), 161. Franklin later recalled the Albany plan was rejected because the colonial assemblies thought there was "too much prerogative in it, and in England it was judged to have too much of the democratic"; Abernethy, *Western Lands and the American Revolution,* 22.

2. Land Mad

1. Wainwright, *George Croghan, Wilderness Diplomat,* 202–205; *Pennsylvania Magazine of History and Biography* 73, no. 1 (January 1949): 87–91. Col. George Armstrong, a fellow *Britannia* passenger, recorded the circumstances of the shipwreck in Croghan's notebook, found in the Cadwalader Collection at the Historical Society of Pennsylvania, Philadelphia.

2. Wainwright, *George Croghan, Wilderness Diplomat,* 205–207.

3. Ibid., 211–213; Bouquet to Johnson, 25 January 1765, Bouquet to Thomas Gage, 10 April 1765, in *The Papers of Colonel Henry Bouquet* (Harrisburg: Pennsylvania Historical Commission, 1940), Series 21653, 353, available from the William L. Clements Library, University of Michigan.

4. *Collections of the Illinois State Historical Library* (Springfield, 1916), 2:58; Croghan to Johnson, 12 July 1765; Sir William Johnson, *The Papers of Sir William Johnson,* 13 vol., ed. Milton W. Hamilton and Allen Corey (Albany: University of the State of New York), 11:836–841.

5. Croghan to Johnson, 12 July 1765, in Johnson, *Papers of Sir William Johnson,* 11:849–850; James McDonald to Johnson, November 1765, in *Collections of the Illinois State Library,* 2:53.

6. Cadwalader Collection, Historical Society of Pennsylvania.

7. Prior to 1763, the French considered this area to be part of their Louisiana claim.

8. Prevost Jr. was the son of General Augustin Prevost, who commanded British troops at the battle of Savannah. The son joined his father in Pennsylvania as a fourteen-year-old ensign. Abernethy, *Western Lands,* 28–30. Original Illinois Company stockholders were Croghan, Johnson, Benjamin and William Franklin, Samuel, Thomas and Charles Wharton, Joseph Galloway, John Hughes, John Baynton, and George Morgan. William Franklin to Benjamin Franklin, 30 April 1766, in Clarence W. Alvord and Clarence Carter, eds., *The New Regime 1765–1766, Collections of the Illinois State Historical Library* (Springfield, 1916),

11:144–146; George Croghan to Sir William Johnson, 30 March 1766, Johnson, *Papers of Sir William Johnson,* ed. Alexander Flick, 5:129.

9. James Alton James, *Oliver Pollock: The Life and Times of an Unknown Patriot* (New York: Appleton-Century, 1937), 22–23; *Journal of the Illinois State Historical Society* 6, no. 1 (April 1913): 58–71. Fort de Chartres was built to serve as the center of French government in the Illinois, and between 1734 and 1736, Fort Kaskaskia was built on higher ground to relieve Chartres.

10. Benjamin Franklin to George Croghan, 14 April 1767, Cadwalader Collection, Historical Society of Pennsylvania. Original Indiana Company stockholders included Samuel Wharton, William Trent, William Franklin, Joseph Simon, David Franks, Levi Levy, George Morgan, George Croghan, John Baynton, John Gibson, and Evan Shelby, McAllister Collection, Library Company of Philadelphia.

11. William Henry Egle, ed., *Notes and Queries: Historical, Biographical and Genealogical: Relating Chiefly to Interior Pennsylvania* (Harrisburg, PA: Pennsylvania State Library, 1891), 3rd ser., 2:119–121; *Pennsylvania Archives* (Philadelphia: Joseph Severns & Co., 1853), 1st ser., 4:395.

12. Wainwright, *George Croghan, Wilderness Diplomat,* 254–258.

13. Slick, *William Trent and the West,* 139; Charles Augustus Hanna, *The Wilderness Trail* (New York: G.P. Putnam's Sons, 1911), 84; Croghan to Thomas Wharton, 30 May 1769, Walter O'Conner Private Collection. (O'Conner's private collection was sold at auction in 2018.)

14. Wainwright, *George Croghan, Wilderness Diplomat,* 249–250; *Quarterly Journal of the New-York State Historical Association* 12, no. 2 (April 1931): 309–324. "The Great Croghan Patent" of 109,000 acres was issued to George Croghan and ninety-nine others by George III on 30 November 1769. Other patentees conveyed their interests to Croghan for 5 shillings each on 2 December; Nicholas Croghan to George Croghan, 17 July 1769, George Croghan Papers, Historical Society of Pennsylvania; Francis Whiting Halsey, ed., *Richard Smith, A Tour of Four Great Rivers: The Hudson, Mohawk, Susquehanna and Delaware in 1769* (New York: Charles Scribner's Sons, 1906), 47.

15. American general James Clinton's eighteen-hundred-man division camped at Croghan's Forest in the summer of 1779. Erkuries Beatty recorded the arrival on Friday, 2 July 1779. "We . . . camped on the right side of Crohan's house, a very pleasant place. 3 July: . . . made a magazine of Crohan's house." New-York Historical Society, Rare Books and Manuscripts Collection.

16. Abernethy, *Western Lands,* 89; Jared Sparks, ed., *Writings of George Washington* (Boston: Little, Brown and Co., 1853), 2:516.

17. Clarence E. Carter, ed., *The Correspondence of General Thomas Gage with the Secretaries of State, 1763–1772* (New Haven: Yale University Press, 1931), 1:176;

Gage to Capt. Charles Edmonstone, 31 August 1772, Gage Papers Manuscripts, William L. Clements Library, University of Michigan; *Pennsylvania Archives,* 3:544. Washington visited McKee's large eight-room log home during his 1770 tour.

18. Wainwright, *George Croghan, Wilderness Diplomat,* 288; Barnard Gratz to Michael Gratz, 3 June 1774, McAllister Manuscripts, Library Company of Philadelphia. William Henry Smith, ed., *St. Clair Papers* (Cincinnati, OH: Robert Clarke, 1882), 1:304: "There is no news here, though I have been told this day here that George Croghan has gone down to the Mississippi."

19. William Vincent Byars, *B. and M. Gratz: Merchants in Philadelphia, 1754–1798* (Jefferson City, MO: Hugh Stephens, 1916), 350; *An Account of the Proceedings of the Illinois and Ouabache Land Companies* (Philadelphia: William Young, 1796), 49.

20. Wainwright, *George Croghan, Wilderness Diplomat,* 274. Abernethy, *Western Lands,* 238–239.

21. Barnard Gratz to George Croghan, 1 August 1773. McAllister Manuscripts, Library Company of Philadelphia; Miriam Simon Gratz to Michael Gratz, 22 July 1774, Etting Manuscripts, Historical Society of Pennsylvania [hereafter cited as Etting MSS].

22. Wainwright, *George Croghan, Wilderness Diplomat,* 301–306.

23. William Croghan to Barnard Gratz, 26 March 1779, Etting MSS; Wainwright, *George Croghan, Wilderness Diplomat,* 282.

24. Virginia Court for Ohio County Minute Book 2:72, Carnegie Library, New York.

25. Etting MSS. George Croghan's will was recorded 3 September 1782 at Philadelphia; George Croghan's estate appraisal, 6 September 1782, No. 156, Office of the Recorder of Deeds, Philadelphia, per Nicholas B. Wainwright to George Swetnam, 20 May 1970; Wainwright, *George Croghan, Wilderness Diplomat,* 310.

26. For a complete summary of the Croghan estate law suit, see Albert T. Volwiler, *George Croghan and the Westward Movement, 1741–1782* (Cleveland, OH: Arthur H. Clark, 1926).

3. George Rogers Clark

1. Julie M. Fenster, *Jefferson's America: The President, the Purchase, and the Explorers Who Transformed a Nation* (New York: Random House, 2016), 22. Illinois governor John Reynolds (1831–1834) is quoted as having described Clark as "nature's favorite." *The Christian Traveler* (1828), quoted in John Mack Faragher, *Daniel Boone: The Life and Legend of an American Pioneer* (New York: Henry Holt

and Company, 1992), 71; 4 June 1772, *Journal of Reverend David Jones,* Historical Society of Pennsylvania, Philadelphia; William Hayden English, *Conquest of the Country Northwest of the River Ohio, 1778–1783, and Life of Gen. George Rogers Clark* (Indianapolis: Bowen-Merrill Company, 1897), 60–62.

2. John Croghan to Draper, 17 January 1847, Draper MSS 10J232. Lucy Clark Croghan's son said his mother often talked of the Albemarle farm, but she could not have remembered the site. John and Ann Clark moved their family to a 170-acre Caroline County farm perhaps eight years before her birth. The Clark children were Jonathan, 1750; George Rogers, 1752; Ann, 1755; John, 1757; Richard, 1760; Edmund, 1762; Lucy, 1765; Elizabeth, 1768; William, 1770; and Frances Eleanor, 1773.

3. William R. Nester, *George Rogers Clark: "I Glory in War"* (Norman: University of Oklahoma Press, 2012), 10. John Clark paid tuition of £13 sterling for George Rogers to study mathematics, geography, and history for approximately nine months. The Christopher Clark and John Clark families were related and lived near one another in Louisa and Albemarle counties, Virginia. The Christopher Clark family and John Clark's mother, Elizabeth Wilson Clark Richards, were Quakers.

4. George Rogers Clark to Jonathan Clark, 9 January 1773, in James Alton James, ed., *George Rogers Clark Papers, 1771–1781* (Springfield: Trustees of the Illinois State Historical Library, 1926), 1:2.

5. Sarah Hughes, *Surveyors and Statesmen, Land Measuring in Colonial Virginia* (Richmond: Virginia Surveyors Foundation, 1979), 99–100; Samuel Evans, "The Truth concerning the Expedition of George Rogers Clark," *Potter's American Monthly* 5 (December 1875). It was John Connolly and John Campbell who initiated Thomas Bullitt's 1773 survey. Neal O. Hammon and Richard Taylor, *Virginia's Western War, 1775*–1786 (Mechanicsburg, PA: Stackpole, 2002), xvi. Dunmore approved Bullitt's surveying trip to Kentucky.

6. George Yater, *Two Hundred Years at the Falls of the Ohio: A History of Louisville and Jefferson County* (Louisville, KY: Heritage, 1979), 13–14; Byars, *B. and M. Gratz,* 15–16. John Connolly's Louisville patent, dated 16 December 1773, recognized his status as a "surgeon's mate" and awarded him two thousand acres "lying and being in the County of Fincastle, on the South side of the Ohio River opposite the falls," Library of Congress [hereafter cited as LOC]. Byars, *B. and M. Gratz,* 15–16.

7. Wainwright, *George Croghan, Wilderness Diplomat,* 289.

8. Faragher, *Daniel Boone,* 92–96; James William Hagy, "The First Attempt to Settle Kentucky: Boone in Virginia," *Filson Club History Quarterly* 44 (1970): 228.

9. Faragher, *Daniel Boone,* 96–97.

10. Logan's given name is not known. He was the son of Oneida chief Shi-

kellamy, who worked closely with William Penn's colonial secretary, John Logan, which suggests a connection. Nicholas Cresswell, *The Journal of Nicholas Cresswell, 1774–1777* (New York: Lincoln MacVeagh/Dial Press, 1924), 71–78. Cresswell described Shawnee prisoners at Winchester as "tall, manly, well-shaped men, of a Copper colour with black hair, quick, piercing eye, and good features."

11. Kathrine W. Seineke, *The George Rogers Clark Adventure in the Illinois and Selected Documents of the American Revolution at the Frontier Posts* (New Orleans: Polyanthos, 1981), 150–151.

12. Dunmore removed the Crown's gunpowder to the HMS *Magdalen,* moored in the York River, 20 April 1775. He later evacuated his family and Loyalists to the HMS *Fowey* and, in November, formed the Ethiopia Regiment. After smallpox erupted among the regiment, the *Fowey* escaped to New York, leaving the sick and dying soldiers on the bank of the York. Reuben Gold Thwaites and Louise Phelps Kellogg, *Documentary History of Dunmore's War, 1774* (Madison: Wisconsin Historical Society, 1905), 261–266, 269–277. The Shawnees would abandon this Chillicothe location and move the village north after Dunmore's War.

13. Abernethy, *Western Lands,* 111–113. John Tebbel and Keith Jennison, *The American Indian Wars* (New York: Harper and Brothers, 1960), 147–148; Anthony F. C. Wallace, *Jefferson and the Indians* (Cambridge: Harvard University Press, 1999), 53.

14. The Treaty of Camp Charlotte defined the peace terms of Dunmore's War.

15. Thomas Jefferson, *Notes on the state of Virginia* (London: printed for John Stockdale, 1787).

16. Jefferson had written *Notes on the state of Virginia* in 1781; he published it anonymously in Paris in 1785, and in English in 1787. Clark to Samuel Brown, 17 June 1798, in Barbara B. Oberg, ed., *The Papers of Thomas Jefferson,* vol. 30, *January 1798 to 31 January 1799* (Princeton: University of Princeton Press, 2013), 30:513–514.

17. Richard W. Loveless, *Records of the District of West Augusta, Ohio County and Yohogania County, Virginia* (Columbus: Ohio State University, 1970), 1:533; George Rogers Clark to Jonathan Clark, 1 April 1775, Draper MSS 1L16.

18. Otis K. Rice, *Frontier Kentucky* (Lexington: University Press of Kentucky, 1993), 71. Big Bone Lick was known by the earliest European explorers as "Elephant Bone" lick. Cresswell, *Journal of Nicholas Cresswell,* 70–71, 78: "Got to Wheeling Creek. Fort Fincastle on the East side of the River. This is a Quadrangular Picketed Fort on a little hill beside the River, built last Summer by Lord Dunmore, a small garrison in it. Here we took into our Co. a Captn. George Clark," "Clark always behaved well while he stayed with us." English, *Conquest of the Country Northwest of the River Ohio,* 1:68.

19. Clarence Walworth Alvord, "Virginia and the West," *Mississippi Valley Historical Review* 3 (June 1916), 19.

20. Clark's memoir [hereafter cited as *Memoir*] was given to historian Lyman Copeland Draper by Clark's nephew, Dr. John Croghan, more than fifty years after its completion. It originally was placed in volume ten (J) of Draper MSS, conserved at the Wisconsin Historical Society in Madison. Text of memoir available on IN.gov, https://www.in.gov/history/2425.htm.

21. George Rogers Clark, *The Conquest of the Illinois,* ed. Milo Milton Quaife (Carbondale: Southern Illinois University Press, 2001); *Memoir*; Temple Bodley, *George Rogers Clark, His Life and Public Services* (Cambridge: Houghton Mifflin Company, 1926), 30: Patrick Henry, Thomas Jefferson, and John Randolph, the elder, each had represented John Clark in a prolonged land litigation.

22. *Memoir.*

23. Byars, *B. and M. Gratz,* 356.

24. Mark M. Boatner III, *Encyclopedia of the American Revolution* (Mechanicsville, PA: Stackpole, 1966), 432; James, *Oliver Pollock,* 61. Draper MSS 60J277 and 3K88. Colonel John Gibson was neither paid nor recognized by the Continental Congress for his efforts in New Orleans because he had been commissioned by Virginia. Ibid., 68–69.

25. David Shepherd's 1789 affidavit stated, "A certain Lieut William Lin and others from Orleans Delivered at the Mouth of Weelin within this County 10000 Weight or thereabout of gunpowder for the use of the State of Virginia the same was kept there some time and then ordered to the Station of fort pitt by a Continental officer Colo Wm Crawford." Draper MSS 1SS24–28.

26. William Hintzen, *Border Wars of the Upper Ohio Valley (1769–1794)* (Ashland, KY: Jesse Stuart Foundation, 1999), 123; *Memoir*; Draper MSS 48J12.

27. *Memoir*; Draper MSS 47J10.

28. George Rogers Clark to George Mason, 19 November 1779 [hereafter cited as Mason Letter], The Filson Historical Society [hereafter TFHS].

29. Jefferson Papers, Series 2, vol. 67, no. 99, LOC; Mason Letter, TFHS.

30. Slick, *William Trent and the West,* 159.

4. William Croghan

1. James Mills, ed., *Registry of St. Nicholas Without, Dublin, 1694–1739* (Exeter: Parish Register Society, 1912). The parish church operated within the north transept of St. Patrick's Cathedral, the largest Protestant church in Ireland.

2. Nicholas Croghan to George Croghan, 17 July 1769. Historical Society of Pennsylvania; Draper MSS 4S187, "Major Wm. Croghan was in the regular

British service before the Revolution." A published 1772 roster of British officers lists what could be considered an anglicized version of Ens. William Croghan.

3. This James Innes should not be confused with his contemporary, Col. James Innes (Innis) of Will's Creek and, later, North Carolina; Washington County, PA, Will Book 1:129; William Croghan to Virginia General Assembly, 1784, Draper MSS 3N99.

4. M. Lee Minnis, *The First Virginia Regiment of Foot, 1775–1783* (Westminster, MD: Willow Bend Books, 1998), 18. Virginia Continental Line records submitted by James Wood and Edward Davis note Croghan's Tenth Company of the Virginia Eighth Regiment was raised in West Augusta, near Fort Pitt, on 7 or 9 February 1776. Croghan's own record indicates he entered service as a captain in the Eighth Regiment on 17 February 1776.

5. Boatner, *Encyclopedia of the American Revolution,* 798–801; Arthur S. Lefkowitz, *The Long Retreat: The Calamitous American Defense of New Jersey, 1776* (Metuchen, NJ: Upland, 1998), 82.

6. David McCullough, *1776* (New York: Simon & Schuster, 2005), 247–250.

7. Ibid., 255–263. Charles Lee was a former British officer who had fought in the French and Indian War; he sold his services in various European conflicts before he returned to Virginia, where he assumed that he would be named commander-in-chief of the Continental Army.

8. *The Selected Papers of Charles Willson Peale and His Family,* ed. Lillian Miller, vol. 5, *The Autobiography of Charles Willson Peale* (New Haven: Yale University Press, 2000), 5:50; Jared Lobdell, ed., "The Revolutionary War Journal of Sergeant Thomas McCarty," *Proceedings of the New Jersey Historical Society* 82, no. 1 (1964): 29–36; Boatner, *Encyclopedia of the American Revolution,* 784–785.

9. McCullough, *1776,* 285–286.

10. Thomas Paine's "The American Crisis" was published 19 December 1776 as one of a series of patriotic pamphlets published to encourage the American Revolution.

11. Boatner, *Encyclopedia of the American Revolution,* 785–788.

12. Ibid., 785–787; Ron Chernow, *Washington, A Life* (New York: Penguin, 2010), 281; E. M. Sanchez-Saavedra, *A Guide to Virginia Military Organizations in the American Revolution, 1774–1787* (Richmond: Library of Virginia, 1978), 55–56.

13. Chernow, *Washington,* 302.

14. Ibid., 304–305; Boatner, *Encyclopedia of the American Revolution,* 105–110; Douglas Southall Freeman, *George Washington* (New York: Charles Scribner's Sons, 1948), 4:488; IN.gov, Indiana Historical Bureau, "Jonathan Clark Diary," TFHS special collections.

15. James Thomas Flexner, *George Washington* (New York: Little, Brown and Co., 1965), 2:241, and repeated in Chernow, *Washington,* 306.

16. Thomas J. McGuire, *Battle of Paoli* (Mechanicsburg, PA: Stackpole, 2000), 145–146.

17. Edward G. Lengel, *General George Washington: A Military Life* (New York: Random House, 2005), 251.

18. Boatner, *Encyclopedia of the American Revolution,* 427–429; "Jonathan Clark Diary."

5. The Illinois

1. Sanchez-Saavedra, *A Guide to Virginia Military Organizations,* 128.

2. Orders from P. Henry to Lieut. Colonel George Rogers Clark, 2 January 1778, Indiana Historical Society Library, Indianapolis.

3. Henry to Clark, 15 January 1778, Draper MSS 48J17. Bowman was the cousin of Clark's future sister-in-law, Sarah Hite, granddaughter of Jost Hite; English, *Conquest of the Country Northwest,* 1:112; *Memoir.*

4. Mason Letter, TFHS.

5. Clark wrote Mason that there were about twenty families who followed him. Dr. Henry McMurtrie identified the families of James Patton, Richard Chenoweth, John Tuel, William Faith, and John McManness in his 1819 *Sketches of Louisville and Its Environs* (Louisville, 1819). Reuben T. Durrett added Jacob Reager, Edward Worthington, James Graham, John Donne, Isaac Kimbley, Joseph Hunter, Neal Dougherty, Samuel Perkins, John Sinclair, and Robert Travis to the list in his *The Centenary of Louisville, Saturday, May 1, 1880* (Louisville, 1893), 40; English translation of Clark to O'Hara, 15 July 1778. File 2370, Cuban Papers Collection, General Archives of the Indies, Seville, Spain.

6. *Memoir.* He left the date of departure blank in the *Memoir.* In his 1779 report to Mason, he specified 26 June, but wrote he "set sail" on 24 June in his 15 July 1778 letter to James O'Hara.

7. William H. Denny, *The Record of the Court at Upland . . . and* A *Military Journal Kept by Major Ebenezer Denny* (Philadelphia: Lippincott & Co., 1860) [hereafter cited as *Denny Journal*]; Samuel W. Thomas, "William Clark's 1795 and 1797 Journals and Their Significance," *Bulletin of the Missouri Historical Society* 25, no. 4, pt. 1 (July 1969): 289. "Sixty-five families, besides merchants, casual people, and slaves" lived in Kaskaskia in 1766; in 1797, William Clark described the "once flourishing Town," as "now nothing more then a heap of ruins"; Mason Letter, TFHS. British officers threw a picket around the deserted Jesuit school and named the place after Thomas Gage after Kaskakians burned down their fort.

8. Lawrence Kinnaird, ed., "Clark–Leyba Papers," *American Historical Re-*

view 41, no. 1 (1935–1936): 95 and 97. St. Louis had been founded in 1764 by Pierre de Laclede; Mason Letter, TFHS.

9. Ibid.

10. Larry L. Nelson, "Clark's Kaskaskia Expedition, June 24–July 4, 1778," in *The Life of George Rogers Clark 1752–1818: Triumphs and Tragedies,* ed. Kenneth C. Carstens and Nancy Son Carstens (Westport, CT: Praeger, 2004), 28–29; Nester, *George Rogers Clark,* 99. Clark and his officers acquired a number of the Rocheblave slaves and sold some in New Orleans.

11. Mason Letter, TFHS.

12. Willing to Clark, 1 September 1778, Draper MSS 48J36; John Dodge to George Rogers Clark, 3 March 1783, Draper MSS 52J78.

13. Henry to Virginia delegates, 16 November 1778, Draper MSS 14S128. Fort Chartres had been abandoned several years before Clark appeared in the area, and was in collapse by 1778.

14. *Memoir.* Clark did not mention issuing this order in his report to Mason.

15. Byars, *B. and M. Gratz,* 191–95. Campbell would be captured by McKee and Girty in October 1779 and presumed dead, but he continued through the Revolution to be considered the founder of Louisville by the few pioneers who lived in the area.

16. John D. Barnhart, *Henry Hamilton and George Rogers Clark in the American Revolution* (Crawfordsville, IN: R.E. Banta, 1951), 41.

17. Ibid., 110.

18. Henry to Clark, 12 December 1778. H. R. McIlwaine, ed., *Official Letters of the Governors of the State of Virginia* (Richmond: Library of Virginia [Virginia State Library], 1926), 1:338–340; Julian Boyd, ed., *The Papers of Thomas Jefferson* (Princeton: Princeton University Press, 1951), 11:258.

19. *Memoir.* Pen Bogert, "Clark, the Slave Trade and the Illinois Regiment," in *The Life of George Rogers Clark, 1752–1818: Triumphs and Tragedies,* ed. Carstens and Carstens, 137–147. Clark brought Lewis, Charles, and three other slaves to the Illinois. The only known black soldier was artificer, Caesar, who belonged to the estate of James Robertson and was on the *Willing* at Vincennes. At his death in 1836, Louisvillian Henry Beard wrote that Caesar was a "strict Methodist and I have no fear for his soul"; Nester, *George Rogers Clark,* 100–102.

20. Helm to Clark, 17 December 1778. National Archives of Canada. Letter was confiscated. Printed in the *American Historical Review* 1 (1895): 90–91.

21. James, *Oliver Pollock,* 138–139. An Italian by birth, Vigo had served in the Spanish army, and when he was discharged at New Orleans he became acquainted with Oliver Pollock. He established branch stores in the Illinois villages and furnished supplies to Clark; *Memoir.*

22. Barnhart, *Hamilton and Clark,* 68; Draper MSS 3J101. J. R. Underwood

sent a copy of the letter to the *National Intelligencer* on 14 February 1837 and noted: "My situation on the Committee on Revolutionary Claims has made me acquainted with the Original Letter."

23. Library of Virginia. Reprinted, *Commonwealth* (Frankfort), 8 March 1837.

24. Bogert, "Slave Trade," 138.

25. John Rogers was the son of George Rogers, brother of George Rogers Clark's mother, Ann Rogers Clark; Mason Letter, TFHS.

26. See Edwin C. Bearss, *George Rogers Clark: Vincennes Sites Study and Evaluation* (Washington, DC: National Parks Service, 1968), a 327-page aid in the interpretation of the George Rogers Clark National Historical Park. Barnhart, *Hamilton and Clark,* 188.

27. "Joseph Bowman's Journal" in James, ed., *George Rogers Clark Papers, 1771–1781,* 158.

28. Nester, *George Rogers Clark,* 120–121.

29. Barnhart, *Hamilton and Clark,* 180.

30. Nester, *George Rogers Clark,* 145.

31. "Bowman's Journal," 160; Barnhart, *Hamilton and Clark,* 180.

32. "Bowman's Journal," 161.

33. Barnhart, *Hamilton and Clark,* 182–186.

34. Nester, *George Rogers Clark,* 103.

35. Ibid., 147.

36. Mason Letter, TFHS.

37. Barnhart, *Hamilton and Clark,* 183; Mason Letter, TFHS.

38. James, *Clark Papers,* 1:194; Barnhart, *Hamilton and Clark,* 185–186.

39. James, *Clark Papers,* 1:191.

40. "The Haldimand Papers," *Michigan Pioneer and Historical Collections,* 9:370–383; George M. Waller, *The American Revolution in the West* (Chicago: Nelson-Hall, 1976), 56 and 63; Brian Leigh Dunnigan, "Detroit: Clark's Obsession," in *The Life of George Rogers Clark, 1752–1818: Triumphs and Tragedies,* ed. Carstens and Carstens, 101–111.

41. George Rogers Clark to John Clark, 15 June 1779, Draper MSS 49J53.

42. Deposition of George Rogers Clark, 27 April 1805, Draper MSS 54J44–46.

6. Washington's Soldier

1. George Weedon, *Valley Forge Orderly Book of General George Weedon of the Continental Army under Command of General George Washington* (New York: Dodd, Mead, 1902), 254–255; Allen McLane Papers, New-York Historical Society, New York; "The Women Present at Valley Forge," Valley Forge National Historic Park,

Pennsylvania, National Park Service, last modified 7 September 2015, https://www.nps.gov/vafo/learn/historyculture/valleyforgewomen.htm.

2. The Muster Roll Project, Valley Forge Park Alliance, Valley Forge National Historic Park, last modified 3 March 2019, http://valleyforgemusterroll.org/muster.asp?id=VA14034; "Jonathan Clark Diary," TFHS special collections.

3. Chernow, *Washington,* 339. Lieutenant-General Sir Henry Clinton, son of a New York Colonial governor, was a veteran of the Coldstream and Grenadier guards. "18 June 1778 . . . Enemy left Philadelphia," in "Jonathan Clark Diary," TFHS special collections.

4. Flexner, *Washington,* 120.

5. Chernow, *Washington,* 342; Boatner, *Encyclopedia of the American Revolution,* 717–718.

6. Boatner, *Encyclopedia of the American Revolution,* 719–725.

7. Nancy Isenberg, *Fallen Founder: The Life of Aaron Burr* (New York: Viking, 2007), 64–68.

8. William Croghan to Barnard Gratz, 1 March 1779; Croghan to Michael Gratz, 13 September 1779, Etting MSS. "We arrived in these disagreeable mountains about two weeks ago. . . . Our chief employment is to repair roads," in "The Revolutionary War Diary of Major William Croghan [1779 81]," Draper MSS 3N.

9. Ibid., 7 August 1779.

10. William Livingston to Timothy Johnes, National Parks Service, Morristown, NJ.

11. "Revolutionary War Diary of Major William Croghan," Draper MSS 3N.

12. William Croghan to Michael Gratz, 7 February 1780, New York Public Library; Sanchez-Saavedra, *A Guide to Virginia Military Organizations,* 34–35. Major Charles Pelham was assigned to the Second Virginia Regiment under Lt. Colonel Richard Taylor.

13. "Revolutionary War Diary of Major William Croghan," Draper MSS 3N.

14. Boatner, *Encyclopedia of the American Revolution,* 993–994; Charles Scott to Barnard Gratz, 20 October 1780, Historical Society of Pennsylvania.

15. Croghan to Michael Gratz, 8 April 1780, New York Public Library; R. W. Gibbes, ed., *Documentary History of the American Revolution* (New York: Appleton, 1857).

16. Boatner, *Encyclopedia of the American Revolution,* 213–214. Historians accept the American losses in the Battle of Charleston as about 90 killed and 145 wounded; British losses were reported as about 265 killed and wounded.

17. Croghan to Michael Gratz, 18 May 1780, in Byars, *B. and M. Gratz,* 199. Lt. Col. Jacques Marcus Prevost had married Theodosia Bartow on 28 July 1763 at Trinity Church in Manhattan. For correspondence between William Croghan and the Prevost family, see the Haldimand Papers, fol. 105, British Library, London.

18. William Croghan to George Croghan, 10 June 1780, Historical Society of Pennsylvania.

19. Disease killed most of the men, with smallpox epidemics and tuberculosis leading the way; "Revolutionary War Diary of Major William Croghan," Draper MSS 3N.

20. "Jonathan Clark Diary," TFHS special collections. Croghan applied for parole on 30 January 1781; Jonathan Clark received parole on 22 January.

21. Boatner, *Encyclopedia of the American Revolution,* 1230–1232.

22. Robert Selig, *The Washington-Rochambeau Revolutionary Route,* Resource Study and Environmental Assessment (Washington, DC: National Park Service, 2006).

23. William B. Willcox, ed., *The American Rebellion: Sir Henry Clinton's Narrative of his Campaigns, 1775–1782* (New Haven: Yale University Press, 1954), 530–531.

24. Boatner, *Encyclopedia of the American Revolution,* 1235–1236.

25. Ibid., 1236–1237; Chernow, *Washington,* 408–413.

26. Harlow Giles Unger, *Lafayette* (Hoboken: John Wiley & Sons, 2002), 153; Flexner, *Washington,* 2:454; Chernow, *Washington,* 412–415.

27. Richard M. Ketchum, *Victory at Yorktown: The Campaign that Won the Revolution* (New York: Henry Holt and Co., 2004), 208; Chernow, *Washington,* 413–417.

28. William Hague, *William Pitt the Younger: A Biography* (New York: HarperCollins, 2004), 67; Boatner, *Encyclopedia of the American Revolution,* 1246. Laurens was Hamilton's closest revolutionary friend. Louis Marie Antoine de Noailles was Lafayette's brother-in-law, married to Anne Jeanne Baptiste Louise, sister to Marie Adrienne Francoise de Noailles du Motier, Marquise de La Fayette. Adrienne's grandmother, mother, and sister were guillotined in Paris on 22 July 1794, but she was saved through the intervention of James Monroe while Lafayette was an Austrian prisoner.

29. Chernow, *Washington,* 417–419.

30. William Croghan to William Davies, 30 November 1781, Library of Virginia.

7. Detroit

1. James Alton James, "George Rogers Clark and Detroit, 1780–1781," *Proceedings, Mississippi Valley Historical Association* 2 (1915): 295; Clark to Thomas Nelson, 1 October 1781, Draper MSS 14S64; Draper MSS 2B188; quoted in Faragher, *Daniel Boone,* 81; Clark to Richard Lernoult, 16 March 1779; James, *Clark Papers,* 1:306–307.

2. Henry to Galvez, 18 October 1777, Clark Manuscripts, Library of Virginia, Richmond; Thomas Jefferson to Joseph Martin, 24 January 1780, Draper MSS 46J57.

3. Kenneth Carstens, "George Rogers Clark's Fort Jefferson, 1780–81," *Filson Club History Quarterly* 71 (July 1997): 259–284; James, *Clark Papers,* 996–997 and 496–497; Jefferson to Clark, 29 January 1780, Draper MSS 50J7; Robert George to Oliver Pollock, 1 January 1781, *Journal of the House of Delegates of the Commonwealth of Virginia* (Virginia General Assembly, 1835), 14. Captain Philip Barbour inflated the cost of goods he delivered to Fort Jefferson in 1780 from $25,000 to $230,000.

4. Nancy Son Carstens, "Making of a Myth: George Rogers Clark and Teresa de Leyba," *Filson History Quarterly* 76 (Spring 2002): 126–127, and 139. De Leyba died a month after the St. Louis attack.

5. Todd to Clark, 3 October 1779, Draper MSS 49J77; Carstens, "Making of a Myth," 126–127. For additional information, see Lawrence Kinnaird, "The Western Fringe of Revolution," *Western Historical Quarterly* (July 1976): 252. A copy of the will is in the Leyba Papers, Missouri History Museum, St. Louis.

6. Draper MSS 7J109. See Carstens, "Making of a Myth," and *Clark: Triumphs and Tragedies,* ed. Carstens and Carstens, for a summary of the Clark–de Leyba saga.

7. Draper MSS 50J72; Jefferson to Clark, 1 January 1780, in Boyd, *Jefferson Papers,* 3:258.

8. Shawnee chief Cornstalk had gone to Point Pleasant to discuss ways to bring an end to the frontier war. Local backwoodsmen took his son and him hostage and subsequently murdered them.

9. *John Bradford's & Etc. Historical Notes on Kentucky,* ed. Douglas S. Watson (San Francisco: Grabhorn, 1932), 41.

10. Col. John Bowman was brother to Clark's major Joseph Bowman and Col. Abraham Bowman of the Virginia Eighth Regiment. The value of the three hundred horses was $32,000. The death of Blackfish left the Shawnees without a strong leader as they faced Clark's 1780 raid.

11. Draper MSS 50J19; Martin West, "Clark's 1780 Shawnee Expedition," in *Clark: Triumphs and Tragedies,* ed. Carstens and Carstens, 178; Jefferson to Clark, 19 March 1780, in Boyd, *Jefferson Papers,* 19:316–317; Clark to Fleming, 4 April 1780, Draper MSS 46J54.

12. Brodhead to Clark, 20 May 1780, Draper MSS 50J39.

13. Draper MSS 9J21; for a fuller account, see West, "Clark's 1780 Shawnee Expedition," 178–186. Piqua, also known to pioneers as Pickowee, Pekowi Town, and Pickaway, was a group of three villages surrounded by a stockade. Old Chillicothe stood twelve miles south of Piqua.

14. Draper MSS 8J156–57; Clark to Jefferson, 22 August 1780, *Virginia Gazette* (4 October 1780).

15. Report of John Clairy, American deserter, 5 August 1780, Haldimand Collection, Public Archives of Canada, Ottawa, B100, 443.

16. *Clark's Shawnee Campaign of 1780—Contemporary Accounts* (Springfield, OH: Clark County Historical Society, 1975), 14; Draper MSS 8J142, 9J28, 8J142, 8J145; Clark to Jefferson, 22 August 1780, Draper MSS 9J28; West, "Clark's 1780 Shawnee Expedition," 188–189.

17. Draper MSS 9J28–30, 9J95–6, 8J141, 145; West, "Clark's 1780 Shawnee Expedition," 190–191.

18. George Rogers Clark to John Clark, 23 August 1780, TFHS.

19. When the Virginia Assembly offered to place its western lands under federal authority in exchange for military support, it did so with the proviso that the Indiana grant and those of William Murray (the Illinois Company) should "be deemed and declared absolutely void." The Virginia legislature officially surrendered its Northwest Territory on 20 October 1783.

20. Jefferson to Clark, 25 December 1780, *Letter Book of Thomas Jefferson, 1781,* Library of Virginia, 10. Lt. John Clark had been captured at the Battle of Germantown.

21. Johann Ewald, *Diary of the American War: A Hessian Journal,* ed. and trans. Joseph P. Tustin (New Haven: Yale University Press, 1979), 271–272.

22. Jefferson to Virginia delegates, 18 January 1781, Boyd, *Jefferson Papers,* 4:399; George Rogers Clark to Thomas Jefferson, 18 January 1781, Clark Manuscripts, Library of Virginia.

23. George Washington to Daniel Brodhead, 29 December 1780, Sparks, *Writings of Washington,* 7:344–345.

24. Edgar Hassler, *Old Westmoreland: A History of Western Pennsylvania during the Revolution* (1900; repr., Bowie, MD: Heritage, 1998), 132; Draper MSS 1K82–90; Samuel Evans, "The Truth concerning the Expedition of George Rogers Clark," *Potters American Monthly* 6 (March 1876); Sanchez-Saavedra, *Guide to Virginia Military Organizations,* 199.

25. The resolution to end the Detroit campaign was made by Patrick Henry. Opinion is divided as to whether Virginia's release of the Northwest Territory, or Henry's late enmity with Jefferson, who claimed the Detroit campaign as his initiative, prompted the action. Bodley, *George Rogers Clark,* 174; Clark to Washington, 20 May 1781, LOC, Washington Papers.

26. Clark to Jefferson, 4 August 1781, Clark Manuscripts, Library of Virginia.

27. Partnership Agreement between Barnard and Michael Gratz and John Gibson, 21 May 1781, Barnard Gratz to Michael Gratz, 10 June 1784, John Gib-

son to Barnard and Michael Gratz, 23 July 1783, Gibson to M. Gratz, 9 March 1784, Etting MSS; Byars, *B. and M. Gratz,* 217 and 226.

28. William Croghan to William Davies, 18 August 1781, Virginia State Library.

29. Kelsay, *Brant,* 276–277; Barnhart, *Hamilton and Clark,* 164; George Washington Papers, 1741–1799, Series 4, LOC, General Correspondence.

30. John Macombe to Daniel Claus, 14 September 1781, Daniel Claus Papers, vol. 3, Public Archives of Canada, Ottawa.

31. Tebbel and Jennison, *Indian Wars,* 59. The Miamis (Twightwees) were a loose confederation of western tribes that lived along the Miami and Wabash rivers; Vincent J. Akers, "Long Run Massacre (Boone's Defeat) and Floyd's Defeat," in *The New History of Shelby County, Kentucky* (Prospect, KY: Harmony House, 2003), 40–46. Also, see Blaine A. Guthrie Jr., "Captain Richard Chenoweth: A Founding Father of Louisville," *Filson Club History Quarterly* 46 (April 1972): 147–160.

8. Frontier Wars

1. National Archives of Canada, Ottawa, NAC MG 21: Haldimand Papers; *The Calendar of Virginia State Papers* (Richmond: James E. Goode, 1881) 2:294, https://books.google.com/books?id=fOsxAQAAMAAJ&printsec=frontcover&source=gbs_ge_summary_r&cad=0#v=onepage&q&f=false. Clark wrote from Wheeling on his way to the Falls of the Ohio; Clark to Fleming, 12 June 1781, James, ed., *Clark Papers,* 565.

2. John Todd Jr., to Governor Thomas Nelson, 21 October 1781, *Calendar of Virginia State Papers,* 2:562–564. Nelson served briefly as governor in 1781; Harrison to Clark, 20 December 1781. James, *Clark Papers,* 19–20.

3. Harrison to Fleming, 29 January 1782, Draper MSS 46J69; Clark to Jefferson, 20 February 1782. Jefferson Papers, Massachusetts Historical Society, Boston.

4. Robert George to John Todd Jr., 19 May 1782, Draper MSS 52J25; *Calendar of Virginia State Papers,* 3:150.

5. David Zeisberger, *Schoenbrunn Story: Excerpts from the Diary of the Reverend David Zeisberger, 1772–1777, at Schoenbrunn in the Ohio Country* (Columbus: Ohio History Connection, 1972).

6. Tecumseh's Speech to William Henry Harrison, 11 August 1810, Indiana Historical Society, Indianapolis.

7. William Croghan to Michael Gratz, 20 April 1782, Historical Society of Pennsylvania.

8. Crawford met Washington in 1749, and after the French and Indian War he served as his primary surveyor. He was colonel of the Seventh Virginia Regiment before he was transferred to the Western Department in 1777.

9. William Croghan to William Davies, 6 June 1782, Indiana Historical Society.

10. Hammon and Taylor, *Virginia's Western War,* 155.

11. Faragher, *Daniel Boone,* 217–219.

12. Draper MSS 22C36.

13. Faragher, *Daniel Boone,* 220–222; Hammon and Taylor, *Virginia's Western War,* 158–164.

14. Harrison to Fleming, 16 October 1782, James, *Clark Papers,* 132.

15. Boone et al. to Benjamin Harrison, 11 September 1782; James, *Clark Papers,* 113–114.

16. Clark to Benjamin Harrison, 27 November 1782; James, *Clark Papers,* 157; Hammon and Taylor, *Virginia's Western War,* 170; Irvine to Clark, 7 November 1782, Draper MSS 52J55.

17. Brant to John Johnson, 25 December 1782, Haldimand Papers, B 115:47, British Museum and Library, London; Kelsay, *Brant,* 332–333.

18. Clark to Harrison, 8 March 1783, Library of Virginia.

19. "Journal of Western Commissioners," in James, *Clark Papers,* 362 and 401. The records were found in the basement of the Virginia State Library and archived by E. G. Swem; the photostated collection is at The Filson Historical Society.

20. Harrison to Clark, 2 July 1783, Draper MSS 52J88.

9. End of Glory

1. Jefferson to Clark, 26 November 1782, Jefferson Papers, LOC; Croghan to B. Gratz, 31 January 1783, Etting MSS.

2. William Croghan to Barnard Gratz, 7 August 1779 and 26 March 1779, Etting MSS.

3. Ibid., William Croghan to Barnard Gratz, 31 January 1783.

4. Bryce Metcalf, *Original Members and other Officers Eligible to the Society of the Cincinnati 1783–1938* (Strasburg, VA: Shenandoah, 1938), 97. Original membership was open to about 5,500 officers who had served three years in the Continental Army or Navy, and to French officers who had participated in the American Revolution. Of that number, about 2,150 officers joined within the first year. Although militiamen were excluded from membership, some leaders, including George Rogers Clark, were invited to join. Clark declined.

5. Clark to Jefferson, 12 October 1783, Historic Locust Grove, Inc. Brigadier generals in both the militia and Continental services reverted to their previous com-

mission status at the conclusion of the war. Although Clark officially was a retired lieutenant colonel, he was referred to as a general for the remainder of his life.

6. Jefferson to Clark, 4 December 1783, Draper MSS 52J93; Clark to Jefferson, 8 February 1784, Virginia Historical Society.

7. Mason Letter, TFHS; Mason to Joseph Jones, 27 July 1780, Robert A. Rutland, ed., *The Papers of George Mason 1725–1792* (Chapel Hill: University of North Carolina Press, 1970), 2:657. Jones, an uncle of James Monroe, worked with Mason concerning the cession of Virginia lands to Congress.

8. English, *Conquest of the Country Northwest of the River Ohio,* 2:839–855; *Collections of the Illinois State Historical Library,* vol. 8, *Virginia Series,* vol. 3, *George Rogers Clark Papers, 1771–1790* (Springfield: Trustees of the Illinois State Historical Library, 1912), 8:151–153.

9. The Rev. James Madison, eighth president of the College of William and Mary and a cousin to future president James Madison, made the appointment. By law, the college received a portion of all fees collected by Virginia surveyors. Clark's appointment by a "deputation" committee was made on 17 December 1783, Draper MSS 32J93; *Calendar of the Virginia State Papers* 3:550; Draper MSS 53J3.

10. "Richmond. Thursday last Col. Richard C. Anderson and Major Wm. Croghan set off from this city on their way to the back country, being appointed by the general assembly at their last sitting, to survey and lay off the officers' and soldiers' lands for their services during the late war," *Pennsylvania Packet,* 26 February 1784, 2.

11. The first entry in the book kept by Croghan was dated 2 August 1784, Louisville Metro Archives, LouisvilleKY.gov.

12. Clark's cousin, William Clark, son of Benjamin Clark, should not be confused with his brother. Harrison to Clark, 17 August 1784, Draper MSS 53J14.

13. Harrison to Clark, 17 August 1784. Draper MSS 53J14. Muhlenberg to Thomas Miflin, 5 July 1784. *State Records of North Carolina, 1781-1785* (Goldsboro: Nash Brothers, 1899), 17:159–161, https://babel.hathitrust.org/cgi/pt?id=inu.30000128792045;view=1up;seq=7. Muhlenberg County, Kentucky, was named for him.

14. Mifflin to Clark, 6 March 1784, Draper MSS 53J7; Jefferson to Clark, 4 March. Draper MSS 53J5; Clark to James O'Hara, 25 August 1787. Darlington Memorial Library, University of Pittsburgh.

15. Treaties made at Ft. Stanwix, New York, in 1784 and at Ft. McIntosh, Pennsylvania, in 1785.

16. Butler to Clark, 21 July 1785, Draper MSS 53J17; Resolution of Commissioners, 31 July 1785, Draper MSS 53J18. Proclamation to Western District Nations, 31 July 1785, Indiana Historical Society. Clark and Butler to Chippewas and Ottawas, 30 July 1785.

17. Croghan to Clark, 3 November 1785, Draper MSS 53J21. Ft. Finney was located at the confluence of the Great Miami River and the Ohio. A second Ft. Finney (Fort Steuben) was built near the future Jeffersonville, Indiana.

18. *Denny Journal,* 71 and 267. Ebenezer Denny was Pittsburgh's first mayor; his son, Harmar, was brother-in-law to William Croghan Jr.

19. Journal of General Richard Butler, 1785–1786, 2:489, Reuben T. Durrett Collection on Kentucky and the Ohio River Valley, University of Chicago.

20. *Denny Journal,* 277, 73.

21. Alan S. Brown, "The Role of the Army in Western Settlement: Josiah Harmar's Command, 1785–1790," *Pennsylvania Magazine of History and Biography* 43 (April 1969): 167; Clark to Henry in William Croghan's hand, April or May 1786, Yale University Library; Resolution of Clark, Butler, and Parsons, 8 February 1786, National Archives, College Park, MD, RG 360.

22. John Small to Clark, 23 June 1786, Draper MSS 55J36; Logan to Henry, 19 April 1786, Library of Virginia.

23. Clark to Henry in William Croghan's hand, April or May 1786, Yale University Library.

24. Clark to Richard H. Lee, April or May 1786, National Archives RG 360.

25. Jacob P. Dunn, *Indiana and Indianans, a History of Aboriginal and Territorial Indiana and the Century of Statehood* (Chicago: American Historical Society, 1919), 170–171.

26. English, *Conquest of the Country Northwest of the River Ohio,* 2:799. May would be killed by natives in 1790. The town of Maysville was established on land owned by May and Simon Kenton.

27. Nester, *Clark,* 272; Chapline to Clark, 26 July 1786, Draper MSS 53J40.

28. Resolutions of the Officers of the Kentucky District, 2 August 1786, Draper MSS 53J42.

29. Ibid.; Benjamin Logan to Edmund Randolph, 13 December 1786, Library of Virginia.

30. In addition to her two known Indian husbands, Nonhelema is linked to Alexander McKee, by whom she gave birth to a son, Thomas McKee, and to Richard Butler and George Morgan. She died at Fort Pitt in December 1786.

31. *Denny Journal,* 94.

32. "Papers respecting the Seizure of Property at Post St. Vincennes," Draper MSS 53J59–61; Thomas Green to Governor, Council and Legislature of Georgia, 3 December 1786, Draper MSS 53J58.

33. Unsigned letter of 12 December 1786, *Calendar of Virginia State Papers,* 4:202.

34. Lowell H. Harrison, *Kentucky's Road to Statehood* (Lexington: University

Press of Kentucky, 1992), 46. Future president James Madison was a classmate of Clark's at Robertson's school.

35. Committee Report, 19 and 20 December 1786, Draper MSS 53J59–61.

36. Ibid; Memorial to Edmund Randolph, 22 December 1786, Library of Virginia.

37. Proclamation, 28 February 1787; Draper MSS 53J65; Clark to Edmund Randolph, 11 May 1787, Library of Virginia.

38. Clark to Randolph, 8 October 1787, Library of Virginia.

10. Wilkinson

1. Thomas Robson Hay and M. R. Werner, *The Admirable Trumpeteer: A Biography of General James Wilkinson* (Garden City, NY: Doubleday, Doran, 1941), 109; Andro Linklater, *An Artist in Treason: The Extraordinary Double Life of General James Wilkinson* (New York: Walker, 2009), 111; Jefferson to Clark, 26 November 1782, LOC, Jefferson Papers.

2. *Denny Journal,* 12; Linklater, *An Artist in Treason,* 72.

3. Harrison, *Kentucky's Road,* 19–20; R. S. Cotterill, *History of Pioneer Kentucky* (Cincinnati: Johnson and Hardin, 1917), 210–211; Harrison, *Kentucky's Road,* 21–22.

4. Harrison, *Kentucky's Road,* 34–35.

5. Proof of Wilkinson's role as Agent 13 was not known by the public until Charles Gayarré published the correspondence between Wilkinson and Miró in 1854, long after the deaths of both men.

6. Linklater, *An Artist in Treason,* 152. Wilkinson would receive another $9,640 from Spain in 1795 to renew his Spanish contract.

7. Ibid., 87–88.

8. David O. Stewart, *The Summer of 1787: The Men Who Invented the Constitution* (New York: Simon & Schuster, 2007), 82.

9. Harrison, *Kentucky's Road,* 50, 57; Charles Gayarré, *History of Louisiana* (New Orleans: F.F. Hansell & Bro., Ltd., 1903), 3:194–195, 241; Stuart Seely Sprague, "Senator John Brown of Kentucky, 1757–1837: A Political Biography" (PhD diss., New York University, 1972). Sebastian was named executor in John Clark's 1799 will and served as judge in Kentucky's appellate court from 1792 until 1806, when he was removed after discovery of his involvement in the Spanish Conspiracy.

10. Mary K. Bonsteel Tachau, *Federal Courts in the Early Republic: Kentucky, 1789–1816* (Princeton: Princeton University Press, 1978); Harrison, *Kentucky's Road,* 57–61. One Bourbon County (Kentucky) delegate did not vote. Harry

Innes, a Caroline County, Virginia, lawyer educated by Donald Robertson, moved to Kentucky in 1783.

11. Harry Innes to Edmund Randolph, 1787, in Thomas Marshall Green, *The Spanish Conspiracy* (Cincinnati: Robert Clarke & Co., 1891), 83.

12. Clark to Clark, 20 April 1788, Draper MSS 2L26.

13. Clark to Don Diego de Gardoqui, 15 March 1788, University of Chicago Library.

14. Harrison, *Kentucky's Road,* 84. In September 1789, Wilkinson demanded $7,000 from Spain and presented a list of Kentuckians whose interests in Spain could be purchased. Among the Kentuckians recommended for $1,000 annual pensions were Sebastian, Innes, and Brown, while Logan and Shelby were placed in an $800 category.

15. Draper MSS 2L46.

16. Gayarré, *History of Louisiana,* 3:278–79.

17. Linklater, *An Artist in Treason,* 158–162; Draper MSS 44J230, as reported by Mann Butler.

18. Innes to Jefferson, 30 May 1791, LOC, Innes Papers.

19. Brown to Clark, 5 July 1789, Draper MSS 53J80.

20. Clark to Brown, 20 August 1789, printed in the *Commonwealth* (Frankfort), 25 July 1838.

21. Ibid., Clark to Brown, 30 January 1790. For more information, see Samuel W. Thomas and Eugene H. Conner, "George Rogers Clark [1752–1818]: Natural Scientist and Historian," *Filson Club History Quarterly* 41 (July 1967): 206–207.

22. Clark's mound builders essay was uncovered by Draper and sent to Henry Rowe Schoolcraft, who published it in his *Archives of Aboriginal Knowledge* (Philadelphia: J. B. Lippincott, 1860), 4:133–136.

23. Draper MSS 53J81; James, "Clark and the Mound Builders," appendix 11 in *The Life of George Rogers Clark,* 495–499.

24. Clark to Brown, 15 July 1790, printed in the *Commonwealth* (Frankfort), 25 July 1838.

25. John Pope, *A Tour Through the Southern and Western Territories of the United States of North America; the Spanish Dominions on the River Mississippi, and the Floridas; The Countries of the Creek Nations; and Many Uninhabited Parts* (Richmond, VA: John Dixon, 1792), 19–20.

26. Jefferson to Innes, 7 March 1791, Thomas Jefferson, *The Writings of Jefferson. Published by the Order of the Joint Committee of Congress on the Library, from the Original Manuscripts, Deposited in the Department of State* (New York: J.C. Riker, 1853), 3:217–218.

27. Draper MSS 34J20–23; Missouri History Museum, St. Louis, Manu-

script Collection; John Carl Parish, *The Westward Movement* (Los Angeles and Berkeley: University of California Press, 1943), 79–80.

28. O'Fallon to Gardoqui, 26 May 1788, Gardoqui Papers, 1:198–200, Reuben T. Durrett Collection, University of Chicago Library. O'Fallon promised to collect twenty thousand men, "the best material," for the colony, most of whom would be Irish, and all of whom would be Catholics.

29. Gayarré, *History of Louisiana,* 289.

30. Ibid., 293.

31. Ibid., 290–291.The Georgia legislature made grants to three land companies in 1790: the South Carolina Yazoo Company, Tennessee Company, and Virginia Company, the last of which involved Patrick Henry. Gayarré, *History of Louisiana,* 3:272–273; John Carl Parish, "The Intrigues of Dr. James O'Fallon," *Mississippi Valley Historical Review* 17, no. 2 (1930): 245; Linklater, *An Artist in Treason,* 108; Parish, *Westward Movement,* 95–97.

32. Parish, *Western Movement,* 100. O'Fallon had ingratiated himself to the Clarks by writing to Jonathan to assume credit for George Rogers's sobriety and advising John and Ann to wear red flannel underwear for joint pain.

11. French Major General

1. Isaac Shelby to Jefferson, 13 January 1794, Martin Hardin Family Papers, Chicago History Museum; John Adams to Jefferson, 30 June 1813, in Lester J. Cappon, ed., *The Adams-Jefferson Letters* (Chapel Hill: University of North Carolina Press, 1959), 2:346–347.

2. Draper MSS 53J91; Clark to Jonathan Clark, 11 May 1792, Virginia Historical Society.

3. O'Fallon to Captain Herron, 18 October 1793, in M. D. Conway, *The Life of Thomas Paine* (New York: B. Blom, 1892), 2:156.

4. Clark to Paine, 5 February 1793, in hand of James O'Fallon, Draper MSS 55J1.

5. Paine to O'Fallon, 17 February 1793, Draper MSS 12J60. The letter was addressed to "Dr. James OFallon, Physician near Louisville in Kentucky, United States of America," and was published by Louise Phelps Kellogg in the *American Historical Review* 29 (April 1924): 501–505.

6. Draper MSS 42J(A)114; Parish, *Western Movement,* 93. O'Fallon wrote that Clark accused him of forging a letter allegedly written by Anthony Wayne, inviting him to join his campaign. The family, too, according to O'Fallon, suspected him of poisoning his son, Johnny, and killing his former wife.

7. André Michaux to Clark, 7 October 1793, Draper MSS 55J4. "Only I

inquire for . . . money of many Merchants at Lexings and they promise to me as much as they could give me in the time. M. Brown was very much informed of our affairs. He desire it could be effected."

8. Genêt to Clark, 12 July 1793, American Historical Association, *Annual Report* (Washington, DC: Government Printing Office, 1897), 1:986.

9. Boyd, *Papers of Jefferson,* 26:651–53 and 27:196.

10. Jefferson to Shelby, 29 August 1793, Martin Hardin Family Papers, Chicago History Museum.

11. Clark to Citizen Genêt, 3 October 1793, Draper MSS 11J202–205, 55J4–5.

12. Carondelet to Alcudia, 27 September 1793, Draper MSS 42J83–89.

13. Elijah Clarke was a militia lieutenant colonel who fought with Henry Lee; they defeated Banastre Tarleton and recaptured Augusta in 1781. As a general, he led the Georgia militia against the Creek and Cherokee nations, and established the Republic of Georgia (Transoconee Republic) in May 1794. In *Burr, Hamilton, and Jefferson: A Study in Character* (New York: Oxford University Press, 1999), 125, Roger G. Kennedy writes without citation that Elijah Clarke was a kinsman of George Rogers Clark. Draper, too, assumed there was a connection stemming from the Christopher Clark family of Albemarle and Louisa counties in Virginia, but was unable to find proof beyond family tradition.

14. Lt. Col. John Montgomery had explored the Cumberland River before the Revolution. Montgomery was killed in an Indian attack in 1794 and was buried near Smithland, on property he acquired with William Croghan, John Rogers, and Mayo Carrington in 1784 at "the iron banks" of the Ohio River. Logan to Clark, 31 December 1793, Draper MSS 55J6 and 55J9.

15. Gayoso de Lemos to Alcudia, 1 January 1794, Draper MSS 42J106–07.

16. Isaac Shelby to Jefferson, 13 January 1794, Letters from Governors of States, 1790–1812, National Archives, ASP, Foreign Relations, 1:455–456.

17. Wilkinson to Wayne, 2 February 1794, University of Kentucky Library, Lexington.

18. St. Clair was a Scot assigned to Britain's Royal American Regiment during the French and Indian War; he served as a Continental Army major-general during the Revolution and was appointed first governor of the Northwest Territory in 1788. His 1791 Wabash campaign was overwhelmed by forces led by Miami chief Little Turtle and Shawnee chief Blue Jacket; William E. Foley, *Wilderness Journey: The Life of William Clark* (Columbia: University of Missouri Press, 2004), 36–40; Anthony Wayne to Henry Knox, 1794, quoted in Thomas P. Slaughter, *The Whiskey Rebellion* (New York: Oxford University Press, 1986), 176.

19. Paul David Nelson, "The Battle of Fallen Timbers," in *The Kentucky En-*

cyclopedia, ed. John E. Kleber (Lexington: University Press of Kentucky, 1992), 304; Slaughter, *Whiskey Rebellion,* 176–177; Charles J. Kappler, ed., *Indian Affairs: Laws and Treaties* (Washington, DC: Government Printing Office, 1904), 2:117–119. William Wells, brother to Anderson neighbor, Samuel Wells, married Little Turtle's daughter.

20. Britain had refused to abandon Northwest Territory forts until Revolutionary War prisoners were returned and all American debts owed to British citizens paid.

21. *American Historical Review* 18, no. 4 (July 1913): 781–782. Marston Green Clark was the son of John Clark's brother, Benjamin.

22. Draper MSS 55J20 and 55J33.

23. Draper MSS 55J24.

24. R. Hunter to Anthony Wayne, 1794, Historical Society of Pennsylvania; Samuel W. Thomas, "William Clark's 1795 and 1797 Journals and Their Significance," *Missouri Historical Society Bulletin* (July 1969), 278–281; William Clark to Jonathan Clark, 25 May 1794, Draper MSS 2L33; William Clark Papers, Missouri History Museum; Foley, *Wilderness Journey,* 30, 38–39. Foley cites an unsigned document to Wayne in William Clark's hand, 4 November 1795.

25. Victor Collot, *A Journey in North America* (Paris: Arthus Bertrand, 1826), 1:152–155.

26. The Library of Virginia to Samuel W. Thomas, 16 March 1970. One parcel amounted to 36,962 acres and the other, 37,000 acres. The original document was witnessed by John Clark and James Carnes.

27. Power of Attorney dated 15 August 1796, recorded 5 October 1796 in Jefferson County (KY) Bond and Power of Attorney Book 1:181.

28. William Clark to Edmund Clark, 18 August 1797 and 14 December 1797, Draper MSS 2L45–46.

29. Mann Butler, *A History of the Commonwealth of Kentucky* (1834; repr., Berea, KY: Oscar Rucker, Jr., 1968), 282.

30. Thomas Fleming, *The Louisiana Purchase* (Hoboken, NJ: Wiley, 2003), 1; Thomas D. Clark, ed., *The Voice of the Frontier: John Bradford's Notes on Kentucky* (Lexington: University Press of Kentucky, 1993), 197. Between 1798 and 1800, France captured and sacked $12 million ($200 million in today's market) of American goods at sea. Charles Maurice de Talleyrand-Perigord became France's foreign minister in 1797.

31. Marc de Villiers du Terrage, *Les Dernieres Annees de la Louisiane Francaise* (Paris: Librarie Orientale et Americaine, 1904), 362–363, translation.

32. James Alton James, *The Life of George Rogers Clark* (Chicago: University of Chicago Press, 1929), 511–513, translation. Daniel Boone would settle in Missou-

ri in 1799 before the territory's acquisition by the United States, which indicates that Clark would not have been alone in the territory.

33. Clark to the Minister of External Affairs, St. Louis, 10 September 1798, translation, in James, *The Life of George Rogers Clark,* 513.

12. Country Houses

1. John Francis McDermott, ed., "The Western Journals of Dr. George Hunter, 1796–1805," *Transactions of the American Philosophical Society* 53 (July 1963): 26.

2. Deed from heirs of George Meriwether to John Clark, 29 August 1785; Louisville Metro Archives, Jefferson County Deed Book 1:48 [hereafter cited JCDB]; Ernest Ellison, *Mulberry Hill Plantation: The Clark Family Home in Louisville, Kentucky* (Privately printed, 1991); John Frederick Dorman III, "Descendants of General Jonathan Clark, Jefferson County, Kentucky 1750–1811," *Filson Club History Quarterly* 23 (January 1949): 26; George Rogers Clark to Edmund Clark, 2 September 1791, Draper MSS 34J7. James J. Holmberg, ed., *Dear Brother: Letters of William Clark to Jonathan Clark* (New Haven: Yale University Press, 2002), 32–33. The core of Mulberry Hill today is owned by Metro Louisville and is managed as George Rogers Clark Park. The graves of John and Ann Clark remain at the park. David Meriwether to father, William Meriwether, 14 September 1785, TFHS.

3. James, *Clark Papers,* 335; In.gov, Indiana Historical Bureau. John Clark was held initially in Philadelphia, but was transferred to Long Island upon Britain's desertion of the city. His last year of captivity was spent upon a prison ship.

4. Will dated 24 July 1799. Jefferson County Will Book 1:86, Louisville Metro Archives. Bill of Sale to William Clark, 10 January 1799, Jefferson County Bond and Power of Attorney 2:56. This transfer might have occurred in January 1800. Meriwether Lewis Clark Sr. reported his father returned them to George Rogers Clark in 1803, Draper MSS 2J100.

5. *Richmond Whig,* undated; Draper MSS 2K88; "Major Anderson," *Daily Louisville Commercial,* 9 January 1879.

6. "A Guide to the Society of the Cincinnati in the State of Virginia, Records, 1778–1941," a collection in the Library of Virginia, accession no. 26102, http://ead.lib.virginia.edu/vivaxtf/view?docId=lva/vi00902.xml. The Virginia Military District was situated in today's south central Kentucky, below the Green River, and in south central Ohio.

7. JCDB 1:78; Allen Tischendorf and E. Taylor Parks, eds., *The Diary and Journal of Richard Clough Anderson, Jr., 1814–1826* (Durham: Duke University Press, 1964), 3. With the acquisition of surrounding tracts, Soldier's Retreat to-

taled 952 acres. Sarah Marshall Anderson was a cousin to Humphrey Marshall and Chief Justice John Marshall. Her mother, Ann, was the daughter of Torquil McLeod and Ann Clark, sister to John Clark, father of Elizabeth Clark Anderson.

8. John Cleves Symmes to Richard Clough Anderson, 27 June 1787, TFHS. Symmes (1741–1814) was a Continental congressman and Supreme Court justice in New Jersey before he purchased 311,000 acres in the Ohio Territory. He served as the federal government's Ohio judge from 1788 to 1803.

9. Jefferson County Marriage records, TFHS.

10. Deposition, John T. Gray v. Trustees of Louisville, Jefferson Circuit Court case 552 (1817). Croghan was a trustee in the Town of Louisville in 1791. Jefferson County Minute Order Book 2:77, 81; agreement of 4 April 1788 filed in Jefferson County "Old Circuit Court Common Law" case 1954 (1788). Louisville Metro Archives. The stone courthouse was described as "built with some Taste."

11. Wainwright, *George Croghan, Wilderness Diplomat,* 196. Daniel Clark's illegitimate daughter, Myra, would attend the 1822 wedding of William Croghan's eldest daughter in the company of her husband and the groom's best man, General Edmund P. Gaines.

12. Daniel Clark to William Croghan, 14 June 1788, Draper MSS 1N89.

13. William Croghan to [Richard Clough Anderson], 20 November 1788, TFHS.

14. Croghan to Anderson, 20 November 1788, TFHS; Jefferson County Minute Order Book 2:116, 120.

15. *Kentucky Gazette,* 12 April 1790.

16. *Kentucky Gazette,* vol. 4, no. 35, 7 May 1791.

17. Fincastle County Survey Book 5:66, Land Office, Secretary of State, Frankfort. The Peachy and Eustace grants were signed by Jefferson on 12 November 1779. The Peachy grant was surveyed 1 June 1774 and entered posthumously on 23 December for Hancock Taylor, a cousin to Lee, abutting the tract surveyed by Taylor for Hancock Eustace, a mutual cousin to Lee and Taylor. Eustace sold his tract to William Jones, who sold a portion of it to Ambrose Madison. Madison, Abraham Haptonstall, Zachary Taylor, Hancock, and Lee conveyed 360 acres for £10 on 12 March 1792 to Richard Taylor. The deed was verified by Croghan on 7 August 1792, but was not acknowledged by the county clerk until 3 May 1814, Louisville Metro Archives.

18. The deed from Lee to Croghan was recorded on 19 July 1802 in JCDB 6:249. The text attached to the deed notes: "Whereas the aforesaid William Croghan did on the tenth day of April one thousand seven hundred and ninety purchase from the said Hancock Lee the following described tract of land containing three hundred and Eighty seven acres for which he then paid £340." JCDB 3:170. By law, Croghan charged twenty cents for a horse to cross the Ohio

on his ferry. Jefferson County Minute Order Book 5:175, 6 August 1799; William Croghan to Richard Terrell, 18 March 1798, JCDB 10:80. Croghan sold the island acres to Terrell for one hundred "Spanish dollars."

19. William Croghan to James Madison, 7 April 1802, LOC. Deed from James Madison and his wife, Dolley, and Nelly Madison to William Croghan, 27 September 1802, recorded in JCDB 6:544.

20. Deed from Taylor to William Croghan, 18 July 1811, JCDB 9:150.

21. J. Blaine Hudson, "Slavery in Early Louisville and Jefferson County," *Filson Club History Quarterly* 73 (July 1999): 269. Hudson cited Jefferson County Tax Lists, 1780–1820 and United States Bureau of the Census, *Historical Statistics,* 8–15; *The Port Folio* (March 1815): 216; Croghan family Bible kept by Serena L. Croghan, with dates copied by R. C. B. Thruston, with permission of Serena Croghan Rodgers, TFHS.

22. John Frederick Dorman III, "Descendants of General Jonathan Clark, Jefferson County, Kentucky, 1750–1811," *Filson Club History Quarterly* 23 (January 1949): 26–27; Holmberg, *Dear Brother,* 8–9.

23. William Clark to Jonathan Clark, 13 October 1801, 2 March 1802, and 5 April 1802, TFHS. Clark reported he arrived in Louisville on 23 February, "Jonathan Clark Diary," TFHS; Holmberg, *Dear Brother,* 38–44, 55.

24. Interview of Meriwether Lewis Clark by Draper, 25–26 November 1868, Draper MSS 2J99. Holmberg, *Dear Brother,* 9; Deed to Jonathan Clark, 2 May 1803, JCDB 6:431; Deed to Edmund Clark, 2 May 1803, JCDB 6:432.

25. Holmberg, *Dear Brother,* 35; Clark County (IN) Deed Book 13:100; Sarah Jane Gamble to Draper, 14 June 1889, Draper MSS 10J352–357.

26. McDermott, "Western Journals," 26; George P. Garrison, "A Memorandum of M. Austin's Journey," *American Historical Review* 5, no. 3 (1900): 527.

13. The Expedition

1. Bernard DeVoto, ed., *The Journals of Lewis and Clark* (Boston: Houghton Mifflin, 1953), 279. The Treaty of San Idlefonso was signed secretly in October 1800.

2. Fleming, *Louisiana Purchase,* 23–25.

3. Ibid., 81.

4. Robert R. Livingston to James Madison, 3 April 1803, Historic New Orleans Collection, MSS 321.

5. Fleming, *Louisiana Purchase,* 34–43, and 110. Napoleon informed his ministers of his inclination to sell Louisiana on Easter Sunday. Meriwether Lewis to William Clark, 19 June 1803, William Clark Papers, Missouri History Museum. Jefferson had written Clark on 21 June on the same subject.

6. Paul Russell Cutright, "Jefferson's Instructions to Lewis and Clark," *Bulletin of the Missouri Historical Society* 22 (1966): 302–320; Donald Jackson, ed., *Letters of the Lewis and Clark Expedition, with Related Documents, 1783–1854* (Urbana: University of Illinois Press, 1962), 1:10–14. The Lewis and Clark Expedition would cost $39,000.

7. The 1803 purchase price of $15,000,000 equaled approximately three cents per acre paid for Louisiana. In 2016 currency, Louisiana was purchased from France for about $240,000,000; Louisiana Purchase Agreement, Chicago History Museum.

8. Foley, *Wilderness Journey,* 46.

9. George Rogers Clark to Jefferson, 12 December 1802, LOC.

10. Jo Ann Trogdon, *The Unknown Travels and Dubious Pursuits of William Clark* (Columbia: University of Missouri Press, 2015), 53–55.

11. Donald Dean Jackson, ed., *Letters of the Lewis and Clark Expedition; With Related Documents, 1783–1854* (Champaign: University of Illinois Press, 1962), 1:57–60.

12. Jackson, *Letters of the Lewis and Clark Expedition,* 1:44; Jefferson to Lewis, 27 April 1803; Foley, *Wilderness Journey,* 53–54: Jefferson read of Alexander Mackenzie's Canadian exploration in *Voyages from Montreal.*

13. Clark to Lewis, 18 July 1803, William Clark Papers, Missouri History Museum.

14. Lewis to Clark, 3 August 1803, William Clark Papers, Missouri History Museum; Roy E. Appleman, "Joseph and Reubin Field, Kentucky Frontiersmen of the Lewis and Clark Expedition and their Father, Abraham," *Filson Club History Quarterly* 49, no. 1 (January 1975): 5–36.

15. "Jonathan Clark Diary," TFHS; William Clark to William Croghan, 15 January 1804 and 21 May 1804, Missouri History Museum.

16. Clark to Croghan, 2 April 1805, Draper MSS12J4.

17. DeVoto, *Journals of Lewis and Clark,* 279.

18. Stephen E. Ambrose, *Lewis & Clark: Voyage of Discovery* (Washington, DC: National Geographic Society, 1998), 175–177; Gary Moulton, ed., *The Journals of the Lewis and Clark Expedition* (Lincoln: University of Nebraska Press, 2002), 8:369–370; William Clark to Jonathan Clark, 24 September 1806, TFHS; Holmberg, *Dear Brother,* 115; Jackson, *Letters of the Lewis and Clark Expedition,* 1:329.

19. Holmberg, *Dear Brother,* 122; Croghan Papers, Historical Society of Pennsylvania; Jackson, *Letters of the Lewis and Clark Expedition,* 1:358–360.

20. Linklater, *An Artist in Treason,* 207–209; Kennedy, *Burr, Hamilton, and Jefferson,* 282.

21. Ibid., 206–207. All of Louisiana officially was turned over to the United

States on 4 March 1804. Jefferson secretly revealed the expedition's true mission to Congress in January 1804. Linklater, *An Artist in Treason,* 208–210. For more information concerning Wilkinson's connection to Spain between 1804 and 1825, see works of Isaac J. Cox and Arthur P. Whitaker. Charles Floyd died on 20 August 1804 near today's Sioux City, Iowa.

22. A list of "these gigantic remains" is provided in McMurtrie, *Sketches of Louisville and its Environs,* 83. Big Bone Lick is located in today's Boone County, Kentucky, near the Ohio River. Jefferson thought he had received the bones of an unknown lion, but later, scientists convinced him it was the remains of a giant sloth. Jefferson to Clark, 19 December 1807, LOC, Jefferson Papers.

23. John Croghan to Major William Croghan, 27 April 1807, Draper MSS 3N86–87.

14. Burr

1. Draper MSS 10J215.

2. Draper MSS 10J308 and 25S136; Ann Clark Thruston Farrar to Draper, 15 August 1869; interview of Lucy Green Clark, 1868.

3. Josiah Espy, *Memorandums of a Tour made by Josiah Espy in the States of Ohio and Kentucky and Indiana Territory in 1805* (Cincinnati: Robert Clarke and Company, 1870), 14.

4. Dunn, *Indiana and Indianans,* 382–386. The southern route eventually was selected, and the former Shippingport settlement today is an abandoned island lying adjacent to Louisville's Portland neighborhood.

5. Joseph Brant, who admired Prevost extraordinarily, provided the colonel with a new wool uniform upon his departure for Jamaica.

6. The Prevosts, originally from Poitou, France, emigrated to Geneva during the Reformation. In the family tradition, Augustin Jr. attended military school in England before joining the Royal American Regiment. Burr fathered two children with an East Indian servant during the 1790s, each of whom married into well-educated African American families who were strong advocates for abolition. George Prevost, brother of Augustin Jr., rose in rank to lieutenant general and later became the governor general of Canada.

7. Isenberg, *Fallen Founder,* 279–281; Aaron Burr to Theodosia Alston, 13 April 1805, in Matthew L. Davis, *Memoirs of Aaron Burr with Miscellaneous Selections from his Correspondence* (New York: Harper, 1836–1837), 2:368; Thomas Perkins Abernethy, *The Burr Conspiracy* (New York: Oxford University Press, 1954), 27.

8. Isenberg, *Fallen Founder,* 293. Jonathan Dayton was a lawyer and Revo-

lutionary officer before he was elected to Congress in 1791. He served as the US Congress's Speaker of the House from 1795–1799, at which time he was elected as a Federalist to the US Senate.

9. Draper MSS 25S221: "Mr. Burr, as both Mr. Bullitt & Mrs. Key remember, did visit Louisville (1805) & Mr. B. says . . . dined at Maj. Croghan's." Draper spoke of William C. Bullitt, whose home abutted the western boundary of Locust Grove, and Helen Key, his sister; "An Act to Incorporate the Indiana Canal Company," *Kentucky Gazette,* 7 October 1805.

10. Stuart Seely Sprague, "The Louisville Canal: Key to Aaron Burr's Western Trip of 1805," *Register of the Kentucky Historical Society* 71 (January 1973): 78–79; Kennedy, *Burr, Hamilton, and Jefferson,* 262–263. The Bastrop Tract was given to Philip Hendrick Nering Bogel, who adopted the name of Neri and the title of Baron de Bastrop when he fled to America after he was accused of embezzlement in Holland. Ownership of the Bastrop Tract remained in litigation for decades, which made Burr's purchase worthless during his lifetime.

11. From the *Oxford English Dictionary,* the word was first used in the Americas by Spaniards, who defined private military adventurers as "filibusteros." Isenberg recommends Amy S. Greenberg, *Manifest Manhood and the Antebellum American Empire* (New York: Cambridge University Press, 2005), 5.

12. Isenberg, *Fallen Founder,* 303. Dayton received $2,500.

13. Ibid., 301. Anonymous, received 1 December and 5 December 1805 in The Papers of Thomas Jefferson, microfilm. Thomas Jefferson's Notes on the Spanish Treaty, 1805, LOC.

14. Mary-Jo Kline and Joanne Wood Ryan, eds., *Political Correspondence and Public Papers of Aaron Burr* (Princeton: Princeton University Press, 1983), 2:1039.

15. Wilkinson to Adair, 28 September 1806, Wilkinson to Smith, 26 September 1806, Walter F. McCaleb, *The Aaron Burr Conspiracy* (New York: Dodd, Mead, 1903), 204–209; Isenberg, *Fallen Founder,* 305.

16. Isenberg, *Fallen Founder,* 305. Theodosia Burr married future South Carolina governor, Joseph Alston, in 1801 at the age of eighteen. She would die under mysterious circumstances at twenty-nine, lost at sea en route to New York.

17. Ibid., 308; Andrew A. Lipscomb and Albert Ellery Bergh, eds., *The Writings of Thomas Jefferson* (Washington, DC: Thomas Jefferson Association of the United States, 1903), 1:460–461.

18. Kline and Ryan, *Correspondence of Aaron Burr,* 2:974–985; Isenberg, *Fallen Founder,* 314–315.

19. See Kennedy, *Burr, Hamilton, and Jefferson,* 280–283, for a discussion of Jefferson's post-1806 behavior toward Burr.

20. Holmberg, *Dear Brother,* 119.

21. Kline and Ryan, *Correspondence of Aaron Burr,* 2:982; "Special Message to Congress, January 22, 1807." Clark either misdated his letter to Jonathan Clark, or did not know Congress would take up Jefferson's request on the day of its writing.

22. Kline and Ryan, *Correspondence of Aaron Burr,* 2:1007–1016; Isenberg, *Fallen Founder,* 316, 319–320.

23. Thomas Perkins Abernethy, "Aaron Burr in Mississippi," *Journal of Southern History, Southern History Association* 15, no. 1 (February 1949).

24. Daniel Clark Jr., *Proofs of the Corruption of General James Wilkinson and His Connexion with Aaron Burr* (Philadelphia: William Hall, Jr. & Geo. W. Pierie, 1809).

25. David Robertson, *Report of the Trials of Colonel Aaron Burr* (Philadelphia: Hopkins and Earle, Fry and Kammerer, 1808), 1:78.

26. Burr to Theodosia Burr Alston, 29 March 1805, in Matthew L. Davis, *Memoirs of Aaron Burr* (New York: Harper and Brothers, 1836), 2:366–367.

27. The Logan Act, passed in 1799, prohibited private negotiations with the nation's enemies.

28. Wilkinson was investigated twice by Congress following Burr's trial, but he was reactivated as a major general during the War of 1812. After leading two failed campaigns, he was removed from duty and discharged from the army in 1815.

29. "From the Palladium," *Kentucky Gazette,* 19 December 1805.

30. Gwathmey to Clark, 16 September 1808, Draper MSS 55J63; Fitzhugh to Clark, 30 August 1808, Draper MSS 55J62; Clark to Fitzhugh, 3 September 1808 and 17 December 1808, Clark Family Papers, TFHS. Fitzhugh owned a Louisville store and was a justice of the peace by 1819.

31. TFHS; Draper MSS 25S153–56.

32. Board of Trustees, Town of Clarksville Minute Book 1:32, Clark County, Indiana, courthouse. Julia Hancock and William Clark were married at her father's home in Fincastle, Virginia, on 5 January 1808.

15. Clark's Death

1. W. B. Gwathmey to Draper, 25 January 1847. Draper MSS 10J181; interview of Samuel Gwathmey, fall 1846, Draper MSS 10J215; interview of George W. Clark, 27 November 1868, Draper MSS 10J344–345; Sarah Jane Gamble to Draper, 3 June 1889, Draper MSS 10J352–357.

2. Tal. P. Shaffner to Draper, 27 November 1846, Draper MSS 10J182.

3. Ann Clark Thruston Farrar to Draper, 15 August 1869, Draper MSS 10J308. Today, the Fifth and Main Street site of Clark's amputation is the headquarters of the Humana Corporation. See Julia C. Parke, "Clark's Last Years," in *The Life of George Rogers Clark, 1752–1818: Triumphs and Tragedies,* ed. Carstens and Carstens, for additional information.

4. Durrett Collection, University of Chicago.

5. William Croghan's Ledger Book B: 31, University of Chicago; Sarah Jane Gamble to Draper, 3 June 1889, Draper MSS 10J352–57; statement of Richard Ferguson, MD, 2 December 1809, Draper MSS 55J67; Durrett Collection, University of Chicago.

6. An extensive research and renovation program took place at Locust Grove between 2008 and 2010, and the house interior was scientifically restored to its ca. 1810 appearance. George W. Clark to Draper, 27 November 1868, Draper MSS 10J344.

7. Missouri History Museum, dated 31 March 1818.

8. James Harrison to Draper, 21 March 1883, Draper MSS 12J121; interview of Dr. William Clark by Draper, 7 December 1868, Draper MSS 10J324–335; James Harrison to Draper, 30 March 1883, Draper MSS 12J123. Kitt was not mentioned in George Rogers Clark's will, dated 5 November 1815.

9. Draper MSS 2J100 and 10J324–35.

10. Interview of James Harrison, 18 November 1868, Draper MSS 25S188–89; James J. Holmberg, "The Historical Portraits of George Rogers Clark," in *George Rogers Clark, 1752–1818: Triumphs and Tragedies,* ed. Carstens and Carstens, 295–299.

11. Harry Innes to John Gwathmey, 30 January 1810, Draper MSS 55J70; Jonathan Clark to George Rogers Clark, 3 February 1810, Draper MSS 55J71. Charles Fenton Mercer was an originator of the American Colonization Society, formed to export the United States' free Africans. Mercer to Draper, 1 September 1848, Draper MSS 12J36, printed in the *Kentucky Gazette,* 10 March 1812.

12. University of Virginia; George Rogers Clark's sword today is displayed to the public at Locust Grove in Louisville.

13. Mercer to Draper, 1 September 1848, Draper MSS 12J36; interview of Mercer by Draper, Draper MSS 25S213. The interview took place between 1848 and Mercer's death in 1858.

14. William Croghan Ledger Book B: 141, University of Chicago.

15. Ibid., 10J330–331. William Croghan apparently constructed a small brick structure for use as a home for Clark and Kitt before 1815.

16. Mann Butler, *Valley of the Ohio,* ed. G. Glenn Clift and Hambleton Tapp (Frankfort: Kentucky Historical Society, 1971), 245–246; D. R. Poignaud to Draper, August 1869, Draper MSS 35J78.

17. Reuben Durrett to Draper, 10 July 1883, Draper MSS 2J94, published in the *Courier-Journal.* Affidavit of James Ann Pearce Pindell, 3 December 1887, Historic Locust Grove, Inc. The Bush portrait is the property of Historic Locust Grove, Inc. and is displayed in the museum.

18. Jonathan Clark had died at Trough Spring on 25 November 1811, fol-

lowed by Edmund Clark in 1815. The varied life of Fanny Clark O'Fallon Thruston Fitzhugh, "the great black-eyed beauty of Kentucky," came to an end in St. Louis on 19 June 1825.

19. W. B. Gwathmey to Draper, 25 January 1847, Draper MSS 10J181.

20. Poignard to Draper, August 1869, Draper MSS 35J78; Vincennes *Western Sun,* 7 March 1818; G. W. Clark to Draper, 27 November 1868, Draper MSS 10J344; John Bakeless, *Background to Glory: The Life of George Rogers Clark* (Philadelphia: Lippincott, 1957), 359. Bodley's citation, referenced by Bakeless, has not been found. The Presbyterian Rev. Daniel Chapman Banks was the grandson of Burr's aunt.

21. William Clark to Draper, 7 December 1868, Draper MSS 10J333.

22. "Commissioner's Sale" *Louisville Public Advertiser,* 5 July 1826; Report of Commissioner Samuel Dickinson, 25 October 1826; Jefferson Circuit Court case 1845. The plat is reproduced in John E. L. Robertson, *Paducah: A Pictorial History* (St. Louis: G. Bradley, 1988), 12. The word, *Paducah,* chosen by Clark for his town, probably derives from *Padouca,* the Spanish name for Comanche.

23. Jefferson County Minute Order Book, 15:369; Jefferson County Inventory and Settlement Book, 16:239, Louisville Metro Archives.

24. *Western Sun,* 7 March 1818.

25. James Fisher, "A Forgotten Hero Remembered, Revered and Revised," in *The Life of George Rogers Clark, 1752–1818: Triumphs and Tragedies,* ed. Carstens and Carstens, 280.

26. *Western Sun,* 7 March 1818.

16. William and Lucy Clark Croghan

1. Zachary Taylor to John O'Fallon, 25 October 1818, in William Hyde and Howard L. Conrad, eds., *Encyclopedia of the History of St. Louis* (New York: Southern History Company, 1899), 3:1664–1665.

2. *Kentucky Herald and Mercantile Advertiser,* 30 June 1819.

3. *The Port Folio* 5 (March 1815): 214. The battle, led by The Prophet near the confluence of the Wabash and Tippecanoe rivers, elevated tensions between the Shawnees, now led by Tecumseh, and the American army.

4. Croghan to Harrison, 30 July 1813, *Indiana Historical Collections,* 7:503; George Croghan to William Croghan Sr., 11 September 1813, Draper MSS 3N175; Anderson Chenault Quisenberry, *Kentucky in the War of 1812* (Frankfort: Kentucky Historical Society, 1915), 72; Croghan to Jackson, 13 May 1816, LOC, Jackson Papers.

5. Croghan to Jackson, 9 July 1816 and 22 July 1822, LOC, Jackson Papers;

James Gilliam, "A Trip North," in "The 1816 Journal of James Gilliam, Esq.," Library of Virginia; Croghan to Robert Butler, 18 October and 4 December 1816, LOC; George Croghan to unknown recipient, 27 February 1817, LOC, Jesup Papers. The September–October 1816 court-martial of Gaines concluded in an acquittal.

6. *New York Post,* 10 May 1817; Stratford Hall Archives; Stratford Hall blog, citing M. A. Weatherspoon, "1815–1819: Prelude to Irving's Sketchbook," *American Literature* 42 (1969–1970). St. John's was a chapel of Trinity Church, located on Varick Street in what was then the newest area of wealthy Manhattan development and is today known as Tribeca. Serena was born on 25 August 1794 in New York City. She bore seven children, but only Mary Angelica (Wyatt), St. George Louis Livingston, and Serena (Rodgers) survived to adulthood.

7. Jefferson County Marriage Book 1:35, Louisville Metro Archives. Presbyterian minister Daniel Chapman Banks also presided at Clark's funeral. He was the grandson of Aaron Burr's aunt. His successor, Rev. Daniel Smith, conducted the marriage of Ann Croghan and Thomas Jesup.

8. George and Julia Hancock were children of Col. George Hancock and Margaret Strother of Virginia. Margaret Hancock's sister was Sarah Dabney Strother, wife of Richard Taylor, mother of future president, Zachary Taylor, and next-door neighbor to the Croghans. Jefferson County Marriage Book 1:135. Zachary Taylor to John O'Fallon, 25 October 1818. Hyde and Conrad, *Encyclopedia of the History of St. Louis,* 3:1664. Jarvis was a New York acquaintance of Croghan and Serena.

9. Croghan Jr. to Archibald Woods, 15 January 1820; Archibald Woods Papers, College of William and Mary; Edmund Croghan to Lucy Clark, 17 July 1821, LOC, Jesup Papers; *Louisville Public Advertiser,* 3:22, 22 September 1821.

10. Thomas Sidney Jesup was born December 1788, in Berkeley County, Virginia (West Virginia). For more on Jesup, see Chester L. Kieffer, *Maligned General: A Biography of Thomas S. Jesup* (San Rafael: Presidio, 1979).

11. Croghan Jr. to Croghan Sr., 18 May 1822, Historical Society of Western Pennsylvania.

12. *National Intelligencer,* 9 October 1822.

13. Croghan's will was dated 27 August 1822 and recorded in Jefferson County Will Book 2:229. Lucy received the house at Fifth and Main Streets in Louisville (city lot no. 80). Henry B. Reager had deeded the building to Samuel Gwathmey in 1805, and Gwathmey deeded it to William Croghan on 24 May 1806 for $1,500, JCDB 7:506.

14. *Pittsburg Mercury,* 4 February 1823.

15. Samuel W. Thomas, "William Croghan, Jr. (1794–1850): A Prominent

Pittsburgh Lawyer from Kentucky," *Western Pennsylvania Historical Magazine* 51 (July 1968): 215–216; Henry Clay to Richard Rush, 30 March 1817, National Archives; Charles W. Thruston to John O'Fallon, 17 August 1818, TFHS. Croghan and Dunbar were to practice in Kentucky and Indiana. Thomas, "William Croghan, Jr.," 217: "I have just returned from up the coast, having made a purchase of Madam Victnors land." Tapping Reeve was the husband of Aaron Burr's sister, Sally.

16. John Croghan to Jesup, 10 April 1825, LOC, Jesup Papers; Cuthbert Bullitt, "Tale of Two Cities," *Courier-Journal,* 6 September 1891; John Croghan to Jesup, 20 May 1825, LOC, Jesup Papers.

17. William Croghan III was born in March 1824; *Louisville Public Advertiser,* vol. 7, 16 July 1825; George Croghan to T. S. Jesup, 19 August 1825 and John Croghan to Thomas S. Jesup, 27 October 1832, LOC, Jesup Papers: "It is my painful duty to announce to you the death of our beloved Charles. He died on the night of the 21st and was interred in the cemetery of Pere La Chaise on the 23rd." Fanny Clark Fitzhugh died at the St. Louis home of her son, Col. John O'Fallon. Charles's house was not the mid-nineteenth-century house that stands today in Louisville at the corner of Blankenbaker Lane and River Road.

18. Croghan to Jesup, 1 August 1826, LOC, Jesup Papers.

19. Thomas Cushing, ed., *History of Allegheny County, Pennsylvania* (Chicago: A. Warner & Co., 1889), 2:775. Mary Elizabeth Croghan's published birth date of 27 April 1826 is incorrect as her sister would have been six months old at the time. Croghan Jr. to Jesup, 22 November 1827, LOC, Jesup Papers. Elizabeth Denny was the wife of Harmar, son of Clark's 1786 companion, Ebenezer Denny. William Croghan III died at the home of his aunt and uncle Denny in Pittsburgh on 25 April 1828. The sale of Locust Grove was not recorded in Jefferson County, but was implied in Hancock's letter to Croghan, 15 December 1828, Darlington Collection, University of Pittsburgh Library.

20. Pic Nic was not permanently occupied after William Croghan's death, although his staff remained in place and his daughter and her family lived there periodically in the 1850s and early 1860s. It was razed in 1955 when the estate became a golf course.

21. Eugene H. Conner and Samuel W. Thomas, "John Croghan [1790–1849]: An Enterprising Kentucky Physician," *Filson Club History Quarterly* 40 (July 1966): 210–211. John Croghan attended William and Mary from 1807 to 1809. His medical school senior thesis was "Diabetes."

22. *Louisville Public Advertizer,* 20 September 1820; C. M. McGee, "The Great American Oil Well, Burkesville, Kentucky (1829)," *Filson Club History Quarterly* 33 (October 1959): 318–326; John Croghan to Thomas S. Jesup, 20 May 1825, LOC, Jesup Papers.

23. Ibid., 17 February 1826, LOC, Jesup Papers; Croghan Jr. to Ann Jesup, 27 December 1829, LOC, Jesup Papers.

24. Hancock considered buying the Louisville property known as Spring Station in 1827. George Hancock Jr. to Croghan Jr., 15 December 1828, Darlington Collection, University of Pittsburgh Library.

25. Hancock to Jesup, 26 October 1832, LOC, Jesup Papers; Croghan Papers, TFHS.

26. Hancock to Jesup, 24 October 1833, LOC, Jesup Papers.

27. The 1834 transfer of Locust Grove remained private, but the terms were outlined by Hancock to Jesup in a December 1838 letter found in the LOC, Jesup Papers. William Croghan Jr., who held the deed from his father's estate, transferred it to Dr. John Croghan on 4 April 1840. JCDB 55:444.

28. The Jesup children were Lucy Ann, born 1823, Mary Serena, 1825, Jane Findlay, 1827, William Croghan, 1833, Charles Edward, 1835, and Julia Clark, 1840.

29. John Croghan to Thomas Sidney Jesup, 22 January 1837, LOC, Jesup Papers. Osceola was arrested in October 1837 near St. Augustine, Florida.

30. Croghan to Jesup, 22 January and 20 May 1837, LOC, Jesup Papers. Dr. Croghan built "a small room adjoining the house as a chamber for my Mother." Probably constructed as a bath and dressing room (roughly 17 feet by 9 feet), the new room was accessible through the northeast ground floor room. The addition was razed during the 1960s restoration of Locust Grove.

17. Emancipation

1. John Croghan to Jesup, 28 January 1848, LOC, Jesup Papers.

2. Tischendorf and Parks, *Diary and Journal of Richard Clough Anderson, Jr.*

3. Thomas McArthur Anderson, "A Monograph of the Anderson, Clark, Marshall and McArthur Connection," 1900. Anderson's grandmother told him Sarah Anderson considered Little Turtle to be a great man and that he had received a set of pistols at Soldier's Retreat and met George Rogers Clark there. Charles Anderson, "The Story of Soldier's Retreat: A Memoir, 1814–1895," TFHS; Charles Snow Guthrie, "Richard Clough Anderson, Jr.," and George Yater, "Robert Anderson" in *The Kentucky Encyclopedia,* 21; Anderson Family Papers, 1810–1848, Huntington Library, San Marino, California.

4. Samuel W. Thomas, Eugene H. Conner, and Harold Meloy, "A History of Mammoth Cave, Emphasizing Tourist Development and Medical Experimentation under Dr. John Croghan," *Register of the Kentucky Historical Society* 68, no. 4 (October 1970). Croghan purchased Mammoth Cave for $10,000; Croghan Jr. to Jesup, 15 November 1839, LOC, Jesup Papers.

5. Maria Audubon, ed., *Audubon and His Journals* (New York: Charles Scribner's Sons, 1897), 1:271. The 1826–1838 edition of *Birds of America* generally is referred to as the "double-elephant folio."

6. Emily M. Bullitt, "Alexander Clark Bullitt, A Bit of Louisville History," *Filson Club History Quarterly* 33 (October 1959): 315. George Croghan's 1842 journal: 6 January, "Have had Stephen busily employed drawing a pencil map of the Mammoth Cave [at Locust Grove]," TFHS. Croghan inked Stephen's pencil drawing on the evening of 15 January. Croghan's journal records that he had spent the previous day reading Alexander Hamilton's pamphlet, in which the former treasury secretary admitted he had "*been intimate with the wife of a certain Mr. Reynolds . . . with the knowledge of her husband*" (italics added). Hamilton had published the pamphlet himself in 1797 and Monroe, who was central to the public announcement of the Reynolds affair, had spent three days at Locust Grove in 1819.

7. Franklin Gorin to W. Stump Forwood, in Harold Meloy, "The Stephen Bishop Story: The Man and the Legend," files of Mammoth Cave, Kentucky (1974 manuscript).

8. Caroline Butler Bell to Edward G. W. Butler, 18 January and 23 February 1824, Historic New Orleans Collection; Gwendolyn Midlo Hall, *Louisiana Slave Records 1719–1820* (www.ibiblio.org/laslave). Nathaniel Evans bought enslaved men, Bob, twenty-five years old, and Amos and Lamb, each twenty, sold by John Croghan for $3,000 in Louisiana in April 1818. The sale probably was driven by his father's desire to help George Croghan purchase the Louisiana plantation, as Lamb, at least, became a member of the colonel's plantation population.

9. Croghan Jr. to Jesup, 1 August and 30 December 1826, LOC, Jesup Papers; Bell to Butler, 28 January 1827, Butler Family Papers.

10. George Croghan to Lucy Croghan, 19 July 1829, Darlington Collection, University of Pittsburgh Library; Winfield Scott to T. S. Jesup, 8 October 1830, Historic Locust Grove, Inc.

11. The medal and sword are owned by Historic Locust Grove, Inc. Charles Richard Williams, "George Croghan," *Ohio Archaeological and Historical Publications* 12 (1903): 375–409; Thomas W. Parsons, "George Croghan in the War of 1812," *Northwest Ohio Quarterly* 20 (1948): 192–202; Col. George Croghan's journal, 1 January–1 May 1842, Historic Locust Grove, Inc. The 1840 Federal Census places George Croghan at Locust Grove with an emancipated female servant and a younger enslaved couple.

12. Alberta McLean to Charles W. Shetler, 29 May 1949, Darlington Autograph Files, 1610–1914, University of Pittsburgh; Sandhurst Collection, Royal Military Academy, Sandhurst, England; Charles Dalton, *The Waterloo Roll Call* (1904; repr., London: Arms and Armour, 1978); Gerald Edmond Boyle, ed., *The*

Rifle Brigade Century: An Alphabetical List of the Officers of the Rifle Brigade from 1800–1905 (London: Wm. Clowes and Sons, 1905); UK Census reports indicate Schenley was born in 1798, and the Athenry Parish Register in County Galway, Ireland, recorded the baptism of William Henry Shanly on 22 April 1798; Gwynne Tuell Potts, "Edward Wyndham Harrington Schenley and Mary Elizabeth Croghan" (unpublished paper presented at Locust Grove, 2015).

13. Joanne Craig, Hertfordshire, UK, to author: Uphall Parish Death Records, 1828. R. A. Humphreys, *The Diplomatic History of British Honduras, 1638–1901* (London: Oxford University Press, 1961), 21, 31; *Gentleman's Magazine,* London, 25 April 1837; Schenley to Henry Lynch, January 1842, Darlington Autograph Files, University of Pittsburgh.

14. William Croghan Jr. to Thomas Jesup, 6 May 1845, LOC, Jesup Papers.

15. W. H. Denny to T. S. Jesup, 27 September 1850, LOC, Jesup Papers; "Mary Schenley," *Pittsburgh Sun-Telegraph,* 15 September 1941; Potts, "Schenley and Croghan."

16. Mary left wills in England, the United States, and Italy.

17. John Croghan to Jesup, 10 November 1842 and 20 November 1843, LOC, Jesup Papers

18. John Croghan to Thomas S. Jesup, 25 December 1844, LOC, Jesup Papers; John Croghan to William Croghan Jesup, 16 January 1846, William Croghan Family Papers, TFHS. Mary Serena Jesup married Navy Lt. James Blair on 14 January 1846 at her parents' Washington home, one block from the home of the groom's parents, *Washington Globe* publisher, Francis Preston Blair, and his wife, Violet Gist. First Lady, Sarah Polk, attended. Blair had participated in Com. Charles Wilkes's 1838–1842 Antarctica exploration.

19. Charles Bird King to Jesup, November 1846, LOC, Jesup Papers. "The two portraits will be 140 dollars which I hope you will not think too high when you take into consideration the numberless repaintings I made both in the face and dress of the larger picture." One of the King portraits of Ann Heron Croghan Jesup is owned and exhibited by Historic Locust Grove, Inc; Janin Family Papers, Huntington Library.

20. John Croghan to Thomas Jesup, 4 January 1848, LOC, Jesup Papers.

21. George C. Gwathmey to Thomas Jesup, 18 January 1849, LOC, Jesup Papers.

22. Will of John Croghan, Jefferson County Will Book 4:121. "I direct my Executor to Emancipate & set free from bondage immediately my slave Isaac, who has served me so faithfully"; Jefferson County (KY) Inventory and Settlement Book 13:230–233 and 244–247; Jefferson County (KY) Minute Order Book 21:393–397. Stephen Bishop's tombstone was provided by a tourist who had admired Bishop, but the year of his death was incorrectly inscribed as 1857. See Joy

Medley Lyons, *Making Their Mark: The Signature of Slavery at Mammoth Cave* (Ft. Washington, PA: Eastern National Park and Monument Association, 2003) for additional information about the African American guides at Mammoth Cave.

23. Thomas S. Jesup to James E. Jesup, 19 May 1853; William Croghan Family Papers, TFHS; William C. Jesup to Lucy Ann Sitgreaves, 14 May 1857, author's private collection.

24. William Croghan Family Papers, TFHS; Thomas S. Jesup to Charles Jesup, 25 July 1858, LOC, Jesup Papers.

25. The daughters of Ann Croghan and Thomas Sidney Jesup reinterred their parents' bodies in Georgetown's Oak Hill Cemetery in April 1862. See Kieffer, *Maligned General.*

Epilogue

1. US Military and Naval Academies, Cadet Records; William Croghan Family Papers, TFHS. The Ohio River property was left by Charles Croghan to Serena and her children, who ceded their interest to St. George in 1845. Cornelia Ridgely was the daughter of Cornelia Louisiana Livingston and Commodore Charles Goodwin Ridgely. Cornelia Livingston Croghan, 1847–1878, was born at Locust Grove. Ulster County, New York, Deed 73204 recorded on 14 October 1848. George and Margaret Ketchum sold St. George Croghan 86.5 acres at Flatbush for $4,000.

2. Jefferson County (KY) Inventory and Settlement Book 13:230–233 and 244–247. The Locust Grove inventory was made on 5 July 1849 and the Mammoth Cave inventory on 13 August 1849. *Louisville Daily Journal,* Thursday, 2 August 1849: "A sale of the personal estate of the late Dr. John Croghan will take place at his farm, 5 miles above the city of Louisville, on Thursday morning next, at 10 o'clock A.M." After her son's death, Serena Livingston Croghan would sail, with Clark's sword, via the horn of South America to San Francisco, where it descended in this family to Virginia Rodgers Murphy Wheaton, who presented it to Historic Locust Grove, 19 November 1992.

3. Croghan Family Papers, TFHS; Lucy Serena Croghan Browne tombstone, Mountain View Cemetery, Oakland, California.

4. JCDB 83:310; Croghan included Locust Grove furniture, animals, and the crops as collateral against the loan from Thruston, which was repaid on 22 September 1852, Croghan Family Papers, TFHS; St. George and Cornelia Croghan brought thirty-two suits in Ulster County, New York, between 1853 and 1857 to break Cornelia's mother's will. George Croghan was born at Locust Grove on 27 March 1852, and last child, Elizabeth Augusta (Lillie), was born at the Flatbush house on 31 July 1854. Dutchess (NY) Surrogate Court, 7 October

1851: J. R. Livingston died on 25 September 1851, leaving Serena a house at 168 Duane Street, New York City, and a portion of his residual properties. Between 1820 and his death, Livingston owned more than thirty Fifth Ward houses, most of which functioned as brothels.

5. Joseph Rogers Underwood, trustee, to George Croghan, son of St. George Croghan and ward of Rev. Christopher B. Wyatt, 28 September 1868, JCDB 139:485; George Croghan and Wyatt to W. O. Harris, 28 April 1873, JCDB 201:35; George Croghan to John H. Ward, 5 August 1878, JCDB 218:620.

6. Croghan Papers, TFHS; Bela Estvan, in *War Pictures from the South* (New York: Appleton, 1863), wrote that "thousands of citizens came forth" in Richmond to greet the returning Confederate army . . . and that "a carriage, with two ladies in deep mourning, moved silently along, conveying the mother and intended bride of Colonel Croghan"; JCDB 139:485; *Daily Louisville Commercial,* 28 April 1876; JCDB 221:549. Serena Croghan lived with daughter Serena (Tinie) Rodgers until her death on 16 January 1884. She is buried with her family at Mountain View Cemetery, Oakland, plot 16. Clark's sword passed through Tinie Rodgers's descendants and family portraits through Mary Angelica Wyatt's family. JCDB 221:549 and 551.

7. JCDB 221:549.

8. Christopher C. Graham to Lyman C. Draper, 15 November 1882, Draper MSS 35J146; "Historic Excursion," *Courier-Journal,* 10 July 1883.

9. Etta Paul to Richard Waters, 1 October 1883, JCDB 263:563; Etta L. Paul, widow of James Paul Jr., affirmed the deed, JCDB 291:2; Richard Waters to Lucy Mary Jane Waters et al., 5 November 1891, recorded in JCDB 381:232; Articles of Incorporation, 29 December 1906, Jefferson County Corporation Book 16:142.

10. John Baylor Temple to Lyman C. Draper, 19 September 1867, Draper MSS 10J32. Temple was a grandson of Gen. Jonathan Clark; Alfred Pirtle, "The Death of General George Rogers Clark," *Evening Post,* 13 February 1922.

11. Cave Hill Cemetery, Lot 146, Section T, May 1916.

Index